Transitions:

How Women Embrace Change and Celebrate Life

Transitions:

How Women Embrace Change and Celebrate Life

Abigail Brenner, M.D.

To Ray

One's whole life is like a ritual or a ceremony. . . . Sacredness is everywhere. . . . Genuine heartfelt ritual helps us reconnect with power and vision as well as the sadness and pain of the human condition.

—Pema Chodron

CAMPBELL: The myths and rites were means of putting the mind in accord with the body and the way of life in accord with the way that nature dictates.

MOYERS: So these old stories live in us?

CAMPBELL: They do indeed. The stages of human development are the same today as they were in the ancient times.

MOYERS: And these myths tell me how others have made the passage, and how I can make the passage?

CAMPBELL: Yes, and also what are the beauties of the way.

—Joseph Campbell and Bill Moyers, *The Power of Myth*

Contents

x ～ Contents

Acknowledgments

For years, people had been asking, "So where's the book?" Friends even envisioned the finished product. Although I felt honored that people thought I had something of value to say, the idea of actually sitting down and writing seemed a daunting task. Finally, after many more years and conversations, I committed myself to giving life creatively to an idea that just wouldn't go away.

So here's the book. And what a journey it's been. I really mean that now, although much of the time along the way I seriously questioned my good sense and judgment. There was so much I didn't know and had to learn, and that wasn't just about writing a book either.

There have been so many people throughout it all who have encouraged, supported, and just listened to me while I thought out loud. There are those individuals who have taken an active role, offering assistance, making introductions, and generally opening doors. I am so grateful for your interest and kindness.

My friend and colleague, Sylvia Karasu, MD, and her husband, T. Byram Karasu, MD, went the extra mile for me. Thank you for believing in me.

Kathy Chetkovich provided valuable editorial insights when the book was just beginning to take shape.

With simplicity and elegance, Ruth Greenstein showed me the difference between writing and how to write a book.

This book would never have been what it is without the women who contributed their beautiful stories. All I did was ask, and there was this outpouring, this pure willingness to share the intimate moments and experiences that make up a life. Your generosity overwhelms me, and your stories, every time I read them, touch me deeply. Each story affirms how interconnected we all are and how universal are the themes of life, yet each story highlights how unique and special each storyteller is. You inspire me. Thank you from the bottom of my heart—Bruria Obstbaum Aviram; Lisa Berg; Alice Berry; Jamie Brenner; Debra Cibilich; Susan Cohn; Els Cortens; Elise Cummiskey; Carol Futterman; Monique Guffey; Deborah Hamolsky; Patti Hawn; Maggie Hinders; Sheilaa Hite; Eve Isaacson; Tuija Itkonen; Julie Johnson; Katie Kessler; Lorraine Klagsbrun; Barbara Kramer; Barbara Lipkin-Luther; Mary Joan Mandel; Sr. Joan Marshall; Dunya Dianne McPherson; Terry Merrill; Sheryl Miller; Meredith Narissi; Dr. Rebecca Nystrom, DC; Angela Oh; Sylvia Ragoonath; Dr. Christine Ranck; Natalie Rogers; Gladys Roij; Deborah Roth; Cheryl Rothman; Danielle Rothman; Martha Schut; Jackie Schwartz; Susan Shils; Arielle Silverman; Rita Battat Silverman; Karlin Sloan; Mary Spring; Pam van Summern; Lucille Vaz; Patricia Suarez Weiss; and Doris Kamp White.

Thanks to more wonderful friends and supporters—Helen Adrienne, Alice Finley, Lenore Graham, Roberta Halpern, Latifa Mitchell-Stephens, and Melynda Taylor.

I'm blessed with an amazing family. My children David and Robbie have grown up to be all that a parent could ever have wished for—warm, intelligent, loving, and compassionate individuals who have been fortunate enough to have found their equals in their partners, Jamie and Aaron. All have been present for me through the process of writing this book, lending advice and encouraging me every step of the way.

My husband, friend, and partner of forty years, Ray Brenner, has had more to do with this book than anyone else. He has seen me through the good, the bad, and the ugly, through the sublime and the ridiculous. He has been my confidante and adviser, my legal counsel, my therapist, and my computer techie (when I was totally computer illiterate and convinced that hitting the wrong key would vanish my manuscript), and has provided stability, sanity, balance, and a much-needed sense of humor through it all.

And to all those others I've met by chance, by accident, in foreign and often strange places, thanks for being there. You helped more than you'll ever know.

~

Opening the Door

My Passage

In December 1991, my husband had one of those serendipitous conversations that can change a life. It was at his company's annual Christmas party in New York. When one of his West Coast colleagues grumbled about having to leave home for this annual occasion, my husband simply replied, "If I lived in San Francisco, I wouldn't complain so much." A few weeks later, my husband's boss, reminding him of this comment, approached him about relocating to California. The West Coast colleague was about to retire, and the position needed to be filled.

To my husband's way of thinking, all of us are given only so much time on this earth to accomplish whatever we want or need. This window of opportunity was what he called "the last clear chance"—an opportunity to change the course of his life. I was intrigued but also apprehensive about a potential move: I'd never lived outside of the New York metropolitan area. I had a very solid psychiatric practice in the city, one it had taken me years of schooling and work to build. My children, in their last years of college, had stayed close to home.

But I also knew I was feeling stuck at that point in my life. Although the sum total of my living experience could be described as successful and satisfactory on many levels, I no longer felt sure of what my purpose was. What was my mission? What else was I supposed to be doing with my life?

So when my children laughed at my worries about "leaving" them (they'd already left home years before, after all) and encouraged me to "Do it, Mom!" I did. Perhaps on some level I knew that making this physical move was actually the first step of a much larger reorienting of my whole life—a

1

far more radical shift than I could have ever imagined. Perhaps that was why I was simultaneously so eager to do it and so resistant. In essence, I was subconsciously encouraging myself to embark upon one of the great journeys of my life—and part of me was loath to give up the safety of the home port I'd known for so long.

I closed my practice, left my hospital affiliation of many years, sold my little house in Connecticut, and left behind family and many dear friends. Essentially, except for my husband, none of the "externals" with which I identified was making the journey west with me. Looked at one way, I was free; looked at another, I had lost my home.

For the first time in longer than I could remember, I had a lot of time on my hands. In my new home, the only people I knew were one or two acquaintances I had previously met through my husband's company. Immersing myself immediately in work was out of the question, since California has its own licensing requirements for physicians. Without the comfort of all my old roles—doctor, mother, daughter, friend—I was suddenly "just" a person.

Wandering anonymously around San Francisco, I often asked myself, "Who are you now?" There was an exhilarating freedom in not having to meet anyone's expectations for who I should be or what I should do, but it was also disquieting and disorienting to be thrown so totally back on myself. Loneliness can be painful. Several times during the first years after our move, the "dark night of the soul" visited me. Issues I was sure I was done with found their way back to me with a vengeance. These unresolved conflicts, accompanied by acute anxiety, reemerged in both my waking life and my dreams, washing over me like a series of relentless waves, sometimes barely allowing me time to catch my breath between them. My symptoms often bordered on panic, and sometimes even sheer terror. I felt overwhelmed by a force I had not experienced since my late teens and early twenties. Clearly, something was happening to me; it was a process I myself had initiated, but I no longer felt in conscious control of it.

Aside from learning to just be with myself, I began venturing beyond, finding healers of every kind and opening up to new modalities of "healing through" a problem. As a traditionally trained psychiatrist, I had always had a healthy curiosity about alternative, "unconventional" methods of healing; now, for the first time, I had both the opportunity and the strong desire to learn more about these methods. Thanks to the disruption of my old life and the soul-searching that resulted from it, I was about to learn to see the world in some very new ways.

Everyone I met had a story to tell, and I began to see that my own uncertain search had opened me up to listening in a new way. I had occasion to meet a woman getting a divorce and choosing to celebrate it with a group of friends. Two special women, aided by various practitioners and rites designed to honor the darkness they were traversing, managed to heal themselves of life-threatening disease. I met one woman who had lost a son in an automobile accident and who felt a sorrow beyond name, a sadness that ran about as deeply as any I had ever witnessed. Isolating herself in her misery, she seemed to be caving in upon herself, her own spirit withering away. Everyone I came in contact with seemed to be at a crossroads. I was struck both by those who seemed able to move on and by those who didn't.

As a therapist, of course, much of this was familiar territory to me. Indeed, my interest in milestone events could probably be traced back to my childhood as an "MK" (minister's kid). To my father, a spiritual leader in the community, births, weddings, and funerals were part of the everyday routine, not exceptional events. In that context, too, I had been taught to keep other people's secrets, especially about those "unfortunate" happenings that often aren't acknowledged in "polite" conversation: physical and mental illnesses, accidents, addictions, overdoses, suicides, losses of job or fortune, and divorces.

In one way or another, I'd long been exposed to or directly focused on the problem of how people got themselves through the big moments (both happy and sad, planned for and unexpected) in their lives. But, for the first time, I found myself thinking about that territory in a new way. *What was it that enabled some people to cope with the big changes in their lives while others seemed undone by them?* Of course, many factors contribute to the mix, but it seemed to me that when individuals could find a conscious, meaningful structure to encompass the events of their lives, they could take more responsibility and feel less lost in the dark.

By the time I finally returned to live in New York, almost four years later, I was a much different person than I had been when I left. I couldn't resume seeing patients from a strictly clinical point of view, as I had been trained to do; it no longer was enough. Beyond analysis of the psyche, people seemed to be longing for connection and for a sense of meaning in life. Their emerging spirit was expressing itself through the therapeutic process, attempting to come to their aid for a deeper understanding of their true essence.

When the phrase "rite of passage" first took up residence in my brain, shortly after my arrival in California, I didn't understand what it was doing there. Some ideas, even words or symbols, just seem to appear randomly, but I've learned that it's worth paying attention to them, for they are the voice of your inner knowing, providing access to the deepest recesses of your self. So I began to do a little reading, and a little led to a lot; gradually I began to see that the phenomenon I had been observing in other people and in myself could be described by this somewhat old-fashioned-sounding expression. By *not just surviving but actively accepting and acknowledging the turning points in our lives, we could begin to find what so many people I knew (myself included) were looking for: a life of greater meaning and fulfillment.*

A Brief History

As microcosms that mirror life itself, rites of passage are intimately tied to cycles, or stages, of life. In their study of adult life, *The Seasons of a Man's Life*, Daniel J. Levinson and his associates address the idea of the universal quality of life cycles. The literatures of many cultures, going back thousands of years, speak to these same stages: "The Sayings of Our Fathers" in the Talmud cover the ages of man, Confucius marked man's life in six steps, and Solon identified ten separate stages. "Unfortunately," as Levinson pointedly notes, "all of them refer to males; the neglect of the female life cycle has a long history."[1]

Presenting a far more balanced view, Carl G. Jung, widely considered the father of the modern study of adult development, based his theories on wisdom both masculine and feminine in nature. He divined his philosophies by tapping into anthropological, religious, and mythological sources, as well as relevant clinical data. His strong belief in the concept of the individuation process included the important idea that midlife transition comes with a new developmental impetus to express the self. Using historical, biographical, sociological, psychological, and anthropological sources, Erik H. Erikson broadened the study of adult development by defining eight ego stages of the life cycle. Both of these men knew what the ancients knew: there is an order to the life of man, and the deeper and more complete our understanding of that order is, the richer our lives will be.

In a well-timed "karmic confluence," Jung's brilliant theory of the stages of life emerged around the time that Dutch anthropologist Arnold van Gennep published his now-classic text *Les Rites de Passage* (1908). This coming together of disciplines allowed for a more complete understanding of how humans in various cultures mark their life cycles. The 1970s brought renewed interest in, and a revisiting of, the study of adult development. The popularity of Daniel Levinson's *The Seasons of a Man's Life* and Gail Sheehy's *Passages*, both dealing with life stages and cycles, speaks of people's fascination with understanding how life unfolds and a real desire to know what to expect along the way. *Surprisingly absent from these pivotal texts, however, is virtually any discussion of the essential rites that serve as significant landmarks and invaluable road signs along our lives' paths. Clearly, understanding passages is vital to our evolution; the necessary next step is toward an understanding of the rites that mark these passages.*

In a related development around the same time, the feminist movement brought with it a fascination with anything connected to the Goddess or the Divine Feminine. Every aspect of "her" life and expression was explored in countless ways by women eager to reconnect with an essential female energy. Meanwhile, in the 1980s, books like Joseph Campbell's *The Power of Myth* (as well as the subsequent television series with Campbell and Bill Moyers) reintroduced and popularized the concepts of myth, archetype, ritual, rite, and the hero's journey—topics that by then had all but disappeared from the forefront of our collective consciousness. As consciousness tends to spiral around, what's old becomes new.

Because ritual has its roots in religion, a study of religious literature was also undertaken, and there, a profoundly discouraging story was found: evidence that the Goddess, in one form or another, had been revered in cultures prior to the waves of invasions from the Russian steppes by Indo-European peoples (4500–2500 BC) and in occasional subsequent eras, but that in general, the long march of the patriarchal religions of Christianity, Judaism, and Islam had significantly devalued and disempowered not only the Goddess, but all things feminine. This was a key piece of the puzzle. Couldn't this be part of the reason why the masculine and feminine energies of our contemporary society feel so out of balance with each other, and why, even though women have "caught up" with men in so many ways, we're left searching for the vehicle to express the process of coming into our own? Isn't it possible that a very fundamental piece, from way back, is missing?

Putting together what I had learned led me to several conclusions. First, rites of passage are psychologically and culturally necessary to help us move forward in our lives and to invest our lives with meaning. However, the loss of a vibrant culture of ritual that encompassed rites of passage, coupled with the loss of reverence for those traits symbolized by the Divine Feminine, has made it hard for all of us—but especially women—to find the meaning and sense of "rightness" that so many of us are looking for in our lives. Because women have been cut off from our inherent, intuitive ways of knowing and have been taught to look outside ourselves for the answers to life's questions, we need the freedom and encouragement to design our own rites as a form of finding the answers within. And we need the tools to do so. Where can we look to find these?

This is what I was searching for. Yet in all my reading on the subjects of myth, ritual, and passages, I found remarkably little on the subject of women's rites of passage, and nothing that offered examples and analysis of rites of passage in the lives of women today, or guidance on their creation and use. For a culture as dedicated to personal growth and self-improvement as ours is, this seemed peculiar—and worth pursuing.

About This Book

Transitions grew out of my desire to answer some fundamental questions about the role of rites of passage in contemporary women's lives. What kinds of passages are most significant to women today? Do we consciously recognize and mark these passages? If so, how? And how does this affect our lives? Drawing upon my extensive research in the fields of anthropology, sociology, psychology, mythology, archeology, history, philosophy, and religion, my aim was to distill the best of the scholarly material that would interest a mainstream audience, combine this with personal stories from a wide range of women, and complete the perspective with my own observations, analysis, anecdotes, and guidance as a practicing psychiatrist and healer of many years. I wanted to create a book that would reconnect women to their important life transitions while giving them the tools to honor those transitions and understand their significance in the broader scheme of their lives.

Fueled by this mission, I took my questions and hypotheses back into the world to see what kind of feedback I would get. I designed a questionnaire asking women to identify the important events in their lives and to describe those they viewed as "rites of passage." I asked them how they chose particular rites, and what lasting effect, if any, these rites had on their lives. I distributed the questionnaire to approximately fifty women. Although not a formal or scientific social study, I looked for diversity in my sample, seeking women of different ages and backgrounds, from many walks of life and from different parts of the country and the world. I expected a few interesting responses and perhaps some shrugs and blank looks. What I got far exceeded what I imagined: a flood of stories, each distinct, each giving voice to the energy of a major life transition and the meaning found in it. Even without formal knowledge of a sacred tradition, these women seemed to almost organically understand the need to mark the important events in their lives. The original sources of knowing and relating, which had long been dormant or sup-pressed, seemed to spring up of their own accord when women got in touch with what was meaningful to them. By borrowing from one tradition or another, or by following their own instinct for what the moment called for, women had fashioned their own rites of passage. If necessity is the mother of invention, then perhaps this was one of the happier by-products of women's historical exclusion from so much of the tradition of public ritual. Whether the resulting "rite" was a consciously created ritual or simply an instance of heightened consciousness, the effect was the same: a "momentous moment" of awareness and transformation in a woman's life.

In *The Cultural Creatives*, Ray and Anderson note that "each person's path is unique, but true stories can be maps of some of the major landmarks and compass settings for the journey."[2] The stories gathered here form a map of many kinds of passages, from leaving home to leaving a husband, from camp-ing alone in the wilderness to alternative healing, from coping with depres-sion to changing careers. They are candid, revelatory, and moving—and are an important tool for learning by doing and by example. Many of the women who participated in this project told me how grateful they were to have had the opportunity to thoughtfully process and write about their lives. Some even sent their stories to other women. When we share the stories of our initiations and transformations, we inform each other about the journey. By telling our own story, we see things we didn't see before. And by listening empathically to someone else's story, imagining ourselves in her shoes, our world is expanded. As a therapist, I have always said that my patients are my best teachers. Bearing witness to another's life story has not only broadened my own compassion but has allowed me to live through the experience vicar-iously, informing me without the necessity of going through it myself.

In analyzing the collected stories, certain trends emerged. Women were interested in two kinds of passages: those surrounding the life cycle, whether biologically or relationally oriented, and those pertaining to their individual development. The passages and the rites they used to mark them were both traditionally and personally defined. Moreover, in consciously creating their rituals, women discovered and drew upon a surprising array of resources and tools.

The structure of this book reflects these findings and is framed by my own perspective. It is divided into two main parts. The first part, "The Passages," begins with an overview that defines and categorizes passages, analyzes the historical movement from societally prescribed passages to individually desig-nated passages, looks at the traditional limits of women's rites of passage, and sets forth general principles and goals of conscious passage making. The three chapters that follow focus on the major types of passages identified above: passages of the body (menstruation, sexual initiation, childbirth, menopause, illness, etc.) and passages of the self (marriages, birthdays, and personal milestones), with a separate chapter on the special challenges of passages through loss (breakups, divorce, and death). The second part, "The Tools," investigates the resources that women use to make and mark their passages. The five chapters each correspond to a main category of these, including myths and symbols, journeys, creative projects, religious and spiritual traditions, and communities.

Each chapter includes a provocative discussion of the topic at large, including its historical and conceptual underpinnings; edifying and inspiring examples of particular passages or rites drawn from the many stories I gathered; an analysis of the principles and lessons of these stories; my further observations and anecdotes; and exercises designed to help readers bring conscious ritual into their own lives. An introduction describes my own midlife passage, my study of the field, the genesis of this project, and the organization of this book. The conclusion discusses how rites of passage can elucidate the structure of our lives and help us to find and follow our life's themes.

Life is the thing that happens when you're making other plans, we're often told. This book is dedicated to helping you avoid that trap by learning to identify, respond to, and honor your own moments of growth and transformation. One definition of the word *passage* is "the power to move freely." A rite of passage both honors that power and helps to create it. What makes a rite meaningful is your own involvement in creating it. It's not about following a set of directions; it's about learning how to recognize and respond to the particulars of your own life. This is what I hope this book will teach. Designing your own rites of passage gives credence to what is intuitively understood and allows for the creative expression that strengthens the individuation process. Over time, your cumulative rites of passage—and, more importantly, your ability to look at life through this lens—will help you to map a path of greater fulfillment and meaning.

I don't promise that *Transitions* will change your life, but it *will* help you recognize and navigate the life in which you find yourself. After all, you already have what you need. It's a matter of learning to listen to and trust the one true authority in your life: yourself.

PART ONE

THE PASSAGES

CHAPTER ONE

Defining Passages

When brought to birth, man is not yet completed; he must be born a second time, spiritually; he becomes a complete man by passing from an imperfect, embryonic state to a perfect, adult state. In a word, it may be said that human existence attains completion through a series of passage rites, in short, by successive initiations.

—Mircea Eliade

A Little History

Just what is a rite of passage, anyway?

In 1908, Dutch anthropologist Arnold van Gennep published his now classic *The Rites of Passage*, an account of the various cultural celebrations that mark a person's change in status. After looking at ethnographic data gathered from cultures all over the world (including Australia, America, Asia, and Africa), van Gennep concluded that, across all human societies, we see "a wide degree of general similarity among ceremonies of birth, childhood, social puberty, betrothal, marriage, pregnancy, fatherhood, initiation into religious societies, and funerals."[1] All major transitions in life tend to be recognized by ceremonies or rituals that tell the world, and the individual him- or herself, that a change has taken place. Since "man's life resembles nature, from which neither the individual nor the society stands independent,"[2] van Gennep also included seasonal, annual, and celestial transitions in his list of events that are ritually marked.

The Three Phases: Separation, Transition, Incorporation

According to van Gennep, all rites of passage, wherever they are celebrated and whatever transition they mark, contain the same basic structure. Each

11

entails a three-stage process of separation, transition, and incorporation (or, in van Gennep's terminology, preliminal, liminal, and postliminal phases). In each case, the individual is separated from the known status; undergoes a ritual transition, passing through the unknown dangers of the "threshold"; and is then incorporated back into society with a new status. For example, in male initiatory rites among the various peoples of Australia, initiands are taken from their homes into the bush (separation), where they undergo a series of ordeals as well as religious instruction (transition), before being returned home to be acknowledged by the community as adults or, in some instances, as "those risen from the dead" (incorporation).

Even today, in our relatively secularized society, we can still glimpse van Gennep's structure at work in some of our most trivial rituals. Think about the simple tradition of making a wish and blowing out the candles on a birthday cake. At the heart of that playful and seemingly trivial ritual, celebrated on the turning of each person's personal year, we find a rite-of-passage drama in miniature: leaving the familiar (closing one's eyes), stepping into the unknown (making a wish for the future), and coming back (opening one's eyes and blowing out the candles).

What about Women?

Have women's rites of passage historically followed the same structure as men's? In his landmark book, *Emerging from the Chrysalis* (1981), a cross-cultural study of women's initiation rituals, Bruce Lincoln took up this question and concluded that women's rituals have been marked by the stages of enclosure, metamorphosis (or magnification), and emergence.

What accounted for this difference? According to Lincoln, it was due largely to the fact that in many cultures a woman's status cannot outwardly change, so the rite was focused on her "symbolic" elevation rather than on any real-world advancement. In the initiation rites that Lincoln studied, women did not spatially separate as men do in the classic "territorial passage"; they stayed close to home and in some cultures were even secluded. Magnification, or metamorphosis, described the expansion of a woman's experiences and capabilities, but *only* in the realm of women's biology; she moved from daughter to wife and mother. Unlike men, the threshold phase was never really open to women. Emergence described the process of coming out of seclusion. For example, Tukuna (Northwest Amazon) initiands in the Moca Nova festival are literally described using the metaphor of insect metamorphosis—the caterpillar, the cocoon, and finally the butterfly.[3]

Women did not ritually die to be born anew in traditional rites of passage; rather, they became, through their passages, more developed forms of their original selves. While this may have been true for traditional rites of passage, women today are finding the "male" structure of the ritual—departure, journey, and return—to be both powerful and true to their own process.

The Power of the Passage

All rituals, when performed with intention, are meaningful. When they're alive for us, rituals connect us to something larger than ourselves, to that truth that is, in Joseph Campbell's words, "always and forever." The deliberate, symbolic act of a ritual takes us temporarily out of the flow of daily life and places us in sacred space, where what we know bows to what we don't. In ritual, the borders blur—the worlds of the finite and the infinite touch.

While all rituals have the potential to transport us to that timeless place, rites of passage have the unique power to transform. About sixty years after van Gennep coined the phrase "rite of passage," anthropologist Victor Turner took it one step further by focusing specifically on the liminal, or "threshold," phase. Calling this phase the "betwixt and between," Turner identified it as the crucial stage that distinguishes rites of passage from all other rituals. A ritual that enacts the status quo is merely a ceremony, but for Turner, the real work of a rite of passage is "to evoke creativity and change." As Ronald Grimes, scholar of religion and culture, states it, "To enact any kind of rite is to perform, but to enact a rite of passage is also to transform."[4]

As rites of passage help to move us from one status to another, we can feel the shift in consciousness that results. It's as if we've entered a new room in our inner house; another part of ourselves is revealed. So transformative is the rite of passage that even a single one, as Grimes has noted, "can divide a person's life into 'before and after.' An entire system of such rites organizes a life into stages. . . . These ceremonial occasions inscribe images into the memories of the participants, and they etch values into the cornerstones of social institutions."[5]

Since it is this capacity to transform that makes a rite of passage so significant, it makes sense that its waning power in our contemporary culture could have a devastating effect. As anthropologists have shown us, a rite of passage is not just a *sign* that your life has changed in some way; it is *part* of that change. Saying "I do" and placing a ring on your partner's finger, for example, is not just a symbol of marriage but the actual enactment of it.

Something *happens* in a rite of passage. If such ceremonies have begun to lose their ritual force in our increasingly secularized, "rational" society, we may be losing an important means not just of marking change, but of making it.

Dying to Be Reborn

Every rite of passage involves a death and a rebirth. In order to assume a new status, you must first let go of your old one. In the language of ritual, something dies so that something else can be born.

To those of us reared in a culture that fears and avoids anything to do with death, the idea that death should be an integral part of a ritual intended to reaffirm life may seem strange, even disturbing. But not if we remember that life is a spiral, not a straight line—just as winter gives way to spring, which yields to summer, we must let go of each phase of our lives to embrace the next. Every ending is the stage for another beginning. Rites of passage are the ceremonies that pay tribute to the old while they usher in the new.

When Going through the Motions
Isn't Getting You Anywhere

Sadly, for many of us today, ritual events of all kinds have too often become "rites by rote"—a matter of following a cultural script, often without giving much thought to its symbolic significance. The myths of the primitive world were charged with a reality that is hard to appreciate today. To the ancients, the natural world was a place where the sacred and the transcendent were made manifest; rituals were performed with the full belief that the participants were in fact communicating with their gods—and that their gods were listening.

Each spring, for example, the women of ancient Greece reenacted a portion of the drama of the rape and abduction of Persephone by Hades, the god of the underworld. According to the myth, Demeter pines for her missing daughter and throws the world into cosmic chaos by creating a famine. Only when Persephone is returned to her for a few months each year do the crops grow again (hence winter turns to spring—and eventually back to winter again). In their reenactment of the story, the women would banish men from the temple and ceremonially enter dark caves. Their performance of this ritual and their reemergence into the light was thought to ensure a renewal of the world.[6]

Another example of a myth that had an annual reenactment meant to ensure a specific outcome woven into its magical structure was the planting myth of Inanna from the Sumerian civilization. This symbolic myth, a perennial favorite that follows the cycles of nature, speaks of Inanna descending into the underworld to meet the representation of her own shadow side, her twin sister, Ereshkigal. In this descent, she not only plants seeds in the "womb/tomb" of the fertile ground, which ensures the growth of new life, but she also faces her own darkness, to reemerge whole.[7]

As our scientific knowledge of ourselves and the universe evolved, these myths lost the potency of their magic and mystery. We may still enjoy hearing stories of the Greek gods today, but most of us are more persuaded by the theory that spring arrives when the earth has reached a certain point in its orbit around the sun than that it has to do with Persephone's return from the underworld.

Even rites that have persisted into our own age have largely lost their ability to evoke awe and wonder. Why do we continue to perform them? Because we always have. But what do they *mean*? How do they connect to our lives? In our culture, ritual is identified primarily with organized religion—not a promising place to find meaning for those who aren't practicing members of a church or synagogue. And even for those who are, participation in many religious rituals has become an exercise in tradition, not meaning. Lacking intention and heart, these once-significant rites are often performed in a purely "ritualistic" way—repetitively and habitually, with no real feeling, and, not surprisingly, with no effect. While Christian Communion was once a sacred, meaningful ritual in which people believed that they were uniting with Christ, for many churchgoers today, it is just another part of the Mass, something that a "good Catholic" does.

Once ritual ceases to be alive for us, we are left with seemingly outdated words and actions that make no sense in our modern world. Without this bridge between the symbolic and the concrete, nothing is revealed to us because we cannot connect to the true meaning; we cannot link what our brains know with what our hearts feel. We find ourselves going through the motions but not getting anywhere.

Respecting Tradition, Embracing Change

For ritual to regain its meaning for us, it needs to feel true to our individual lives. But how can we justify modernizing and customizing rites that are sanctified, in some cases by divine law and in other cases by decades or even centuries of tradition? Isn't the whole *point* of ritual that it should be "timeless" and "absolute"? Don't those stately ceremonies derive much of their power precisely from the fact of having been repeated so exactly and so unquestioningly for so long?

While this is not a simple question, and different people will no doubt answer it differently (just as some people will want to stick more closely to traditional patterns in devising their own rituals), it's important to recognize that *no* human tradition is truly static. Even the most conservative of the world's religions have seen changes in the way their rituals are performed over time. It's now fairly rare to find ceremonies conducted exclusively in Latin or Hebrew; at one time, it was much more common. Just as a common language, spoken and understood by all, has become the norm in most houses of worship, so too are lay ministers and members of the congregation more involved in religious services than they once were. Although women are still not allowed to become priests in the Catholic Church (a particularly ironic fact when one considers the vaunted status of priestesses in ancient times), in many faiths, the "gender gap" has closed to the point where women can perform all the religious duties of their male counterparts.

Clearly, change is part of our tradition. And for a rite to be powerful, it must not only evoke a sense of continuity with the past, but it must also feel relevant to the present. Rituals are not, as theologian and cultural historian Tom Driver notes, only instruments of transformation; they are also "themselves transformed by the process of which they are a part."[8]

For women, who have historically been excluded from leading and often even from participating in rituals, the move to transform that tradition is even more liberating—and even more necessary. Consider what it means for a Jewish woman, long accustomed to not even being counted in the minyan (or quorum) needed for prayer, to be able to recite the mourner's kaddish led by a female rabbi.

The longer we continue to do certain things because "that's the way they've always been done," the longer we reinforce the idea that there's something unquestionably right, something "absolute" and "timeless," about excluding women from celebrating Mass in the Catholic Church or from being called up to read the Torah. The flip side of the power of rites, of course, is that they can wrap social inequality in a mantle of tradition. If we're excluded from the process of choosing the colors and weaving the threads, it should come as no surprise when we find ourselves feeling as though we're wearing clothes that were made for someone else.

The invitation to create meaningful rites for ourselves, then, is a radical one. It is an invitation to move freely into our own spiritual lives, to take charge of marking the passages that *we* find significant, in the ways that *we* deem meaningful. As the stories in this book illustrate, the experience of doing this for the first time can be exhilarating indeed.

And if something has been lost in our becoming a less tradition-bound culture, something equally valuable has also been gained: the freedom to take responsibility for the direction and meaning of our own lives. The task is to seize and shape this freedom—consciously, deliberately, and joyfully. As the narratives that follow show, rites of passage are one way of doing that.

Every rite of passage is an act of becoming, an act of taking responsibility for the self we are *choosing* to become. A meaningful rite weds knowledge to action, intention to expression, doing to being. For women, this is a matter of bringing the drive of the Masculine to the heart of the Feminine. "I am here," a rite of passage says. "I am present in my life."

Reimagining Rites of Passage

So, how do we do it? How do we go about designing our own rites of passage, and how do we know when we've done it right?

In thinking about how to design rites that better fit our lives, it's easy to feel overwhelmed by what can sometimes feel like a trip to the spiritual shopping mall. It all seems to be out there—tarot, astrology, yoga, Eastern religions, and the ancient arts of divination. And that's just one shelf of the local bookstore! While all these tools can be powerful, they're the means, not the end. The tool isn't the answer; a greater understanding of the self is, and ultimately that comes from within. So let yourself be drawn to the guides and symbols that speak to you, and remember that any number of them can take you where you need to go. Those methods are the vehicle, but your own intuition is the key.

Reimagining ritual is, first and foremost, a creative undertaking; it is sacred play. Ronald Grimes describes the process this way: "When we invent [ritual], we give teeth to what we imagine. Ritual, like art, is a child of imagination, but the ritual imagination requires an invention, a constantly renewed structure, on the basis of which a bodily and community enactment is possible."[9] In practical terms, Grimes suggests placing an imagined ritual next to a traditional one and looking for ways to blend the two. Most of us will find, for example, that we need to go beyond the text and symbols of the Judeo-Christian tradition to create a ritual that adequately represents us. Many of us want that earlier tradition to play a role in our ritual too. Or,

apart from the traditional, just allow spirit to guide you in the perfect creation of your own sacred act.

Improvisation is the first step, Grimes advises. Begin by letting your intuition guide you, and watch what spontaneously develops. Later you can go
back and develop a more "linear" script to follow. Overall, our task is to find
the symbols and language that feel sacred to us, that give us that shiver or
flash of recognition. Just as you know that certain things are true "in your
gut," the right ritual elements, when you settle on them, will just *feel* right.

Regardless of the form you choose, remember that the goal of any rite is
to bring your fullest attention to the moment. Ideally, your mind, body, and
spirit will all be involved in the ritual, and you will feel spiritually, socially,
and psychologically engaged. The stories and exercises you'll find in this
book can inspire you to move in that direction.

CHAPTER TWO

~

Passages of the Body

The question that comes—always, always—is "What about the woman's journey?" The woman's life, if she is following the biologically grounded norm, is that of life in the world, in one relationship or another to a family. . . . The woman brings forth life in one way or another, either biologically or socially, and then, in the latter stages, is life-fostering and life-guiding.

—Joseph Campbell

The cycle of life encompasses all creatures, from the smallest organism to the most highly evolved. For humans in the West, four moments in the life cycle are widely considered to be primary: birth, puberty, marriage, and death. But for women, the life cycle is also determined by changes in female physiology. Traditionally, a woman's life cycle was divided according to what are classically termed the "three blood mysteries": menarche, childbirth, and menopause. The Feminine archetype, which carries across cultures and time, echoes these blood mysteries in its representations of the Child-Maiden (the girl approaching menarche), the Mother (the bearer and nurturer of life), and the Crone (the keeper of wisdom). Today we recognize that women's bodies transit through birth, menarche, childbirth, motherhood, menopause, and death. On top of these, our bodies make the passage through sexual initiation, and often through such unplanned events as miscarriage, abortion, and major illness and injury.

This chapter focuses primarily on female-specific passages, but also on those physical transitions that, as humans, happen to us all. I have chosen to call the passages dealt with here *entering* (menarche), *awakening* (sexual initiation), *conceiving* and *birthing*, *mothering*, *healing* (from major illness and injury), and *guiding* (menopause). After a brief history of women's life-cycle

19

events and the rituals surrounding them, this chapter will examine the stories of contemporary women to understand how they experience, view, and honor the passages of their bodies, and how these passages have informed their lives.

In ancient times, ceremonies around everything feminine abounded, and women celebrated the various stages of life. In *Women Who Run with the Wolves*, Clarissa Pinkola Estes notes, "During old Pagan celebrations, women practiced ritual cleansing of the feminine body and the feminine soul/spirit in preparation for figurative and literal new life in the coming spring. These rites might have included group grieving for childbearing loss, including the death of a child or miscarriage, stillbirth, abortion, and other important events in women's sexual and reproductive lives from the old year."[1] But, as this egalitarian society was replaced by a male-centered one, all things belonging to part of the sacred and hallowed feminine mystery came to be feared and diminished. Men created their own elaborate purification rituals for women, whom they now viewed as defiled and untouchable. With religion in those days being the domain of male theologians and scholars, the Talmud, expanding on Scripture, provided several volumes of rules and laws governing women specifically. "Talmudic law, like the Mohammedan, was man-made law," notes historian Will Durant, "and favored the male so strongly as to suggest . . . a very terror of woman's power."[2]

Among the healthy, natural functions deemed unclean according to Jewish law were sex, menstruation, and childbirth. After giving birth, women were considered unclean for forty days if they had a son, and double that number if they bore a daughter. During menstruation, women were believed to be especially powerful, even dangerously so, not only to others, but to themselves. One taboo suggested that flowers would instantly die if a menstruating woman handled them. In *Restoring the Goddess: Equal Rites for Modern Women*, Barbara Walker refers to the taboo that "forbade man to touch or even look at this awesome blood."[3] Menstruation was turned into an event surrounded by humiliation—and not just the first time, but over and over again through the course of a woman's life.

The church followed suit, denying Communion to menstruating women and to new mothers until forty days after giving birth. Eventually, women took this shame upon themselves, living out a false modesty and feeling that female physiological functions were somehow tainted. Women were pushed into replacing healthy attitudes and beliefs about their bodies with acute senses of shame, fear, and guilt.

In her work on the myths and stories of women, Estes uses the theme of the devil, who "symbolizes anything that corrupts understanding of the feminine processes,"[4] to explain the changes wrought by the patriarchy. "The predator [devil] shapes ideas and feelings in order to steal women's light."[5] In other words, the devil's influence changed society's attitude toward women. As a result, women lost touch with their intuitive knowing and with the generational wisdom passed down from mothers to daughters about their once-celebrated natural functions. The teachings and rituals surrounding their passages into maturation and power ceased to be, and women lost their way.

In much of the world today, the sharing and veneration of women's life-cycle events is sorely lacking. What became of these ritual practices? What happened to this sharing in community? How can we find our way back to the instinctual knowledge that once guided our understanding of our bodies, our lives, and our place in the world? Through the following stories of women's passages across all of the major biological changes, we can consider the many ways that we choose to consciously acknowledge these great life transitions. We will see that they encompass not only the physical, but also the emotional and spiritual passages that inevitably follow.

Entering

Traditionally, the onset of menses marked the beginning of a young woman's initiation into adult status. During this initiation, she may have been separated or even totally segregated from the community, given special clothing to wear and certain foods to eat, and literally "stuck in the hut," with her activity severely restricted. In contrast, young men traditionally embarked upon a "territorial passage" as part of their initiatory ordeal. They were sent away to the bush or the forest to prove themselves, and upon returning were welcomed as full adult members of their community. Since girls were initiated singly, they had scant chance to bond with others over this dramatic passage, while boys, often initiated as a group, enjoyed the benefits of a shared experience. With no sense of community and little mentoring, young women made the passage into adulthood largely unguided. This lack of support kept them isolated and in their place, doing what was expected of them by society.

Today, from a cultural perspective, this seems no longer the case. The broad dissemination of information about women's reproductive and sexual lives has vastly increased our level of awareness of these topics. This in turn has fostered changes in attitudes and a greater emphasis on personal and social responsibility. How do young women today face the initiation into womanhood that begins with menstruation? What do they feel and recall about the event? How do family attitudes color the way they think about their new identities? For some, the legacy of becoming a woman is handed down, almost by rote, from generation to generation. For others, new rites are created, and new roles are acknowledged. Here are four women with four very different "first-blood" experiences. Let's take a look at how this event helped to shape their sense of what it means to become a woman.

"This Awesome Blood"

The shock of being slapped by her mother is what Bruria remembers about getting her first period. "Why did you do that?" she asked her otherwise sweet and loving mother. "Because my mother did that to *me*," her mother replied. In fact, this custom is not peculiar to Bruria's family. Several women of Eastern European heritage have recounted the same experience, though strangely enough no one recalls this custom's origin or meaning. A generation later, when Bruria's own daughter got her period, Bruria decided it was high time to break this tradition. Instead of using a slap as the symbolic gesture to mark the passage into womanhood, Bruria gave her daughter a kiss, acknowledging her daughter's change in status with joy and deep respect. This, she decided, was the new welcoming gesture.

Getting her period on her thirteenth birthday was not the only present Mary received. To this day, she remembers the event with great fondness. As she related the story to me, Mary seemed transported back to that moment, deeply reflective in her recollection, the expression on her face shifting to one of quiet reverence. Returning home from work, Mary's father, a man not easily given to demonstrating emotion, solemnly addressed his daughter, shaking her hand and congratulating her. She remembers that even at thirteen she was fully aware that a change in status had been acknowledged and that a shift in relationship had occurred.

Gladys's first-blood experience suddenly fast-forwarded her life. The potentially serious consequences of physical maturity and the rush to avoid them overshadowed the pride she might have enjoyed had she been given the time to appreciate her new status. Suddenly the hunt was on for that most precious commodity: the husband.

"At the time of my birth, over sixty-five years ago, and in the South American culture in which I was raised, men were elevated and exalted, while women were reminded that they were only as good as the man they were attached to. When I was a little kid, I thought boys had everything.

They were allowed to run impetuously and shout freely. They didn't have to take care of their clothes or be clean. But most of all, if they decided to talk about sex, tell jokes about it, or even do 'it,' not only were they approved of, but they were looked up to because they, of course, were entitled to 'it.' Women, on the other hand, had to be careful, because if they were not attractive enough, their men would leave them and look for other women. And if they were left alone, the women would have to work as clerks or, even worse, as servants.

"I was so inexperienced that when I got my first period, I thought I had dirtied my pants. I was shocked to be told that I was now a young lady, able to become pregnant. Tales meant to instill fear in me were everywhere. Stories of maids that became pregnant and had abortions—some with fatal outcomes—were, in my mother's solemn words, the 'facts of life.' I was barely a woman, with no real sense of who I was, yet there appeared to be countless roles I was expected to take on."

As we will see in chapter 3, Gladys rapidly threw herself into the next stages of her life; by the time she was in her early twenties, she had already gone through several life passages. A generation ago, women reached their biological and familial milestones early on, even if they did not reach psychological and emotional maturity until much later. Women today often postpone the start of their own families in favor of developing greater independence and self-realization, but they run the risk of wearing down their biological clocks.

Jackie had the good fortune of being in the company of other women in her tight-knit family during her first period. Her story illustrates how this significant rite of passage can be a celebratory communal event.

"I was well prepared, intellectually, for the changes that occur in a woman's body. In 'those days,' menstruation was considered a hush-hush topic, at least to my mother. She managed, with the aid of a couple of Modess booklets, to teach me about womanhood—though there's a big difference between what she taught me and the facts of life, about which I knew nothing.

"It's funny how well I remember it, but one Friday afternoon in July, Mom and I were visiting Aunt Grace. Aunt Joan and Aunt Ann were also there. The men were off somewhere that men go off to, and all the younger children were playing outside. How appropriate, now that I think of it. I went to the bathroom, and when I saw blood on my panties, I knew immediately what it was. Having been prepared by my mother, I wasn't afraid, but somehow my heart beat a little faster, my respiration increased, and I knew that I had crossed over the line from childhood to . . . womanhood, whatever that meant.

"'Mom . . . Mommy,' I called in my sing-songy way. Then followed the announcement to my aunts, one of whom was my godmother. There were oohs and ahs, along with words of encouragement and welcoming. Aunt Grace, the youngest of the sisters, contributed the sanitary napkin (they didn't come in sizes then) and belt, which was perfectly appropriate, since I got most of her hand-me-downs anyway. The rest of the afternoon was spent around the kitchen table with the elders in my life talking about their own experiences with menstruation. That may have been the first time I was allowed to have coffee with them and be included as a woman. I was an adult."

What do you remember about your own first-blood experience? Were you told the facts of life and then left on your own to sort out their meaning? What did you learn from your mother and your friends? What did you pass on to your daughters? Were you influenced by old wives' tales that cautioned against swimming or doing any kind of exercise? Did the people close to you view this as a time of being vulnerable and unwell? Did they use expressions like having "the curse" and being "on the rag"? Were the men in your life sensitive and sympathetic, or did they ask if it was "that time of the month" any time you were irritable, emotional, or strongly opinionated?

Menstruation is a normal, healthy, and even joyful function, a reminder of the cyclical rhythm of life and the privilege of being a woman. But, over the centuries, it has become tangled up with negative attitudes and false beliefs. How can we strip away these remnants of negativity, of fear, shame, and obligation? How can we look beyond the physical and sexual to appreciate the sensuality of this experience, an aspect that is typically de-emphasized or totally omitted? Perhaps by sharing these stories and others we can help reframe outmoded ways of thinking and learn to use this defining experience to access our essential womanhood.

Awakening

Attaining physical maturity is only the first step on the way to adulthood; becoming sexually active is the second major marker along this path. Yet the loss of virginity is rarely recognized as a rite of passage in our culture. This seems in part a vestige of our Puritanical heritage and the countless religious and social taboos that still surround this subject. Whether women see their first experience of intercourse as a private and secret event—perhaps even one they should feel guilty about—or as a source of pride depends on the attitude with which they come into their own sexuality. And this is almost always a complicated affair.

Sexual activity is a multilayered experience, and one that is still deeply confusing to women. Physical intimacy does not a relationship make, yet women of all ages often feel that a sexual encounter should somehow mean more. Is a sexual relationship the ultimate intimate experience? Yes and no. This is a riddle that all women struggle with, but for a young woman who brings limited life experience to her sexual awakening, it can be a particularly troubling one. Our biological drive toward sexual union brings our bodies into intimate proximity. But total intimacy—knowing someone through and through—requires a merging of minds and feelings that only comes with time. Presumably this is the kind of love that all of us ultimately seek, yet how many of us are willing to give relationships the work and time they need?

Our high-tech, warp-speed consumer culture is adept at breeding short attention spans, always directing us to the next best thing. On top of that, our psyches seem to be guided by a pleasure principle that seeks to override anything that causes emotional or psychological discomfort and pain. We have become conditioned to gravitate toward that which makes us feel good and gratifies our immediate needs, and we have difficulty staying with that which is painful and anxiety provoking—especially relationships. With sexuality, the trap is to get addicted to the immediate gratification of pleasure, to mistake this for real emotional connection, and to misinterpret what occurs in the intimacy of physical involvement with the intimacy of a relationship developed over time. In addition, there is a probable biochemical reaction that may reinforce this pattern. People become convinced that they have "the real thing" going because a basic need is temporarily satisfied. They tend to want to reinforce this gratifying relationship, regardless of its full nature, and have a hard if not impossible time examining it. If they could, perhaps they would eventually seek out partners that are ultimately more beneficial to their healthy development.

When I invited women to decide for themselves which rite of passage to talk or write about, I found that only a few chose their sexual awakening. Yet, rather than examining the first event, many spoke freely about their ongoing sexual and sensual lives. As women mature, they seem to grow much more comfortable with openly discussing their feelings, attitudes, thoughts, and beliefs about sex and sexuality. Perhaps making the passage into mature,

sexually active adulthood—taking that risk into the unknown—requires several ventures before it is finally complete.

Close Encounters

Jackie's story continues. By the time she was in college some thirty years ago,
she was deeply into religion, having sought solace from some earlier experiences that she thought were sinful and would keep her out of Heaven. "I was
so Mary-like that I had been chosen Queen of the May in high school.
Because of this effort to be pure, I hadn't ever discussed sex with my friends,
and certainly not with my mother. The church had won out, and the fear of
doing sinful things ruled my life."

Then she met Andy, a foreign student from Cyprus, the most handsome
man she had ever seen (even her father agreed). Andy was a star soccer
player, and Jackie was a cheerleader—they seemed to make a perfect couple.
But Andy was a fast mover, and it wasn't long before he crossed the line from
necking to having intercourse. "I didn't want to that first time. I kept saying
no. I cried and kept trying to push him away, to no avail. I had been date
raped and didn't even realize it, thinking that men were supreme. When I
told Andy we just couldn't do it anymore because of the blood and because
he was hurting me, he was astonished that I didn't know. And so my real
education began. I actually married this guy because he told me that I could
never find a man to marry me now that I was no longer a virgin. Looking
back, I can hardly believe I was so naive."

In contrast, here is the story of a young woman whose mother's guidance
and support helped her to have a positive, guilt-free sexual awakening. It had
become apparent to this mother that her seventeen-year-old daughter,
sophisticated and mature beyond her years, and quite knowledgeable in the
ways of men and women, was moving toward an intimate relationship with
a close high school friend of hers for whom she had developed romantic feelings. This mother-daughter pair was fortunate to have an unusually open
relationship. The mother broached the subject, speaking with her daughter
not only about birth control, but also about the seriousness and responsibility
that comes with sexual intimacy and choosing a sexual partner. Although
the mother understood that this young man and her daughter would probably not be the ultimate partners for each other, she sensed that it would be
a positive experience for these two good friends. They have since gone their
separate ways, but the young woman's memories of her friend and the intimacy they shared are still fond ones.

The power of sexual attraction and union is one of life's most compelling highs. As these stories show, it is a power that transcends generation, gender, background, and belief. A young person's first experience can overwhelm the body and senses—can shock them, even. The experience unleashes a complex of heightened emotions—among them fear, guilt, excitement, attachment, confusion, power, love, and pain—that may take years or an entire lifetime to come to grips with. The relationship between sex and love is especially difficult to sort out. Many women today still don't seem to understand the difference between having a strong physical connection as a primary focus and incorporating this connection in the pursuit of a long-term emotional commitment. Our culture romanticizes sexual relationships but rarely illustrates the reality of how such relationships fare over time. Yet it is clear from the many women I've talked to that friendship, initially and ongoing, is what builds and sustains strong partnerships.

Science is just beginning to understand the brain's reactions to sex, love, and attachment. In *Why We Love: The Nature and Chemistry of Romantic Love*, anthropologist Helen Fisher, along with research colleagues at the Albert Einstein College of Medicine and SUNY Stony Brook, studied the brain circuitry and chemistry of romantic love through fMRI brain scanning. As a result of their findings, they proposed that humans exhibit three "primary mating drives": the sex drive, or lust, mediated by androgens and estrogens; attraction or romantic love facilitated by dopamine and norepinephrine; and attachment seemingly sustained by vasopressin and oxytocin. Ultimately, scientific explanation may help us to better understand why we feel the way we do and to put into perspective these often overwhelming and life-altering experiences.

As our attitudes and knowledge continue to evolve, issues surrounding sexual intimacy remain intensely personal and complex. Religious beliefs and social values, health concerns and emotional well-being, are among the many factors that come into play. What are the attitudes and understanding that we bring to our first and subsequent sexual encounters? Do we learn from each experience, or do we recreate relationships that don't satisfy our deeper needs? Consider your own sexual rite of passage. Do you feel that this passage is complete? If so, what marked its completion, and how long did the journey take? Did you need additional time at the end of the passage to understand every aspect of it, to evolve around it, and to learn what is best for you? If you are still in the midst of this journey, consider what you need in order to complete it. And remember, this may well be one of the most challenging passages you make.

Conceiving and Birthing

Pregnancy and childbirth are quintessential initiations for women. The three phases of this rite of passage—ordeal, risk, and transformation—are literal and very real. Far beyond the chronological significance of nine months, the pregnant woman undergoes an archetypal experience equivalent to the hero's journey. It is an experience that transcends time. Passing through this initiation, women contact the Mother (the primal Feminine archetype) and the realm of women's mysteries. Every modality of being is engaged: physical changes, a shift in status, a movement to a higher level of consciousness, and a spiritual unfolding. The experience offers women the ability to access and expand their self-knowledge.

Yet no matter how real the risks that women face during birth, no matter how transformative and miraculous the bearing of life truly is, this event often passes without the full honor and acknowledgement it deserves. In our society, as soon as a woman gives birth, she becomes somebody's mother, yet her own journey, the dramatic passage made by her and her baby, is typically not celebrated. By contrast, cultures that we sometimes deem "primitive" treat this major passage quite differently. In the Todas culture of India, in a ceremony known as "Village We Leave," women in their fifth month of pregnancy are removed to isolated huts where they perform specific rituals. They return home for childbirth, which happens quietly and without special rites. A few days after the birth, both mother and child return to the special hut for protective, initiatory cleansing ceremonies. After drinking a substance called "sacred milk," they return home.[6] As another example, the Hopi celebrate childbirth with rituals that honor the new mother and the new grandmother. The expectant mother remains at home, attended to by her mother. But during the actual birth, the mother leaves, and the woman gives birth alone. Once the child is born, the new grandmother returns to perform the ceremony of carrying the placenta to the "placenta hills" for ritual burial.[7] Rituals such as these are not only helpful and reassuring, but they create containing walls for the mother in which she can honor and celebrate her own transition.

In our culture, ceremonies such as baptisms, circumcisions, and namings are aimed at welcoming the new baby into a specific, often religious, community. But where are our rituals to mark the newborn's entry into the world and the woman's entry into motherhood? Why have we come to treat this sacred rite of passage as largely a medical and technological phenomenon? In *Birth as an American Rite of Passage*, Robbie Davis-Floyd observes that our culture has transformed pregnancy and childbirth into "a male-dominated initiatory rite of passage through which birthing women are taught about the superiority, the necessity, and the 'essential' nature of the relationship between science, technology, patriarchy, and institutions."[8] Among the reasons behind this, Ronald Grimes explains, is the fact that women and their labors have been historically undervalued. If men are viewed as the human norm, then women and children are looked upon as second-class citizens. "Not measuring up, they receive fewer of society's resources, including its ritual ones."[9] Over time, men have come to honor spiritual rebirth (formerly only open to men) over biological birth. In fact, by contrast, most cultures greatly honor and celebrate the initiation rituals of men. "If men gave birth," Grimes concludes, "rites would be cross-culturally widespread and elaborate."[10]

Harking back to one of our earliest sources, the consequence of Eve's actions in the Garden of Eden, as interpreted by male religious scholars, was that all women thereafter would suffer in childbirth: "I will greatly multiply your pain in childbearing; in pain you shall bring forth children, yet your desire shall be for your husband, and he shall rule over you" (Genesis 3:16). It would seem, then, that many of our views about childbirth are holdouts from an era that favored repression of the Feminine. It is important to revisit this concept, which is often confused with the tenets of feminism. When I speak about repression of the Feminine, my perspective is not about evening the score between men and women or blaming men for what has happened to women over centuries. Rather, I am speaking about what happens psychologically and emotionally when the archetype, which normally contains a balance of opposites, has become polarized or "wounded." The Feminine is not just about or for women. Each of us, regardless of gender, carries masculine and feminine aspects within ourselves. The original Mother archetype contained balanced dualities. The problem arose when patriarchal systems overlooked the necessity of utilizing these opposites as a complimentary pair and split them apart, assigning positive aspects to men and negative ones to women. Jung warned that when a society denies or splits off a vital aspect of the archetype, then certain instincts are suppressed, and neurotic, and even psychotic, behaviors may result. How can these vital opposites be reunited? In *Reclaiming the Spirituality of Birth*, Mauger suggests that "healing the collective mother wound means reinstating the Feminine in our culture."[11]

Though sometimes it may seem that we are long past the point of returning to a culture of balanced dualities—one that honors primal archetypes and celebrates the initiation of birth—we may not be so far from it after all.

Consider the following stories of women who have seized the opportunity to celebrate the Feminine and to strengthen their identities through their experiences of pregnancy and childbirth.

Three's a Charm

Advances in modern medicine have made birth safer for women and their babies, and for this we can all be grateful. Over the last few decades, a variety of acutely sensitive tests have emerged that help health practitioners determine the status of the developing fetus and ensure the health of the mother throughout pregnancy, labor, and delivery. At the same time, the medical model has stripped the experience of much of its intimacy and wonderment. It is up to women to restore that. Here is the story of one pioneering woman who did just that.

Mary Joan made the decision to take the road less traveled and have her third baby at home. This was over twenty-five years ago, when home birth was still seen as a foreign and outlandish idea. When she resolved to do this, she had no idea what a major rite of passage the birth of this child would be. Her previous pregnancies had been easy and healthy, and this one seemed on track to be the same. The shock came midway through the third month, when she learned that a new job for her husband meant a move from Texas to New Jersey during her pregnancy.

Once settled in, they were determined to find others who thought as they did—that home birth was the ideal situation: no long separation from other children in the family, and no hospital germs or autocratic hospital routines. Having a baby was a normal part of life, not a medical procedure. Mary Joan began calling local hospitals to try to locate midwives. After several tries, a nurse surreptitiously gave her a phone number for a supportive group called the Home-Oriented Maternity Experience (HOME). Mary Joan and her husband began attending monthly meetings, always at a member's home, and were given free use of the group's library of related materials. They also found a midwife but knew they needed a doctor as well, a qualified ob-gyn to visit on a regular basis and upon whom to rely if they unexpectedly needed to go to a hospital for the birth. In addition, Mary Joan's mother and sister agreed to be with her during the event. "Having my mother there was a direct conduit of love and strength," Mary Joan recalls. "Giving birth is the supreme effort for the woman; everything is strained to its utmost."

Labor began on a spring morning at 3 a.m. The midwife arrived about an hour later and ascertained that Mary Joan was four centimeters dilated. The doctor's service was alerted to the fact that labor had begun and appeared to be proceeding normally. The midwife told Mary Joan that she could do whatever she wanted for the next few hours. "I had laundry I'd planned to finish, so I went up and down the stairs a few times getting loads done. I paused to breathe during contractions but otherwise felt a sense of excitement and well-being." The contractions became increasingly powerful, and at 7 a.m., Mary Joan climbed into bed, approximately eight centimeters dilated. By then, her two children, Aaron, almost ten, and Rachel, almost five, were awake and came in to join the excitement. Her husband coached her with Lamaze breathing techniques. Mary Joan rested between contractions and vocalized during them, which she recalls "was not at all musical!" In the meantime, her son had become very worried and decided, despite reassurances, to wait outside the bedroom door. Her daughter appeared comfortable, perhaps because of all the women in the room.

"Before long, Rachel called out, amazed, 'I see an ear!' All at once, our baby boy was born. What excitement and delight we all felt sharing this miracle, this precious moment together. I saw the sun shining through the bedroom windows facing me. It was 8:05 a.m.

"The midwife asked my mother if she would like to cut the cord. Mom said she would be honored and did so with shining eyes. Words cannot describe this invaluable time, of which mothers and fathers are so routinely deprived in our modern medical institutions. I felt somewhat weary, but also well and happy. I had no pain as I had had with earlier episiotomies; there was no residual discomfort. Our pediatrician, probably aghast at the idea of a home birth, had asked to be called as soon as the baby was born. He actually came right over to make sure our new little one was in good health.

"I dozed and rested with our newborn son. At 10 a.m., I walked downstairs easily, holding the baby, and enjoyed a delectable breakfast that my mother and sister had prepared. I felt wonderful looking around the table at all those I held close to my heart. That day, I felt joined to all mothers and sisters, to the entire community of women around the world. The power we women share, if only we acknowledge it, is astonishing. I felt in touch with that power that day. I will always recall it as one of the very happiest days of my life."

Mary Joan's birth arrangement is only one of many alternative options. I recall a woman I met during my ob-gyn rotation in medical school who, terribly disappointed with her first delivery, had researched alternative methods for her next pregnancy. She read about the French obstetrician Frederick Leboyer, whose delivery techniques (dim lights, soft voices, gently massaging the baby, delay in cutting the umbilical cord) were designed to enable "birth without violence." His ideas appealed to her. Unable to find an obstetrician that practiced this method, she chose a female physician who agreed to include elements of Leboyer in a traditional hospital setting. The result was not only a peaceful, easy delivery, but a corrective emotional experience that helped to resolve past pain.

Childbirth is not only a natural process, but it clearly is one of the most significant and all-encompassing experiences a woman will undergo. How is it that many women find themselves feeling more like spectators than stars of the show? How can women take control of their own bodies, making clear, informed decisions from the perspective not only of what is medically sound, but also of what intuitively rings true? Here are a few pointers:

- Inform yourself of your options in advance so that you can make your own choices rather than having them made for you.
- Consider whether alternative or complementary methods might enhance your experience of pregnancy and birth.
- Determine where you want to give birth: at a birthing center, a hospital, or at home.
- Decide who will oversee your pregnancy and delivery, and who will be present at the birth.
- Using what you've learned from prior experiences of pregnancy, labor, and delivery, as well as what you know about yourself physically and emotionally, what parts of the experience would you keep the same, and what would you like to change?

Twenty-Six Minutes
If we lack compelling rituals to mark pregnancy and childbirth when they unfold in a normal and predictable way, how much more difficult is it to mark—and just as importantly, to heal and move on from—those events that do not go according to plan? Often we find it hard even to talk about such problems, much less to dedicate any kind of ritual or ceremony to them. But those events need to be acknowledged as well. The traumatic aftermath following the birth of Jamie's child helped to teach her this lesson.

Two days after Jamie's daughter was born, she and her husband were informed that the baby had a hole in her heart. The pediatrician was optimistic; the problem was fixable. But when would it be fixed? How would it be fixed? There was no single solution and no timetable. So, instead of learning the new-mommy vocabulary of latch-on, colic, and breast pump, Jamie was consumed with the alien language of congestive heart failure, ventricular septal defect, and Tetralogy of Fallot.

"Somehow, through this bewildering fog came the calls of congratulations—and the cards, and the gifts, and the joy that everyone else was able to feel. All the while, my daughter's birth felt somehow incomplete. While I went through the motions of new motherhood, deep down I could not let go of the superstition I'd bowed to for the nine months I carried her, when I refrained from speaking her name aloud or bringing her baby things into the apartment. Now, even though she'd been born, I still felt deferential to fate, like she wasn't all mine.

"My daughter underwent heart surgery at thirteen weeks. If I thought labor was painful, it paled in comparison to signing the medical waiver and handing my ten-pound infant off to the anesthesiologist who would literally take my daughter's life into her hands.

"Afterward, the surgeon greeted us with good news. She had been on the heart bypass machine for only twenty-six minutes, he said. Nine months of gestation, twelve hours of labor, thirteen weeks of life, and it all came down to twenty-six minutes. When I held her in my arms for the first time in the cardiac intensive care unit, just as vulnerable as she was at the moment of her birth, it was as if the parallel moment three months earlier had never occurred. This felt like her true birth. There was only the triumphant gaze of her brown marble eyes and the relief that she had finally arrived.

"As her first birthday approached, I planned a birthday party, complete with a costumed Barney, a cake, and our friends and family. My daughter wore a pink sweater, ate cake, and laughed. But the first anniversary of her surgery went unmarked. My husband and I flirted with the idea of a party, but we were confounded by the logistics. What would the invitation say? Would people think it was strange? And so the date passed.

"But I haven't forgotten that celebration. My daughter's rebirth was private. I'm sure even the most devoted family members don't remember the date. And yet the anniversary deserves to be marked. I have to be patient, though. The one person who will surely celebrate with us has yet to know the story of her second journey. When she learns, we'll find a way to honor it together."

We are born once, physically. But that is not enough. Classically, the very idea of an initiation or rite of passage is that of a rebirth. But this time, the emphasis is on spiritual birth. Experiencing any life-altering event after which you are transformed or "born again" constitutes a rebirth. Such events may happen by design or by accident—after a physical trauma, for instance:

surviving a harrowing accident or surgery, emerging from a coma, or even having a near-death experience in which one momentarily dies and then returns. In Jamie's case, no conscious effort was made to plan an initiation of this kind. Rather, the necessities of life dictated a particular sequence of events. The spiritual rebirth that followed her baby's physical rebirth only added to the joyousness of the occasion.

The Day My World Changed

Consider this statistic: approximately 35 percent of all conceptions—a full third—do not result in birth. Sometimes problems occur in pregnancy and the longed-for healthy baby never arrives. Sometimes a woman finds herself pregnant when she doesn't want to be and chooses to terminate the pregnancy. In either case, the woman going through such a loss almost surely knows someone else who has had a similar experience. But miscarriage, stillbirth, and abortion have long gone unrecognized in our society. This difficult time is rarely shared, and that makes the experience even more difficult and painful. Often, too, such experiences go unresolved, leaving a residual psychological and emotional impact. The following story brings us a woman who has found her own way.

Terry is not exactly sure if this is a rite of passage she would have chosen, but it is one that changed her life profoundly. August 11, 1995, was the day she stopped thinking like a little girl and started feeling like a woman. It was the day she chose to have an abortion. Although she wanted a child more than anything, and still does, due to the circumstances of her own childhood, she promised herself at a very young age that she would never bring a child into the world if she knew that her relationship was not a lasting one. The man she was living with was not her other half; she had known this for a very long time. But the fear of not finding someone else kept her there, stuck.

"I remember waking up on August 11 and spending the morning talking to the being in my womb. I was explaining to her why I was doing what I was doing. I asked her to please come back when I was ready for such a responsibility—if I ever was. I cried, and yet I knew that the choice I was making was right for me. I shifted with this event. I changed from a scared little girl who was not taking responsibility for her life to a young woman who was. It did not feel good to have an abortion."

In fact, Terry still wonders if that opportunity was her first and last. Should she have had the baby and grown up along with it? Should she have simply gone for it? She wonders where she would be now if she had. She still doesn't know the answers to these questions. But she does know that the day she walked out of the clinic was the day she realized that all of her actions had consequences, good or bad. She knew she never wanted to make that mistake again, because, in spite of the fact that she never knew the little soul inside of her, she nonetheless missed her.

"Every August 11, I sit in silence for the soul I let go. It's a private day. I don't really like to talk about it, but I like to remember it. It keeps me centered on what kind of life I choose to lead, and on what kind of life and world I want to bring a child into. We often look back and wish a choice of some type did not have to be made, but I never look back with regret at the choice I made at twenty-five. It was not a choice I made lightly. It is a choice I honor and will always remember."

Most women do not view abortion as a form of birth control, but rather as a choice they must carefully debate within themselves. Even when the choice is clear, abortion is often accompanied by feelings of sadness, regret, and guilt. Some women feel the need to keep their predicament and decision to themselves. Others fear that they may be judged for their behavior. Most know that after an abortion they will forever carry the memory of what was not to be. Women who experience any kind of pregnancy loss should be encouraged to openly express their feelings. To expect a grieving woman to just "forget about it and move on" is not only unfeeling but is a sure-fire way to leave her unresolved and unhealed. If women can acknowledge such events in a supportive community or through the enactment of ritual, they can respectfully contain the event and perhaps find a sense of closure.

The benefits of using conscious ritual to honor the passages of pregnancy and childbirth are clear. Many women intuitively recognize the positive effects of such rituals, and researchers are likewise confirming them. In *Postpartum Mood Disorders*, edited by psychiatrist Laura J. Miller, it is strongly suggested that, although no direct link has been established between hormonal imbalances and postpartum depression (PPD), even when biological factors may contribute, there are other factors in some societies that seem to protect against PPD. In cultures where new mothers are cared for and supported by community members and relatives, and where rituals are well established, the prevalence of PPD is significantly less. Whether in normal or complicated childbirth, or in pregnancy that for whatever reason does not result in birth, ritual provides a context for recognizing and reflecting upon these powerful female transformations. In this way, it offers a bridge to a time when the initiation of childbirth and its link to the Feminine was simply the way of the world. How much more empowering it is to view conception and birth as part of a woman's great life journey instead of as a punishment or a purely scientific phenomenon. If we can reclaim the marvel of birth, restoring it to its honored place as a sacred rite of passage, perhaps we can learn once again to respect all of life.

Mothering

Giving birth is a dramatic event that instantly separates a woman's life into before and after, but the day-to-day events that turn a woman into a mother are equally significant, if not ultimately more so. Recently, I overheard two young mothers waiting in line for coffee talking about a friend who was about to become a mother for the first time. "She thinks the ultimate challenge, the thing to really gear up for, is labor and delivery. Just wait until she gets home and the *real* fun begins." Peals of laughter followed.

Nothing can fully prepare a woman for being a mother. No amount of reading or research or observation or discussion with women who are already mothers can adequately convey the power of the experience. The joy, the high, and the gratification combine with the unprecedented level of physical stress and strain, creating an overwhelming environment on all fronts. And then there are the hormones. After conception, a woman's normal monthly hormonal cycle shifts in order to sustain the pregnancy. After delivery, the dramatic hormonal shift back to a normal cycle often shocks a woman's emotional core and adds to the stress of the new experience.

Yet the ability to mother is as much an instinctual skill as it is an acquired one. In a recent conversation with a young woman who had just given birth to her second child, the subject of instinct arose. She recalled a *National Geographic* episode where, remarkably, a mother penguin was able to instinctively locate her own baby out of thousands. For humans, as well, the mothering instinct seems to kick in automatically the moment a woman gives birth. From the first smell and the first cry, each baby's uniqueness is imprinted upon its mother—a permanent connection, an extraordinary bond. Instinct is a natural reflex and is a necessity for survival in the animal world. Why have humans lost touch with this native ability? What can motherhood teach us about reconnecting with it and utilizing its power?

Extraordinary Ordinary Moments

Eve was an unlikely mother—a woman who had planned to remain childless. A stormy relationship with her mother had left Eve unsure of her own nurturing abilities, so no one was more surprised than she was when a latent nurturing instinct awakened within her and made her change her mind.

Bearing a child reconnected her with still more of her basic instincts, which she used as building blocks to master the art of mothering.

"I grew up knowing that I would never be a mother. Perhaps because I felt such a lack of love from my parents, I was certain that I would never take on the role myself. As a child, I was frequently told that I was selfish and incapable of thinking about anyone but myself. This, in itself, may be part of a good definition of being a child. As I got older, this comment continued to plague me. Being a parent seemed such a huge responsibility, and my fear that I could not meet the challenges made me sure of my decision. But eventually my idea of myself shifted; my self-esteem grew, opportunities arose, and love came into my life. I began to feel the nurturing, loving, and supportive nature that lived inside of me."

Finally, it seemed that everything had shifted. Every baby seemed compellingly beautiful, and Eve found herself asking every question about them she could think of. She became intensely focused on working through all of her fears of motherhood. And then she became pregnant. Recognizing the difference between instantly becoming a biological parent and the gradual unfolding of true motherhood, Eve studied the task at hand. Her father recalled that as a baby, Eve would watch her older sister, figure out how to do something, and then master it. Faced with the idea of becoming a mother, it seemed as if she was trying to master parenting in the same way.

Eve's delivery was fast (five hours) and painful—"fast and furious," her husband called it. When the midwife told her it was time to push, Eve didn't feel the time was right to deliver her baby. No one had ever suggested to her that a first-time labor could be less than eight hours. Still, she pushed. After five minutes, the midwife gave the okay to let the baby be born. Eve still didn't feel that the moment was right; nonetheless, she reached deep inside herself, let go of her idea of "delivery readiness," and pushed the baby out.

"She was purple, then instantly pink, and when my husband and I pulled her up on my belly, she pushed up onto her arms and looked me squarely in the eyes. I was in love."

Later on, Eve realized that she had subverted her own instincts by listening to the midwife. She had suffered unusually bad tearing in delivery because her tissues hadn't had the time they needed to stretch. The healing process afterward was exceptionally long. Her instincts had informed her that she was not ready, that the baby was fine, and that there was no reason to rush. But the voice of authority had prevailed.

"I learned my lesson that day. In the months that followed, my instincts told me a lot about what my baby needed, and that voice became the voice of my mothering. The extraordinary ordinary moments of my days are what I notice now: the look in Ella's eyes when she laughs, my husband's voice when he is playing with her, the sound of my own laughter filling the air. Sometimes it's as if time stands still and there is nothing but the beauty of the moment."

But the challenges, too, are moment to moment and ongoing: learning patience, finding composure, letting frustration go, and learning to be present even when exhausted. Eve recalls that on days when she felt utterly depleted, when nothing would seem to stop Ella's crying, Eve became scared and insecure. This fear created a distance between mother and child, a negative spiral that was palpable and daunting. "The more I feared her crying, the more she cried, and the more I could feel myself wanting to withdraw. Now I could really understand some of my own mother's feelings about parenting. How terrible it felt to be powerless to help."

As Eve grew to know her daughter, and as Ella began to relate to Eve, a new opening occurred. On good days, Eve was able to feel a tremendous flow of unconditional love and support emanating from within herself, no matter how much her daughter cried. Eventually, they settled into a little relationship of smiles, games, giggles, and finally hugs. Eve says that she has never felt so necessary, important, or useful. Her life now has a purpose beyond her own needs, and she defines this life as the most inspiring, trying, and fulfilling one she can possibly imagine.

"I was not aware of feeling that I was becoming a mother, but I do feel that I am one now. When Ella was born, I loved her instantly, on some biological, primitive level. But she was also a stranger to me. I felt an odd kind of distance, knowing that I loved her for no reason except that when she looked at me, something inside me melted. Now I am thoroughly enjoying her unfolding. I look into her eyes and see the young woman she will someday become, and I look forward to meeting her. As we celebrate her first birthday, a part of me feels that this is *my* first birthday—that some new part of me has been born into the world and is taking shape, just as she is. Together, we are growing."

Eve's story not only encompasses many components of a woman's life as it unfolds to meet new roles and challenges, but it holds valuable insights and lessons as well. Eve was surprised to discover how naturally mothering came to her. And whatever she needed that *didn't* come naturally, she picked up along the way. She learned to trust her inner knowing, to combine it with knowledge gained from experience, and to utilize these tools in every aspect of her life. Inner wisdom reveals itself in many ways. For Eve, subverting her intuition during delivery caused her physical problems down the line and taught her to heed her inner voice. Learn to size up people and situations using both modes of knowing: the one, engaging the mind and senses and interacting with the outside world, and the other, tuned in to an inner sensory awareness—one's intuitive knowing. Learning to access these two kinds of knowing will set you on the path of greatest knowledge, allowing you to view the world more completely, and helping you to make sound decisions and healthy choices.

Healing

Rites heal more effectively than they cure. . . . Cured you are fixed; healed you are reconnected.

—Ronald Grimes, *Deeply into the Bone*

Accidents, illnesses, and other traumatic experiences will inevitably find their way into most of our lives. But this fact of life is not all bad. A physical crisis can also be a healing crisis, a pivotal time to enact a rite of passage, or a period in one's life that may itself become a rite of passage. An acute illness or accident often forces us to take a "time-out" from life. Some believe that in our natural drive toward wholeness, illness arrives to teach us lessons, to release long-held energy patterns that are blocking our progress. Unable to work or relate in the usual way, dependent on others, in pain or discomfort, we typically have far more time than usual to contemplate our lives. As we heal, we may find that the routines of our existence are drastically altered. Or we may return to our normal routines only to find ourselves facing radical shifts in consciousness. We may see our prior lives anew and find them no longer acceptable, appropriate, or useful. Moving toward wholeness, we often change our situations—our jobs, homes, or relationships—to reconnect with aspects of ourselves that had been dormant, or to pursue avenues that we had not sought or known before.

When a doctor becomes a patient, the shift in consciousness may well begin on the examining table. In my own story that follows, a physical crisis triggered a sudden clarity about my priorities in the practical sphere. And my friends in the healing professions delivered support and small miracles that kept me in touch with the whole of me: mind, body, and spirit.

Reweaving My Health, with a Little Help from My Friends

Although a physician, I am first and foremost a woman. Before I could come to grips with being on the receiving end of a serious diagnosis, I had to learn to put away my medical thinking cap and allow myself to be present for the process unfolding before me—I was a human being struggling with a health crisis.

I remember staring into the mirror at myself in the dressing room of the radiologist's office and vowing that I would live, no matter what that meant. I had just been told that the classic picture of DCIS (ductal carcinoma in situ) had unquestionably shown up on my mammogram. This is a very early radiological finding that signifies a change in the cells of the breast, indicating the precondition before cancer as a mass or tumor actually appears. I was in shock. Every cell of my body seemed to be screaming, "*Me?! How could this be happening to me?!*" There was no family history, no prior complications. In a matter of a few short minutes, everything I knew to be true and valid in my life totally overshadowed all the petty garbage that I had somehow thought was important. I got completely clear about what I needed to do and immediately launched into "taking-care-of-business" mode. I also told myself that if I had to lose a breast in order to live, that was a no-brainer.

The next several days and weeks were dedicated to covering all my bases, both traditional and complementary, in order to ensure my health and a successful outcome. Before a lumpectomy and subsequent radiation therapy, which I would eventually undergo, I had other things to do. I am a firm believer that mind, body, and spirit function as a unity. The question was how to honor and balance each of them and to find a way to effectively integrate them for my highest good. As a physician, I understood the problem, but I still sought to fully educate myself before I made my decisions. So much for the body. The mind was still struggling; it seemed stuck somewhere in the middle, not totally grasping the reality, and yet acting as if I fully understood and knew what to do. My spirit told me to give my mind a break, that faith inevitably fills in all the places that elude logic, the things we cannot wrap our brains around.

I asked two healers for help. My friend Ann, a fine therapist who is committed to alternative/complementary healing, asked if she could work on my body through energy work. I was delighted and extremely appreciative. We worked in her home, in her daughter Robin's room. Robin had passed away several years before from a progressive genetic disease that finally overtook her body. Her spirit was there till the end of her life, providing comfort and wisdom to her mother. On that day, Robin was there for me, too. I told this to Ann. The healing was very powerful; there was a palpable energetic shift. As we talked about it afterward, I told Ann that I felt as if a piece of gauzelike material had been laid over the left side of my chest and was energetically reweaving the distorted blueprint that was my cellular disease.

Ann drove me back to my house, where I spotted an unfamiliar car in the driveway—unfamiliar until I saw the license plate: HEAL 1. I knew it was my friend Nigel, then a lay healer and director of the Oratory of the Little Way, a nondenominational retreat center in Connecticut, now an ordained father continuing his healing ministry at Christ the King Spiritual Life Center in Greenwich, New York. He had gotten the message that I was looking for his help. Strangely, I had first met Ann while having a lively (and rather loud) conversation about spirit and healing with Nigel. We were in a local bookstore. Ann just came up to us and introduced herself, comfortably chiming in on our talk. Here at my home, they again greeted each other.

When Ann left, Nigel asked me how I was feeling, what exactly the problem was, and how I was coping with it. I filled him in on the necessary information, giving him enough background to help with my healing. Before he began, he said, "Wait, I have something for you." He reached into his pocket and produced several small gauze squares, handkerchiefs blessed by the archbishop. This is what was inscribed upon them: "God did extraordinary miracles through Paul. Handkerchiefs that had touched him were taken to the sick, and their illnesses were cured" (Acts 19:12). I was astonished, but not surprised. God does work in mysterious ways, and for me, very often through very literal (and often humorous) images. I told Nigel what I had envisioned with Ann. He said, "Then it's done already."

While this part of my healing was done, there was more to follow. I did have a lumpectomy and radiation, followed by a five-year course of Tamoxifen, a medication that blocks the multiplication of estrogen-stimulated cancer cells. That's pretty standard. My own belief is that both forms of treatment are vital. Many people never look beyond traditional medicine. They may heal physically, but other parts of their beings are left behind while their bodies make the passage. Some people insist on having *only* alternative treatment—and sadly, some of them suffer and die. There are miracles some of the time. For me, the "before and after" really hit home when I looked at myself in the mirror. In a few seconds, I weeded out what was important to me and what was definitely not. Although I was in a vulnerable position, my strength came from expanding my identification of self with more than just my body. At the same time, I understood the necessity of having a healthy body and, if I had to, of getting rid of the part that was diseased. I developed a very healthy respect for how the body serves as the vehicle for our essence, the shell that enables us to live out who we are.

If you are facing a serious illness, here are some pointers to help you approach your situation with greater knowledge and control. If you have a loved one who is facing this challenge, consider passing these tips along:

- Tap into your intuitive wisdom about what is most essential to you and your life. Journaling, meditation, or just sitting alone and reflecting may help you do so. Make a list of all the elements that are "nonnegotiables"—anything you deem vital and necessary to consider in taking charge of your healing.
- Clean out your mental closet, discarding all things you no longer need. Lightening your burden can open up a space to think more clearly, free of ideas that confuse and distract.
- Create a plan, a timetable on paper, to organize what you need to do for every aspect of your treatment. How will you ensure that you and your family are cared for while you are recuperating? How can you incorporate into your plans any new insights about the way you choose to live your life moving forward?
- Find ways to strengthen yourself prior to treatment. If alternative healing methods resonate with you—meditation tapes, relaxation and visualization techniques, acupuncture, bodywork, hypnosis, or others— integrate them into your treatment. Enlist the services of dedicated practitioners and doctors for all forms of treatment that you choose.
- Don't let pride, embarrassment, or other such responses stand in the way of your seeking help. Create a network of close friends and family that you can readily count on, those who respect your wishes and decisions completely.

There Are No Accidents
Coincidence or synchronicity? Whatever you believe, life created its own rite of passage for Karen, complete with separation, isolation (with time to reflect), and healing to a higher level of being and consciousness. A serious accident created a pause in Karen's routine that ultimately propelled her into a fulfilling career and life change.

Several years prior to the accident, Karen was irritated and discontent with her job. She was too innovative and independent for the corporate culture within a large architectural firm. Her creative attributes and her quest to improve processes did not bring her rewards. One boss literally said, "You are not a sheep," implying that she didn't fit the mold. In a rage after the ridiculous comment, Karen packed up her desk and planned to quit the next day. She decided to sleep on her decision. When the anger subsided, she realized that quitting her job was not in her best interest. It would only benefit her boss. Karen knew that she would like to start her own business. She began to develop a plan and decided to stay in the firm to get additional training. "I realized that the firm had so much to offer, so I decided to stay and learn about the business before making my departure."

When her ski accident occurred two years later, all focus for Karen was directed at healing her leg. She was required to take a few months off work for physical therapy following her surgery. The separation and focus on healing created a surprising outcome. Karen's goals became very clear. She realized that her long-term plan was ready for implementation. When she returned to work, Karen went back as a part-time employee. She loved working for herself. As Karen approached her fortieth birthday, she was ready to lose the crutch of the company and be fully self-employed. Her fear was overpowered by the desire to be independent.

The shift in daily routine created by the accident was the key to being able to focus inwardly in order to discover a happier life. Turning forty was the final push for Karen to leap into her new future. Karen has never regretted her decision and has successfully been self-employed for twelve years.

If you have had a serious accident or illness, consider what the injury or disease might personally represent to you. In Karen's story, her leg injury prevented her from "running away" from a major life decision. Some believe that physical ailments are outward manifestations of diseases of the spirit. After all, doesn't the body mirror the complexity of everything that makes us uniquely ourselves? However, never accept blame for an illness or accident. It's not about finding fault with yourself or your beliefs—working with spirit excludes guilt and judgment. Rather, pursue your own highest good by accessing what you already know and what you discover along the way.

Why do we wait for change in our lives to come "accidentally"? Consider committing to a scheduled time-out—daily, weekly, or monthly—a time to check in with yourself, consciously creating a space to develop and focus your intention. This might include a daily fifteen minutes to journal or to sit and reflect upon what the day holds for you; a weekly date with yourself to observe and analyze the themes and patterns in your life; or a monthly day off where you turn off the phone, clear away social responsibilities, and focus purposefully on your path, engaging in activities that nurture your spirit. Giving yourself these private focused times will allow your internal creativity to dawn and may help you avoid "rude awakenings."

Guiding

Although no longer a taboo topic, our understanding of the complex process of menopause is still incomplete. Just a generation ago, we were still in the dark ages when it came to women's changing physiology, especially those shifts signaling the end of the childbearing years. "The change" was often thought to signal, as well, a decline into the final stage of life. Menopause was a thing to be endured. Little was shared about it, and there was little to do about it. But with increases in life expectancy, as well as extensive research and technological advances in women's physiology and health in general, we've come to at least a better understanding of what menopause is and what it is not.

Very simply, menopause can be thought of as the cessation of menstruation. But rather than a single point in time, it represents the end of a complex, gradual process that signals the end of ovarian function. For most women, the process extends over several years. We now know that menopause is not just about age. We also know that although there are common changes that many women share, each woman's physiology will determine her own experience of this biological process and its accompanying life-cycle dynamics. Genetics, metabolism, and lifestyle, as well as beliefs and attitudes, will influence and color each woman's experience.

How can we reframe menopause in a way that is contemporary and constructive for women, a way that inspires confidence and creativity as we move forward in our lives? Now that menopause has come out of the closet and stepped into the light of day, women have a broadened perspective of themselves. There's a whole new second half of life to look forward to, that much more time to ourselves, free of the call of our biology. Menopause is a time to look inward, to return to ourselves, to give ourselves the attention that, as caretakers and nurturers, we have given to others for much of our lives. The period often brings a rebirth to a fuller expression of ourselves—a "coalescence," as Sheehy describes it, the mirror image of adolescence. The gift of menopause, then, is a renewal to a higher purpose that encourages us to become, as Joseph Campbell says, "life-fostering and life-guiding."

Kismet's Dance

As always, the sharing of stories goes a long way, educating, supporting, and connecting women to each other. Meredith was a lifelong dancer who did not take easily to the changes that "snuck up" on her body. When it came to the physical, she was accustomed to being in total control. But looking back from this vantage point, it seems that the threads that held her life together were being woven by a grander hand.

"I used to imagine that someday my great-great-grandchildren would take a magical journey up the attic steps to a dusty old trunk, where they would find sparkling, shimmering, fascinating costumes, beads, and coins and veils, along with a very mystical, ancient photo of me—great-great-grandmother as Kismet. This would bring a smile to my lips, as I knew they would think, "*There was a life lived!*"

"I have always loved to dance. As far back as I remember, the joy of 'being in my body' has always been with me. All I know of love and beauty, spirituality and God, has come from my body. It is this intimacy with Nature itself that I honor. It is this intimacy with the divine spark within that has brought me glory and humility."

Meredith's parents encouraged her self-expression. She studied ballet, jazz, and even tap dancing. In high school, the budding student journalists captioned her yearbook photo, "Come Dance with Me." In a family of doctors, she became a teacher with a double master's degree in art and education, earning straight A's and a fellowship. Eventually, she taught fitness and dance.

She married young for love and had two children that she truly wanted. "Natural childbirth and nursing deepened my soul's connection to my body as an instrument of divine expression. I say that the universe borrowed my body to bring forth life. It was, at the time, the most spiritual event I had known."

Although her first husband was brilliant, sensitive, and charismatic, he was also unfaithful. They tried to hold the marriage together, sacrificing their principles "for the sake of the children." Meanwhile, Meredith found solace in becoming Kismet, the beloved one, through Oriental dance. Putting on Cleopatra-like makeup and adorning ancient costumes allowed her to become the veiled beauty who was one with the dance, one with feminine power and grace. Meredith thought belly dancing was fantastically seductive, but what she really learned was that Mother Nature herself was the great seductress. This seduction was not about being a sex object or luring men; it was about the great power of the Feminine.

After twelve years of being a single parent, love came her way again. Only this time, her husband-to-be was brilliant, sensitive, charming, and filled with integrity. Over the years, Meredith's dancing transformed into fitness; her rich career expanded to include owning a fitness studio, where her daughter taught classes and her son worked the front desk and played drums for special workshops. Meredith taught her students the "Sacred Wild

Woman Dance," a compilation of what she had learned about women and movement, even teaching instructors across the country and in Italy. She noticed the hunger in all women as she initiated their remembrance of the feminine legacy we all share.

"Then this rite of passage snuck up on me. This one was different. I thought I had power and control—and then I couldn't sleep at night. Teaching fitness got harder; my whole system seemed to slow down. I spent one Mother's Day reading my children's baby books and crying that they would never be little again. My libido, my all-time connection to truth and life, was lessening. My breasts were becoming bigger and my shape more curvaceous. Who was I in this sauna of a hot flash? If I was not body beautiful, the sexy alluring lover, what was I? I saw images of flowering fallopians dying on the vine, once beautiful, now aging, once fertile, now self-contained. The *change* could not be happening to me!" Meredith talked, wrote poems, talked, meditated, cried, talked, published articles, danced, read, and talked until she was tired of listening to herself. If she took hormones, would she risk breast cancer? If not, would she die of a heart attack? She decided to stay the natural course.

One evening, her husband asked her what was going on. Why was she so different? "All I could scream, through tears and shame, was that *I am not doing this. This is happening to me.* This menopause was a spiritually profound and heavy rite of passage, long and hard, an arduous process of learning to love and cultivate my inner soul, my loving kindness instead of the physical. Could I be loved for my essential self? It all comes together now. Using a yoga analogy, the love energy travels up from the sexual chakra into the heart chakra. I can now love more with my heart."

And what of these hot flashes? she wonders. They are wake-up calls to herald the coming of the next great transformation: death. We lose youth and youth's beauty, and as we experience loss, we may also move toward losing inhibition, anger, and fear. This is a great letting go, not because we are so evolved, but because we have no choice but to surrender.

For Meredith, to be a recipient of such great wisdom—to know secrets only women can know—is a precious thing. Women, the keepers of soulful connection, are called upon to notice soul beauty. "We who know life within us must give birth to beauty and love. It is a deep primal rhythm of cycles and circles to experience with other women and to share with men. My body once again teaches spirit. This dance of menopause transcends, like all great art. It transcends the natural world, the nature of sex, not for procreation, fun, or even love of two, but sacred sex for the union of souls with the

Divine—a practice of acceptance and compassion. Once again, the universe borrowed my body to teach that it brings forth not only life, but love, a gentle and all-forgiving love, one that reminds me to honor my mother and father; to love my daughters and son and their spouses in a wiser and less possessive way; to share and learn from my husband, a great teacher of love himself; to dance with women celebrating our secret experiences of change; and to honor God in my every breath, my every breath until the last.

"A peek into the future—up the attic stairs, into the dusty trunk—little hands open the creaky heavy lid, discovering treasures of their legacy. Did I tell you that in the ancient photo of Kismet, she is smiling? She sees the love and light in her great-great-grandchildren's eyes."

The three-part notion of the female life cycle—menarche, childbirth, and menopause—is clearly a thing of the past. Modern times have brought about changes in women's physiology. It has been proposed that with the advent of electricity, an increased exposure to light, especially over the course of the last century, has had the effect of lowering the production of melatonin, which in turn has been implicated in the much earlier onset of puberty than in past generations. In addition, the average life span increased by approximately thirty years from 1900 to the present. Then, too, radical changes in the fields of female reproduction and female physiology and endocrinology have broadened a woman's perspective on, and involvement in, each key phase of her life cycle. New and sophisticated methods of birth control have helped women make decisions about if and when to have children, and in vitro fertilization has given women the opportunity to have children when they otherwise would have been unable. Some scholars have suggested the introduction of a new phase between the mothering years and elderhood, and indeed many women seem to be living that. Menopause, the passage once suffered in silence, is being talked about, is eased through medical options, and is celebrated as a time of new vitality and possibility.

It is up to each of us to take responsibility for ourselves, to manage our own physical and emotional health and well-being. That we now have the freedom to make our own choices, and a wealth of information to help us make those choices, is an empowering tool for our personal growth. But woman-to-woman guidance and mentoring still lies at the heart of successful passage making. Being encouraged, learning confidence, developing pride, and gaining an ease to comfortably live in our bodies across all the stages of our lives—these valued gifts are passed down through generations of family and community and serve as the basis for a healthy perception of the emerging self.

Body Sense

Know thy body self. If we knew as much about our bodies as we choose to know about our car, flat-screen TV, cell phone, or any of the myriad consumer items available to us, we'd be in great shape. Unfortunately, many of us don't. There seems to be an aversion in our culture to getting up close and personal with our own particulars—or perhaps we are just lazy. How can we care for our most precious possession without knowing its essentials? Why leave the job to outside experts? With the wealth of sources available today—books, videos, workshops, newsletters, and the Internet—there's no excuse not to be informed. Remember, too, that since a number of women's health issues have a genetic component, family history is another vital source.

Listen to the messages of the body. Learn how to detect and decipher the nuances of what your body is telling you. Each new phase of the biological life cycle brings new gifts and challenges. Tuning in to the messages that our ever-evolving bodies send us often provides valuable information, helping us to intuit the most healthful response to the situation at hand. The more we practice this principle, the more we become in touch with our own internal wisdom.

Balance the body's instinctual wisdom with acquired knowledge. Intelligence lies not just within the realm of the brain, but everywhere within our bodies, all the way down to the cellular level. Every experience, every interaction we have, is locked within our bodies. Bodywork and other nontalk modalities may help us access vital information about ourselves that the mind alone cannot reach. One mode of knowing, without the other, presents a lopsided perspective. Honoring and balancing both will ensure that our best efforts for maintaining and developing our whole selves are put forward.

Move with grace into each new stage of life. Every phase of the life cycle is a gift. Learn to appreciate the unique benefits of each of them. Staying vested in past life stages—trying to look and act sixteen when you are actually sixty, for example—not only distorts the sense of the emerging self but hampers our movement forward developmentally. Getting stuck in a physical time warp prevents us from performing the mental, emotional, and spiritual tasks appropriate to, and necessary for, the evolving self.

Celebrate your body's passages; don't just "endure" them. Women's relationships with themselves are multifactored and are not dictated by biology and hormones alone. Attitudes and beliefs about women's roles as they unfold through the life cycle vary greatly from culture to culture and strongly influence how women view themselves. Take a positive attitude about each of your body's passages. Drive away old stereotypes and rejoice in the Feminine. Surround yourself with healthy, natural women who do the same.

Embrace body diversity. The human body, our precious house, comes in many shapes and forms. Why do we continue to squeeze ourselves into society's often wildly unrealistic notions of how women's bodies should look and move? Where would we be without the advances in cultural, racial, and sexual diversity that we've only just begun to make? If each of us embraces body diversity, perhaps we can herald the same kind of advances in our attitudes about the human form.

CHAPTER THREE

Passages of the Self

There is just one life for each of us: our own.

—Euripides

He who knows others is learned;
He who knows himself is wise.

—Lao-tzu, *Tao Te Ching*

Life's big events are not always dictated by our bodies. Birthdays, graduations, and marriages, and personal milestones and achievements such as establishing a new home or restoring a key relationship, also stand among life's great passages. With passages of the self, more than with other types of passages, determining which events hold the greatest significance for us and deciding how to honor them is often a highly personal and idiosyncratic matter. So the responsibility for many passages of the self falls solely to the individual. Because of this, these passages offer perhaps the greatest opportunity for self-definition and self-discovery.

This chapter introduces women whose lives have been transformed by a wide range of events and achievements over the course of the life cycle, from coming into adulthood through community service work, to leaving home, to creating a personalized ceremony of commitment through marriage, to reuniting with a long-lost parent or child, to celebrating milestone birthdays, to honoring one's material and spiritual ideals by creating a home that reflects them.

These life events are described through words that connote activity, highlighting the notion that these transitions can just passively *happen* to us, but they require our active participation in order for them to be truly transforming. They are *emerging* (coming of age, coming into one's own); *merging* (marriage, or the forging of a significant life relationship); *reuniting* and *reconnecting* (finding and reestablishing a long-ago-severed blood tie); *celebrating* and *honoring* milestone events; and *achieving* (acknowledging accomplishments and marking personal growth).

As a young psychiatrist over twenty-five years ago, I was under the simplistic and rather naive impression that most of the work of therapy was accomplished during regular prescribed sessions. Over the years, I've learned that while many of these weekly, or more, sojourns into the terrain of the psyche may prove to be productive, rendering important information and essential insights, many others will seem to be not much more than interesting conversations. Often, individuals think therapy is the hour-long session, once or more a week. Some individuals even feel that this is all that is expected of them or that they are willing to do, and yet they have the expectation that this should be enough to bring about life-altering changes.

One of the major goals and tasks of the therapeutic process, the hallmark of all effective treatment, is to establish and sustain a healthy working alliance. The conflicts and crises that have initially brought an individual into the therapeutic setting and have served as catalysts for change eventually give way to the real heart of the matter—the confrontation with the emerging self. Who we are is why we see things the way we do. What presents itself to us in the course of living may be viewed by some as challenges and opportunities, while others may see the very same things as obstacles or as encounters to be painfully endured. That the self will emerge with or without the benefit of a therapeutic experience is inevitable. But a heightened awareness, a conscious knowledge of our own unfolding evolution, may help increase the possibility for transformation.

Beyond being listener, witness, interpreter, repository of secrets, sharer of sacred stories, and provider of hopefully valuable insights, I've learned that the best I can do to serve individuals is to offer them as many effective and practical tools as possible to help them not just cope but also manage and resolve current issues and problems, as well as those that will inevitably arise in the future.

In my efforts to understand the impossibly complex workings of the psyche, I've searched for the lowest common denominator, that which would seem to explain behavioral and emotional patterns that are universal to all humans. That rites of passage have existed for centuries in virtually every culture, appearing without influence from outside sources, embraces this commonality, this ordering mechanism generated and stored within the collective unconscious, emblematic of our species. This, then, is the basic road map, setting each of us on our course for the journey of a lifetime. This system provides an essentially necessary framework that helps us as individuals to effectively contain our life within the context of the social order in which we will inevitably find ourselves.

But what of the self, that unique essence of our being that distinguishes us from any other human who has ever lived? How do we understand our personal significance in the world, and how do we place our own special mark upon it? How do we imbue our existence with our own sensibility and style? How do we express this evolving self in our own exquisite and elegant way? For women, this process of discovery and the emerging of self has been doubly challenging. Ownership of the self for women was strongly discouraged, and even forbidden, over the course of centuries, since self, for women, traditionally meant assuming roles dictated by, and in the service of, the existing sociopolitical and religious institutions.

In *Women Who Run with the Wolves*, Estes notes that, having swallowed society's sleeping pill up until quite recently, women had been sleepwalking through their lives, only appearing aware and awake as they went through the motions of living. Like popular fairy tales, women had been in a state of "psychic slumber," literally asleep or locked away in some tower, waiting patiently to be rescued. Exercising powerful survival skills behaviorally, women learned more appropriate ways to act in society, and within the family, to ensure continued survival. This survival mode became the state of women's being over centuries. Over time, women learned to craft clever masks suitable for playing the roles they assumed, ensuring that the beauty of their true faces would remain hidden, especially from themselves.

By recognizing the importance of marking significant life passages that are individually and collectively meaningful, and by mindfully creating conscious rituals that honor and celebrate the unique progress of their lives, women today are becoming more fully present to themselves. The simple act of participating actively in our own lives is a giant step toward taking back personal responsibility for how we choose to live, with whom we choose to share our experiences, and for how we choose to define ourselves in our community and in our world. As women do this more for themselves, they will look far less to society to define their initiations and validate their roles.

Emerging

Puberty rites have traditionally marked a dramatic, life-altering change in status. The young person goes through the initiatory ordeal before assuming the identity of a full-fledged member of the tribe or community and becoming an adult. For many cultures, the onset of puberty is the signal of this transition. I want to emphasize this shift in status beyond its biological component by referring to it as coming of age. This broadens the definition and takes into account that, for humans, the adolescent-to-adult passage may take many years to be completed, if it ever truly is. Clearly, it is far more than biology that guides a person's development into mature, responsible adulthood.

The move from childhood to adulthood is one of the most important rites, since it creates a blueprint for responsibility, not only for the self but for the community. Once a child is successfully initiated and welcomed into the community, she or he assumes the status of a healthy, productive, creative adult in a dynamically effective group. But what if the culture doesn't provide the crucial rites of passage for people of all ages, especially for youngsters who so desperately need these springboards to soul growth?

Joseph Campbell and Bill Moyers asked, "What would you find in a society that no longer embraces a powerful mythology?"[1] They strongly suggest that violence and destructive acts would prevail because young people haven't been taught how to behave, and haven't learned their place, within a structured society. "Society has provided them no rituals by which they become members of the tribe, of the community. All children need to be twice born, to learn to function rationally in the present world, leaving childhood behind."[2]

Anthropologist Margaret Mead correlated culture's failure to incorporate effective rites of passage with an increase in social pathology. With an increased need for psychiatric intervention in adolescence, it has been suggested that "serious rites of passage, particularly around puberty and during adolescence, offer healing potentials that are yet inadequately explored."[3]

Creating adolescent rites of passage may encompass selected challenges over a period of time (often a year leading up to an actual celebratory event), a crucial time that marks the transition for the young person. These may include community service, visiting the elderly, helping someone learn to read, collecting money for charity, sponsoring a child in need, creating a family tree or participating in family celebrations, taking a physical challenge such as a vision quest, being welcomed into a group of adults and elders, and countless others.

Recently, in preparation for her change in status within her religious community, Danielle, with the support and encouragement of her mother (who just a few years ago herself chose to retroactively perform this same rite) began participating in community service projects. Both Danielle and her brother have helped their mother deliver food baskets on significant holidays to area residents who could not afford to buy themselves food for the holiday. This proved to be an enlightening experience for Danielle, who quickly realized that not everyone lives the way she does.

"Further opening my eyes was helping to run the Wish Workshop during the holiday season. This project allowed us to anonymously answer letters to Santa asking for holiday gifts. Instead of asking for an X-Box or more Barbie dolls, many children asked for warm clothing for the winter. I helped with organizing the hundreds of letters and shopping for gifts for many of the families. One letter we chose to answer was from a boy who asked only for new sneakers because his had huge holes in them and he was teased every day in school."

Danielle found the time to volunteer at a youth center for underprivileged children on Mondays after school. "This is a place where children who don't have enough money to eat are fed, and where those who are not shown love are nurtured." Along with some friends, she also raised money for multiple sclerosis during a five-mile walk. Danielle still helps her mother with two charities that provide shelter to victims of domestic violence.

I particularly loved hearing Danielle tell the story of how her mother had signed her up to volunteer for the local Special Olympics. Not knowing much about it initially, she was less than enthusiastic about participating. But the job of official "hugger" at the finish line quickly changed her mind. The sheer delight and joy on the faces of those who had just successfully finished the race melted her heart. Her small act of generosity that day had meant so much to so many. Danielle plans on continuing community service into her future life.

Leaving Childhood Behind

Any transition that marks a change in status or identity, separating the life already known from the life that is yet to come, is a perfect time to reflect upon the meaning and the consequences of the decisions and choices made up until that point in time. More specifically, for the period of coming of age, that often-rocky transition from adolescence to adulthood, it is also a time to reflect on how essential guidance is to the growth and healthy development of a child. By giving our children roots, we actually give them wings.

Beyond celebrations of achievement and accomplishment, graduations are just those kinds of events that literally separate one's life into a before and after. The symbolic act of moving a tassel from one side of the required graduate headgear, the mortarboard, to the other signifies the magical moment of change. Graduating from high school was an intense and unanticipated rite of passage for Arielle. The gradual movement toward completion of this phase of her life did not prepare her adequately for the swell of emotion that actually consumed her on that day, and for months afterward.

Her school did provide symbolic traditions for graduating seniors, most especially the "egg drop" project. The idea was to create any object you desired from only three allowable materials: toothpicks, tissue paper, and glue. The object was then released from the roof of the school—with an egg in it. Since for Arielle, flowers had always symbolized her own creativity, she elected once again to use this as the theme of her project. While she enjoyed flowers, she consciously understood that after this event, she was done with them as a symbol of herself. By the way, she did win best in show, and the egg did not break!

"Thinking about graduation, I'd actually been anticipating this shift for about a year. Having a lot of older friends has helped me see their lifestyles, what they're doing after high school. Inch by inch, I've been trying to push toward freedom at home—a later curfew, not always telling my parents where I'm going. Looking forward to college means not having that wall in front of me anymore.

"The graduation ceremony felt like the end; it was one of the scariest days of my life, the last day I'd be in a room with all my classmates. We've all gone through so much together. It's a very bizarre feeling, almost surreal, to be finished with it. I'll be with new people in college, but I don't think it will be the same."

Arielle knows that she's really quite lucky to be going off to the unknown realm of college with a strong foundation, having been reared in a home where there was always a very real commitment to helping others. "Growing up in a house like mine, I was able to open my heart, to see that we really are all the same. Consequently, I am someone who is deeply annoyed by stereotypes, thinking that if someone is stereotyped, they run the risk of making it a self-fulfilling prophesy, actually becoming the stereotype. One place where I've seen similarities is at the Kids Who Care summer camp for performing arts. Kids from around the world attend, and we all get along really well, sharing our experiences, always coming to greater understandings of the world. The arts can break down stereotypes. Seeing a person's gifts somehow makes it seem that if this person has this kind of talent, they must be okay."

In addition, Arielle cofounded a Model United Nations project while in high school. "We learned about the world through researching and talking to people from all over. This, I feel, is the antidote to hatred and bigotry in the world." Her parents founded a not-for-profit organization called We Care USA, which sparked Arielle's interest and involvement. This organization sends essential goods such as clothing, toys, school and sports equipment, and much more to refugee camps. Arielle helped out with typing, organizing, and packing boxes. She relates that she had these toys that she loved as a child, and so she thought very hard before sending them off to Croatia. "Then I got a video of a little girl opening a package containing this one favorite toy. Her face showed me how much she delighted in getting this. For someone with nothing, this was very special. When I saw the video, I knew how blessed I really was. It made me want to send everything to them."

All of Arielle's community activities have helped to broaden her perspective and have given her a certain maturity. In many ways, she feels that she's gained confidence in herself because of the experiences she's encountered, which have included people from many walks of life, religions, socioeconomic groups, and lifestyles. Assessing the problems encountered by young people today, Arielle sums it up this way: they want to learn how to be popular, not how to save the world. "Kids need to connect. I've been to several teen conferences about peace, about helping people. I think a lot of kids have trouble connecting, opening up to that general sense of community. They have difficulty moving beyond their own familiar territory, their own small group, and so leave themselves closed off to anything new.

"I hope someday I'll really be able to make a difference. Whether my impact will be local or global, small or large, the thing that really matters is simply taking action to help. The form doesn't matter, only that we take action. I find myself thinking as I start out on my journey to becoming an adult, that there are no small actions, only small people."

Susan's idea of leaving childhood behind really involves leaving behind childhood dreams. Through the slow and often arduous process of personal introspection, as well as through the often painful yet inevitable realities that confront us all, Susan gained valuable insights into herself as a young person, and, more specifically, into the evolution of herself as a young woman.

"I was a ballet dancer. How could I not be? I had been dancing since I was four." By the time Susan was nine, she was taking classes every day and performing with the local company. As a junior in high school, it dawned on her that she didn't have what it would take; she would never dance at Lincoln Center with the American Ballet Theatre. That hit her hard. "It took me a long time to let go of that part of me. At twenty-one, I still had all my ballet paraphernalia. I was taking ballet classes at NYU where I was a drama major. If you had only seen my bedroom back at my parents' house—it was a shrine to my childhood. My first pair of pointe shoes (I started en pointe when I was nine), practically new, and my last pair, worn when I was eighteen, hung over the ballet mirror and barre that my father had installed for me."

Ages sixteen through twenty-two were very difficult. Susan remembers being depressed. At the start of their junior year of college, her friend Ellen killed herself. Since Ellen had transferred to Brown University after freshman year, Susan and some other friends made the trip to Boston for the memorial service. An extremely talented writer, Ellen's parents read some of her writings. Susan reflects that Ellen did not want to grow up. Neither did she understand adults, nor why most of them were so miserable.

"Everything Ellen had written was everything I was feeling. Later that night on the phone, my best friend Ginny asked how I was feeling. I said I didn't know. When I hung up, it dawned on me that I was jealous. I was jealous that Ellen had actually gone through with it. She didn't have to become an adult. That feeling of jealousy scared me. I started seeing my therapist twice a week."

At some point, her therapist thought Susan should perform some sort of ceremony or ritual for her childhood, but Susan did not understand what this meant at the time. About a year after Ellen's death, Susan visited her parents' home on the Jewish holy day of Yom Kippur. She went out back to where her three cats—Nosey, Muffin, and Elsie, her closest companions from ages five through eighteen—were buried. "I sat under the tree on top of their unmarked graves and read the Jewish prayer for the dead. My father wouldn't let me read it when we had buried each of them.

"Then I thought about Ellen and came to the conclusion that she must have felt that this was the only decision she could make for herself. Everything up until then had somehow been decided for her. That's how I felt. Well, from then on, I declared that all decisions about me were going to be made by me."

That night, after her family had gone to bed, Susan removed her two pairs of pointe shoes from the wall. "I lay down on my bed with them and started crying, which really surprised me. I don't know how long I cried, but when I was done, I wrapped the ribbons around the shoes and wrapped both pairs in some red felt material from a previous ceremony. I thanked my shoes, my parents, and myself the whole time. I laid them in my baby-doll cradle in my closet, said good-bye, and closed the door. I had finally said good-bye to my childhood . . . and its dreams. But that was fine. I had decided it was okay to grow up and be an adult on my own terms."

One of the most turbulent emotional stages that humans pass through is adolescence, with not only its developmental difficulties, but also the added stress of its accompanying fears, insecurities, and sense of inadequacy, magnified by society's inability to safely address these troubling issues in some formal manner. Young people experience the inner turmoil of not just striving to move into adulthood, but of also seeking to find their own identities. Events at the crossroads can take on a life-or-death quality; extremes and excesses may manifest themselves, often with dramatic and even tragic consequences.

It's essential to be fully present for young people at this time of life, for although they may physically look and act appropriate for their age, and although they may seem to be handling life and the accompanying stresses sufficiently well, this may be furthest from the truth. Young people who feel isolated and alone may also feel unable to ask for help. Laboring under the misapprehension that their issues concern only them, and that these are much bigger in importance and consequence than they may actually be, can cause them to take matters into their own hands in order to rescue themselves from a pain and outcome that they imagine to be irreparable.

Merging

When one thinks of rites of passage, marriage is probably the one that most often comes to mind. Having spent a fair number of years exploring the emerging self, many young adults eventually experience the need and the desire to establish an intimate connection with a significant other. That there may be a series of these relationships before "the one" is found most likely describes the norm today. Eventually, this special relationship becomes evident, and a decision about how to move forward as a couple is determined. Some couples will decide to live together without ever entering into a formal contract, while probably the vast majority of individuals will choose to sanction their relationship through the institution of marriage, ultimately binding them together on many different levels.

In *Women's Spirituality and Ritual*, Barbara Walker describes how the rite and the institution of marriage have evolved. In early Christianity, every aspect of marriage was presided over by Roman priestesses of Juno. To the early church fathers, marriage, with its obvious ties to paganism, was viewed as an "unspiritual and sinful state devised by the Goddess."[4] Not until the twelfth century did priests give their blessing to couples just married, but literally only outside of the church, because it was believed that sexuality and lust had no place inside the house of God. Marriage was acknowledged by the sixteenth century, and an acceptable ceremony was ultimately created and sanctioned by the church. Walker notes that, "through most of Christian history, the marriage service was not a Christian sacrament but a secular procedure."[5]

Marriage ceremonies still retain elements of the ancient pagan rites, which emphasized and celebrated fertility. These very familiar customs include throwing rice; "something borrowed," most specifically from a woman who has successfully born several children; and the arrival of the bride and her party on the red carpet, symbolizing the "living blood that could flow through time"—that is, from one generation to the next.[6] Bridget was the moon goddess of wisdom in pre-Christian times. When Christianity rose in popularity among the Celts, Bridget, a still much-loved figure, became Saint Bridget, or Saint Bride. The bridegroom, then, became the one who served the bride.[7]

When performed as a civil ceremony today, marriage may take all of five minutes. Add religion to the mix, and the nuptials may take hours. What is essential and obligatory to all marriage rites are the vows and the formal pronouncement of union by the officiant. Variations on the content of the marriage rite are as diverse as the brides and grooms. Often, what is neglected in the countless decisions around the reception, the guest list, and the flowers is the fact that marriage is a holy institution, a sacred commitment.

Dearly Beloved, We Are Gathered Here—for the Hunt!

Growing up over a half century ago, Gladys's culture not only encouraged but expected young women to actively participate in behavior that would successfully lead to a socially sanctioned shift in status. Since the threshold phase of the classical initiatory rite of passage had been denied to women up until recently in many cultures, and is still denied in some, it is ironic to think that "hunting" for the man, who would then literally carry you over the threshold, became not only expected but required behavior. What is so poignant about Gladys's description of this phase of her life is how readily acceptable stereotypic behaviors were just a generation ago, and how the dictates of a culture could so completely determine the thinking and the affective state of the individuals within it (especially women) about identity, status, and roles.

"My fifteenth birthday, a major milestone in many Latino cultures, was as good an occasion as any to start 'the Hunt.' This meant that my fortunate day would arrive in which I could be saved by rubbing elbows with a man. At sixteen, I started college, but studies were clearly nowhere as important as my desperate search for a mate. By the time I reached the ripe age of seventeen, I felt like a spinster. So I fell in love and got married at eighteen. We had a big wedding, but no rite of passage, unless you're speaking of going from a 'res' (*thing* in Latin) to a real being, the wife of *the man*. Three children quickly followed. But it wasn't until many years later that I began to understand who I was in my own right. Fortunately, my personal evolution coincided with significant changes in the lives of women in general. My own personal journey of self-discovery and growth goes on and on. Pursuing what I feel most passionately about will never cease." Note that, looking back on this event, Gladys does not consider her marriage to be a rite of passage. Perhaps this was merely a "rite by rote," an obligatory passage lacking the deeply personal meaning and the accompanying emotional significance for her.

Marriage can serve as the catalyst for enormous change, not only for the couple but for the individuals involved. That being married and living intimately with another will eventually have an impact on whom we become is fairly certain. The individuals within a marital relationship will inevitably be challenged to encounter and confront numerous complex issues surrounding the establishment and maintenance of their own identity in light of the values and expectations brought to bear by the spouse, by the families of origin, and by the children. The struggle to find and identify self is hard enough for each of us to pursue in our own time and in our own way, but there is no doubt that it is made much more difficult by the external demands that encroach upon our personal territory and demand our attention.

Every life is different and unique. We don't have to identify or even agree with the way one person chooses to live her or his life. But beyond the specifics of a given life, we can identify some things that all humans can relate to. These may include how we make decisions; how we deal with dilemmas; how we resolve conflicts, or, conversely, how we remain mired in conflict that deeply affects and disrupts our lives; how we handle unfolding emotions, and how we learn to stand up and take responsibility for ourselves.

It is vitally important to get to know yourself in every possible way before you move into a committed relationship. Often, individuals go in search of a relationship without this essential knowledge about themselves. How can you ever hope to know another individual if you don't know yourself first? How can you ever address another's needs and desires if you are disconnected from your own? As obvious as these issues may appear to be, and as much as you may feel you understand them intellectually, it should come as no surprise that what seems unimportant initially may take on much greater significance as insights occur over the course of a relationship. In retrospect, some individuals are baffled about their own behavior and expectations in relationships.

Some individuals use the words "supposed to be," "trying to be," and "need to be" in describing how they think they should be viewing and responding to events in their lives in general, and in their relationships specifically, only to find that these are part and parcel of a belief system that does not match with, or is disconnected from, an inner sense of self. But attempting to fit into someone else's mold, even if one's intentions are good, may ultimately be a recipe for disaster. When people have not had the opportunity to explore their own personal terrain—who they are by themselves in their own right—and become frustrated within a marriage, or any committed relationship for that matter, they may go outside to find answers, to satisfy curiosities, or to have their own needs met that have been either ignored, denied, or squashed. Sound familiar? Have you experienced commitments or marriage as a loss of self? Take a moment to assess what you know to be true about yourself as opposed to what others expect of you.

A really good exercise I've asked my patients to do is to write down every partner they've had a significant relationship with. Then, for each partner, list the answers to questions like these: What attracted you to this person initially? Did the attraction last? Was your fantasy about this person, what you imagined or assumed to be true, validated in reality? How long did the relationship last? Did revelations during the course of the relationship change your mind? What was the deal breaker? Do any patterns, similarities from relationship to relationship, emerge?

Learn to ask the hard questions out of the gate, the first or second time you meet, since opinions are not yet solidly formed. Most of us seem to do much better when we have no real expectations of someone, because we hardly know them and are not yet trying to impress them. Watch for red flags. These are indicators that something needs to be questioned or otherwise validated. Often these are clues that something may be trouble in the future. A red flag is a good intuitive image to help you process what you're really feeling. At the end of a difficult relationship, people often say, "He/she told me that he/she was _____ on our first date, but I just didn't listen." Learn to trust what you feel. Your hunch is probably right.

Identifying aspects of a significant relationship—emotional, spiritual, intellectual, or physical—that are important to you is an essential tool to help you determine whether a chosen partner is a good match for you. Going one step further, take the top three to five nonnegotiable aspects—qualities about which you will absolutely not compromise, things you just can't do without—and realistically assess your partner's ability to bring these aspects to the relationship. Honest, clear recognition of each other's needs and abilities from the beginning can provide a healthy backdrop for a good relationship, or can save individuals from future frustration and grief when it is determined that such needs can't be met.

We Are All Sacred—Male and Female

Beyond its religious and secular meaning, marriage for Karlin is an intensely personal, intimate connection that two people share with each other. "I have always been one to search for meaning in every step. The most meaningful markers of time for me have been traditional rites of passage—leaving home, graduating from college, getting my master's degree, becoming an entrepreneur, celebrating milestones in my business, and getting married.

"I chose to focus on marriage because, in our culture, it is the most acceptable and scripted marker of transition for women. I also think that many interpretations of the marriage ceremony are no longer appropriate for women's roles in society, and I believe that the authenticity of the marriage rite has been tainted by an enormous industry that distracts us from the real meaning of commitment to another person. Women in the United States buy millions upon millions of dollars' worth of bridal magazines and bridal books, wedding-planning services, and flowers, cakes, and gowns. Many couples don't even talk about their vows, what they are really promising to each other."

In creating their marriage ceremony, Karlin and Charles were beginning a creative process together in defining their life from a place of respect and love. Karlin felt great joy then and believes that the change after has been subtle. In marriage, Charles and Karlin are not different people, but they recognize that they have been through a wonderful experience together that they created themselves.

"Charles and I were very conscious about marriage; we both wanted to celebrate our partnership and mark our commitment with each other, but we didn't want to involve our community in our sacred ceremony. We felt that the party or community piece was separate from our personal rite of passage together. We designed our ceremony together with elements of many different cultures. We both have Irish heritage, and we drew heavily from a Druid-Celtic tradition. We also incorporated Japanese, Native American, and other components. Charles and I share a name—Charles means "man," and Karlin is the feminine, meaning "woman." We felt that, because our names are so archetypal, as are our personalities in many ways, we would honor the sacred masculine and feminine equally in our ceremony, and our vows would recognize the differences we brought to each other, and the profundity of representing the God and Goddess to one another."

Karlin believes that every rite of passage is unique; each of us experiences change differently, both mentally and physically. Her marriage was a beautiful, celebratory experience for her that was a new beginning and a declaration of love and commitment. "I think that many of us in the West grow up hearing fairy tales that end in marriage, with myths of redemption and wholeness delivered by male saviors, with families who wish their daughters would repeat their rituals and rites of passage. A consciousness of our own desires, of what we are pledging and vowing to another person, is the most important piece of the process. I would never have said that I would obey, and I would never want Charles to pledge his obeisance to me. We thought hard about what we were promising, and that made the promise real."

Reuniting and Reconnecting
Some rites of passage that receive little recognition, if any, address changing roles and identities that don't follow the usual, normal way that life unfolds. What happens when biological parents and children find each other after years apart? What happens when family members separated early in life are reunited? What happens when the "truth" of a life, as one has come to know it, is not the real story at all?

It is impossibly difficult to comprehend the world of the adopted child, whose separation from the birth mother engenders an experience of abandonment and loss so profound as to be likened to a "primal wound." In her research, Nancy Newton Verrier compares this relinquishment to a death, "not only of the mother, but of part of the Self, that core-being or essence of oneself which makes one feel whole."[8]

And what of the birth mother? There is often deep, unresolved pain for her as well, starting from the moment that she gives up her role as mother, assuming the new identity—perhaps really felt and acknowledged only by herself—of stranger. She relinquishes her bond often abruptly, often deeply conflicted, often before she has had a chance to process what is happening and what the potential consequences might be. No one can tell her how she will feel in the years to come. No one will wonder, as she does, about milestones reached, birthdays celebrated, and achievements accomplished, all going on without her.

The affective quality of this experience for the birth mother is difficult for most of us to fathom. There was a child once, but now there is no relationship and no contact; in essence, a death, and yet the child is alive somewhere. How can a woman grieve this separation and loss? This process is often left unresolved because there are no rituals that would enable a woman to properly accept and mourn what she may have reluctantly consented to give away, and yet what she may actually experience as something that was taken from her.

Reunion

Patti waited forty years to find the son that she had adopted away when she was barely a woman herself. Returning to the same agency that had handled the adoption many years before, Patti found herself retracing her steps, seemingly going backward in time. Crossing over the same threshold encountered years before finally enabled her to assume an identity that she was once forced to relinquish. The symbolic act of stepping back through an open doorway once shut to her in the past provided closure to the regret and the unresolved sense of loss that she had carried around with her for so many years.

"Then, in a split second, David is there, standing in the doorway with someone behind him. I feel tears gather in the back of my throat. I rise to my feet, and everyone in the room disappears from my view. He wears glasses, but they don't for a moment obscure his brilliant blue eyes. He's dressed in khakis and a white shirt that is only partially tucked in. He takes a step or two, and I see that he shuffles, moving as though his joints are stiff.

"'I've waited so long to meet you,' I say. 'May I hug you?' David says nothing, but he smiles. And when he does, he is so radiant and his smile so dazzling that I feel blinded by its light. He slides into my arms, and the light stabs my chest, crumbling walls inside of me as if they were made of paper. After forty years of waiting, I feel whole again.

"I immediately feel the need to protect him. From what, I'm not sure, but he appears vulnerable, like a wounded animal inside this tiny room. I instinctively know he's not used to being the center of attention, and today it's as though we are both actors trapped inside a theater-in-the-round: surrounded, once again, by the Greek chorus of long ago. My first impulse is to fill up anything I perceive as uncomfortable with the sound of my voice.

" 'David,' I say, 'It's wonderful to meet you. Let me look at you. I think we look alike. I've brought photos of everyone in my family for you to see.'

"I close my eyes. 'Shut up,' I say to myself. 'Stop jabbering.' What I really want to tell David is how sorry I am. Sorry I gave him away. Sorry he's sick. I want to explain to him that it's not my fault. Nobody in my family has schizophrenia. Maybe I could have saved him from it, though, if only I had kept him—been older, smarter, and better. But of course I say none of these things. Instead, I reach into my purse and pull out a paperback book and continue to jabber.

" 'In your letter, you mentioned that you liked Neil Young, so I brought you this book. Thought you'd get a kick out of it.'

"David takes the book graciously, without ever taking his eyes off my face. He's so calm and composed. Why can't I stop talking?

" 'You know,' I continue, 'I'm going to be here for a few days, so maybe we can see each other, have dinner, or lunch, or just hang out or something. Whatever you like. I live at the beach, but I still have family here, so I come back pretty frequently and—'

" 'I think I look like you,' he interrupts, scrutinizing my face, touching it easily with no trace of self-consciousness. He traces my cheek with the back of his hand in a gesture so gentle that it makes my eyes tear up and finally quiets me. We spend the next minute or so openly staring into each other's faces, saying nothing. It's as though an unspoken agreement has taken place between us to drop unnecessary chatter and simply examine one another.

"We stay chatting easily for a while longer. I show him more pictures of Michael and David and tell him about my house in Manhattan Beach. I'm in the middle of telling him about my job as a movie publicist when suddenly he interrupts me in midsentence, shaking his head in disbelief.

" 'You're my mother,' He murmurs. 'You're really my mother.'

" 'Yes, David,' I say, and my voice drops to a whisper. 'This is true. I really am your mother.'

"It's amazing how every once in a while in our lifetime, if we get lucky for a moment, we get to crawl into each other's light. The peace that this moment brings to me floods over me in a blend of sorrow and tenderness, washing away years of uncertainty."

Coming into My Own
In reconnecting with a long-lost parent, many of the same issues found in the adoption scenario emerge: the sense of loss, the search for self, and the

fantasies, stories, and myths created about the missing parent and about what might have been. For Julie, life without her mother changed the course of the natural progression of her life immeasurably. Deprived of having her biological mother, she had to scramble for herself to fill in the void created by the absence of this life-shaping relationship.

But for Julie, the story was far more complicated. The day her mother "left" divided her life into a "before" and an "after," a profound passage in and of itself, especially for a young child. Imagine the shock when, many years later, Julie was told the details of her mother's self-inflicted disconnection from her own daughter. Finding and reconnecting with her mother required Julie to trust crossing back over the threshold into unknown, often scary territory. But this very courageous act allowed her to access and assimilate pieces of herself that had been lost.

When Julie was about six years old, her mother shot herself in the head as a last attempt to save a faltering marriage. Julie intuitively knew that something ominous was going to happen, but after the accident, she had no memory of it, or of the first six years of her life. All she remembers is the green Impala breaking down with her and her younger sister, Nancy, in the backseat, and being rescued by a Mayflower moving van who picked them up and brought father and daughters to the police station. The first intact memory is being offered Nabisco sugar cookies by the sheriff at the station.

Julie considers herself extremely lucky to have been protected by her father, to have been removed from a difficult situation and given a sense of security until she was ready to learn the truth. When she was twenty-one years old, her father broke the news—her mother was alive, but in such a challenging situation that he had waited this long to tell her. He explained that he had waited until he thought the time was right, when he believed that Julie would not only understand what had happened but could choose to do whatever she wished with the information. Julie credits her father for doing a great job raising her and her sister. Through her stepmother, she came to understand that people would accept and love you unconditionally, even though not biologically related.

But, there were issues. "As a young child, I thought that if I could be good enough, if I could just please enough, I'd be able to have my mother back. Only much later did I come to realize that I had nothing to do with the equation. My mother had been driven to do what she had done as a result of overwhelming issues that became too much for her to live with.

"I also had this problem about someone being present and then not being there. I used to feel inferior, thinking that other families seemed more intact than my own. I would sometimes have a feeling of interruption; I would sense gaps and not know how to bridge them. I was taught to just accept what is and then just get on with it. But I didn't realize that this profound absence of my mother's presence would manifest in a complete absence of my own self-awareness.

"How did I manage all those years without my mother? I was forced into the unknown every day without her, so I had to learn to think on my feet. I took up the cause of needy people and was drawn into taking responsibility for others, sometimes at a cost to myself. Looking at my sister, I saw another way to process what had happened to us. My sister was still angry and remained unresolved about our mother's disappearance. She had embraced motherhood but hadn't forgiven our mother. I see what happened in a more philosophical and, I think, spiritual way. I have no children of my own but have forgiven my mother one hundred percent."

From the time Julie learned about her mother's condition, she couldn't stop thinking about her. Who was this woman? How were they connected to each other? What purpose had her mother served in her life? When Julie first learned where her mother was living, she had the immediate impulse to call her. But she was very apprehensive about pursuing this relationship, because the man her mother had married, a Vietnam vet, was somewhat overbearing on the phone. Julie did not feel that she was strong enough to deal with a face-to-face meeting then. Instead, she started writing to her mother and sending pictures so that she could connect the different chapters of her life, hoping that this would give her mother some clarity emotionally.

Julie's mother moved into a nursing facility when her husband died. In 1997, at age thirty-two, Julie finally felt ready to make the journey to meet her mother. "In the course of just twenty-four hours, I gained a greater understanding of myself. Although we had lived such separate lives, we were connected in so many ways. I see my mother as my guardian angel. Her sacrifice somehow gave me the courage to take more risks in my life.

"Finding the missing pieces has enabled me to see my entire evolution, all that I am and all I have become. I now feel as if I'm embarking on a new journey—as the whole person I was meant to be. The journey back to my source has filled the pages of my passport with the names of places previously unknown."

Honoring and Celebrating

Big Birthdays: Milestone or Millstone?

Every year, we have our own special day to remember who we are and where we come from. But big birthdays, those marking decade changes, have the ability to evoke emotions and feelings about how we have lived, the course of our lives so far. At best, these are times of reflection, review, and resolution. At worst, they are painful reminders of what went wrong, of disappointments, of what never happened, and of unfulfilled expectations, all displayed against the backdrop of the clock ticking away our time.

As noted previously, when the life cycle is examined and broken down into periods or stages, it becomes apparent that there are critical themes and concurrent tasks that mark each successive step, and it is the job of each of us to confront and tackle the key issues relevant to our development at each new stage or phase of life. Beyond review and resolution, though, performing an actual ritual to mark these major life passages, to provide closure on the past and to set the intention for the future, may be a necessary step to clear the way to an opening onto a new stage of our lives.

Forging Ahead at Forty

Kathleen experienced becoming forty as yet another turning point. Leaving home and coming to New York City at age eighteen to start a new life had left her precious little time to be an adolescent. With a "who-cares" attitude and a sense of humor, she allowed herself to be an adolescent at forty. This retroactive rite of passage symbolically helped her to acknowledge a significant period that she had skipped. Getting closure, she could comfortably move on to the rest of her life.

"It was only a month after I'd asked my husband for a separation. That hadn't gone well; he didn't move out of our home. I looked at forty as an important milestone, perhaps even a halfway point in life. I had given my husband a fortieth-birthday party years before for the same reason. I gathered my children and a few very close friends for a festive lunch at the Hard Rock Cafe. The location seemed fitting. Its decor included Elvis and Pat Boone guitars and paraphernalia reminiscent of my teenage years. I was probably experiencing the first blatantly rebellious act of my life."

One More Year to Live

But birthdays are not always celebratory events. Sometimes realizations sneak up and take us by surprise, and these often coincide with milestones in our lives. So revered is youth in our culture that by the time we reach midlife, some of us are certain that life must be over. In actuality, our increased lifespan has broadened the concept to include two separate transitions in midlife—one for reexamining how we've lived up until the present, and the other for reframing how we look at life and ourselves, perhaps finding ways to make changes that may better reflect where we want to go in the future. Instead of thinking of retiring, individuals are considering switching professions, often pursuing something they had only dreamed of doing one day. Instead of slowly coming down the mountain after having reached what they thought was the pinnacle of success in life and career, individuals now seem to have their eye set on new, inviting peaks appearing on the horizon.

"It hit me on my forty-ninth birthday. This was it—only one more year to live. More than half my life was gone, and what had I accomplished? I was still an immature child, for God's sake. I fretted the whole year until my fiftieth birthday." For the first six months, Jackie cried and fell into a horrible depression. Aware that she had to get herself out of it, she began sharing her feelings with everyone she knew. At that time, strangely enough, she was teaching aerobic dance classes to seniors aged sixty to ninety! What better group to share her concerns with? Or so she thought. They just laughed at her, saying, "Oh dearie, just wait until you get to be our age."

Reflecting back to that time, Jackie thinks it must have been an unbearable year for everyone who knew her. For sure, they all knew when her birthday was. Jackie was surprised and pleased that everyone stuck with her; there were words of encouragement amid the jokes. She felt deeply appreciative that the whole world seemed solidly behind her as the fatal day approached.

"The day in February arrived at long last. I got to sleep in. I was aware that I was awake but refused to open my eyes. I did a mental body check. Yep, I was all there. Slowly and carefully, I opened one eye at a time. Why, it was one of those beautiful cold winter days—sunny and clear. I took it as a good sign. I got out of bed, took a few deep breaths, giving thanks that I was alive and well. I vowed to do something meaningful with my life in my remaining years, deciding now to live at least another fifty of them."

That year, Jackie remembers that everyone in the whole world sent her a birthday card. Some friends sent gifts, and even her fitness classes chipped in and collected a money gift. Her God-sent husband, Michael, made sure that the whole day was a wonderful celebration. "It felt great, having been accepted into society not only as an adult but as a crone, though it was another few years before I thought kindly about the crone business. The best gift of all was that I missed my first period that month. Happy birthday to me, and Hallelujah!"

Debby's fiftieth-birthday rite was celebrated with about fifty of the people dearest to her. As she relates it, there was a lot of eye-rolling when she stated the theme of her celebration, requesting that each individual bring something to read that they had either written themselves or that was personally meaningful to them. Debby chose to have the event at a friend's home on an afternoon rather than an evening. What fascinated her was the range of ways in which friends and family were celebrating this life marker of hers.

Friends and family took turns reading, sitting around in a circle. The afternoon wore on, and yet the ritual continued, each one in turn telling a wonderful story, relating thoughts and feelings of their own, or of someone whose words deeply resonated with them. The offerings to Debby were gifts given back to everyone—a chance to revisit, to be reminded about what gives meaning and purpose to the individual life. It was a timeless celebration of all that is sacred in life.

Achieving

Achievements and accomplishments are rites of passage in every imaginable sense. In some ways, marking milestone experiences personally chosen and deeply significant to the individual—apart from those dictated by our own community or society—helps to make these events even more meaningful and satisfying. Beyond the numerous roles and status changes that we will be called upon to assume during the course of our lifetime, the way we choose to define and identify our self separates us from everyone else, giving us our own unique place in the world.

We all know people who want and strive to be different, choosing to separate themselves from everyone else in any number of ways. Some use outward appearances, such as how they dress or how they carry themselves—something we may think of as an expression of individual style. Others choose to define themselves through their behavior, often being viewed as edgy, rebellious, eccentric, and idiosyncratic, sometimes even larger than life. And still others may be singled out for special inherent qualities and gifts, like intelligence or creativity, or for establishing and executing excellence in any number of disciplines.

Setting goals and accomplishing tasks that strengthen self-esteem, encourage independence, and promote a sense of the freedom to continue to choose are the work of our own specially chosen paths. Passage rites celebrate these.

Continuing Education
As a wife and mother, with all its myriad responsibilities and parameters (many self-imposed!), Lorraine made an independent decision that would greatly alter her self-image and the direction her life would take. All of her previous decisions, which had determined her life's direction—getting mar-

ried, having two children, moving to the suburbs—seemed less like decisions than simply following some preordained, societally imposed course of direction.

The first of two such major decisions came about in 1978 when Lorraine was in her late thirties. "Firmly ensconced in a suburban home, with very young children, a very child-centered suburban life, and a supportive, though frequently unavailable husband, I felt my self-image and confidence slowly eroding." Her previous education had ended with an associate in applied science (AAS) degree from the Fashion Institute of Technology, where she had studied fashion illustration, and she had pursued an interesting, lucrative career for many years before her marriage.

"I had always felt a little shaky in terms of my limited formal education, especially compared to a lot of the women I was now meeting. So, at the urging of my therapist, I began to investigate the idea of going back to school. Without discussing this idea with my husband or anyone else, I decided to enroll at Sarah Lawrence, School of Continuing Education."

This turned out to be a fabulous period in Lorraine's life—the people she met, the things she was learning, and her revised sense of self. "To my great surprise, I did very well, and I went on to a master's degree and a career in museum education. I feel that there may have been a negative impact on my family in terms of my not being very available for those years, but retrospectively, I wouldn't have done any differently: it saved my life."

Building a Home, from the Inside Out

I had a lot of problems in my life, but most of them never happened.

—Mark Twain

The initiation, as it has traditionally occurred, glamorizes and reveres the masculine ordeals fought in the "bush," while the everyday experiences of the village green and the kitchen go unnoticed or, worse, are dismissed as not important enough. One needn't go into the bush to realize that life is rich and full; one need only go, intentionally and with eyes wide open, into everyday life.

For women, ritualizing today focuses attention on a new definition of sacred space that is, like the core of all truth, actually very old. Women's rituals and rites of passage attempt "to expand the definition of the sacred horizontally into areas previously considered profane—the home, nature, the workplace."[9]

Rebecca, a highly successful chiropractor in the Bay Area, could easily negotiate everyday life on her own terms—that is, until she was confronted with the reality, and the responsibility, of owning her own home.

"One big rite of passage for me was buying my home in Marin County. For years, I dreamt of living and working there, but I was afraid of spending the hundreds of thousands of dollars I knew it would cost to move. At the time, my two little girls and I were living in a flat in San Francisco, downstairs from a man who was nuts. When I gave one of my daughters a birthday kitten, he went ballistic. 'I'm allergic to fleas!' he shouted at me. I assured him that our cat would never go outdoors, but I knew he wouldn't be satisfied by that answer. And I was right. Shortly after that, the man shot out the windows of my car and my best friend's car."

The next weekend, Rebecca took her girls, and the cat, on a minivacation. On the long drive home on Sunday, the air was beautiful, and by twilight the world around them was magical. Rebecca had a little talk with herself. She told herself it was time to buy that home in Marin. It didn't feel safe, but, she told herself, it would never feel safe, and that was okay. When they got back to their flat, the front door was wide open. Nothing had been disturbed, but the flat itself felt unsafe now, even more unsafe than spending all that money in Marin.

The next week, Rebecca found the perfect home for them. Everything— the deal, the loan, the inspection—went smoothly. She thinks that's because of the internal work she'd done. By buying a home, she was declaring herself in the physical world, in a space that she'd carved out for herself. "But I promptly went into chaos, developing severe vertigo, which meant that the world was spinning around me. At first I fought it, but fighting only made it worse. There's only one way to deal with a spinning world: spin with it. That helped me fill in the space I'd carved out for myself.

"What shifted in my life? I began to trust myself more on the physical and financial plane. I continue to explore this plane and to celebrate it. I celebrated my home by painting it vibrant colors, by living and sleeping on its decks as much as inside it, by gardening, and by sharing it with others. People say, 'Look before you leap,' but I have found that I get comfortable only after I have leapt. So now I don't wait so long before leaping."

We all know that thinking and planning about how we can change our life is worlds apart from actually changing it. Have you ever been confronted with the notion that now was as good a time as any to simply just jump in and do it? If you feel in your bones that the time has come to make a move, you may want to try taking the following actions. Breaking a process down logically and practically into its component parts or steps may help turn a major task from overwhelming into doable.

- Write a priority list containing all of the elements it takes to accomplish the task. Revisit this list frequently, reassessing what is most important.
- Find knowledgeable, supportive advisers (financial advisers, real estate professionals, mentors, and life coaches).
- Trust your intuition. Have you outgrown a place or location, either literally or figuratively? Does the ending of a relationship necessitate a move? Do you just feel insecure or unsafe in your place? Does a financial or personal growth opportunity beckon you?
- Be practical. Consider how you can minimize turning your life upside down while maximizing the benefits, pleasures, and quality of life your new place will bring you.
- Allow yourself to daydream and visualize whatever it is that you wish to accomplish. For example, design your ideal living space. Put down on paper, both in words and through drawings, what you want the rooms, decor, landscaping, and so on to look like. When you are ready to actually pursue your goal in real time, having done the preliminary legwork might help you to zero in on exactly what you are looking for.

The Wall of Fire

As a therapist and public speaking coach for many years, Natalie has given hundreds the ability and the gift of achieving their own personal power. It is often said that you teach best what you know best, and Natalie is a remarkably effective teacher and healer because of her ability to use her own experiences to help others. Throughout her life, she has learned to identify her fears, be present with them, and ultimately conquer them. So it is no surprise that learning to drive in her fifties gave Natalie a new sense of independence, an expanded idea of all the places she could go.

"I had arrived; I felt that I had really earned the weekend house in the mountains that I so wanted to buy. Although the house needed a lot of work, the view from the deck convinced me that this was the right place for me. One problem—how would I get there if I couldn't drive?"

Although she had tried to drive and hadn't succeeded in the past, she knew this time would be different. Lessons, a successful driving test, a car—the next problem was getting behind the wheel and actually driving, which turned out to be far more difficult than she could have imagined. Each new journey seemed to provide its own frustrations and challenges: driving with a flat tire, trying to find the source of a constant beeping noise that accompanied her for an entire trip, attempting to drive when she could not see beyond the windshield in a torrential downpour. On one trip, a friend even sat silently in the front seat, offering no help. In retrospect, this was a good thing. Natalie says that she totally expected her friend to behave like her mother would have, offering to do it for her to alleviate her anxiety.

Driving proved to be a rite of passage in a very literal sense. Not only does your status change from nondriver to driver, but the actual going from "here to there" entails leaving the familiar, going into the unknown, and finally arriving successfully at your destination. The in-between stage is classically where the difficulties occur, but it is also the place where transformation happens. Natalie refers to her personal "betwixt and between" as the wall of fire.

But there is more to the story. On a trip to a conference, Natalie found herself traveling in the wrong direction. More than just frustrating, this proved to be a very big deal for her. Traveling in the right direction meant driving on the side of a curving mountain road where the drop to the bottom was considerable. Anxious beyond words, tensely gripping the steering wheel for dear life, Natalie was suddenly confronted by the face, looming larger than life, of the young man who had molested her when she was eleven. He had left her that day totally humiliated and traumatized, with the warning, "If you tell anyone, I will kill you."

Natalie became enraged. "You son of a bitch! You bastard! You took my life away," she screamed over and over again. The more she vented her anger at him, the better she seemed to feel. As her anxiety lessened, her fear seemed to drop away. She had come through another wall of fire.

I often hear people talk about something they want to have happen or something they want to accomplish, something they feel passionately about and something they fantasize about having in the future. "So own it," I say; "have it." But then the "if-onlys" rush in all too quickly, the myriad reasons, rationalizations, and excuses why this can't happen now and will have to wait for some seemingly better time.

No matter how daunting or how huge something may seem, we can always attempt to approach it slowly, in a piecemeal kind of way, taking small steps forward toward its eventual accomplishment and completion. As in the life larger than life, the mythic one, the great heroes and seekers knew that "going to the mountain," or in search of the Holy Grail, was about much more than arriving at a place or finding a sacred object—it is about our own unique discovery every step of the way, the journey to our heart's desire, to the place of our soul's longing.

Know Thy Self

Seize Responsibility. Whatever happens to you is ultimately up to you. Don't resort to making excuses and inventing reasons why life is too difficult for you to navigate through or manage on your own. Don't assume that what seems comfortable and familiar is always for your greater good. Some individuals in your life may be all too happy to take over, making vital choices and decisions for you, but ultimately this is tantamount to selling your soul.

Take Action. Put your thoughts and feelings into motion. Conscious action has the power to creatively translate your personal, intimate, inner world into a tangible, recognizable process in the world outside of yourself. This is a key way to express your individuality, to present a unique and fresh perspective.

Seek Independence. Personal accountability for yourself and for your actions frees you from outside influences, boosts confidence in your ability to make healthy choices and decisions, and ultimately fosters trust in your own process.

Embrace Change. Change is essential for living a fruitful life. Fear of change, fear of stepping into the unknown, creates a monolithic existence, often dull, narrow in scope, and uninspired. Change creates possibility.

Track Changing Patterns. How do we know when something no longer works for us? How do we know when something is finished or when we are done with it? Learning to identify and chart patterns within your life is a powerful growth tool that you can utilize any time. Creating a graph may serve as a useful visual tool. On the top of a piece of paper, or in your journal, make columns representing topics that are significant to you. These might include special events, people, the arts, travels, dreams, fantasies, and the like. On the left side of the page, create your own timeline, charting when these topics found their way into your conscious life. What at first may seem to be a random event could actually reveal a pattern that may shed light on what has happened in the past and show you how it exerts influence in the present.

Trust Your Instincts. What happens when you subvert your inner knowing, when you ignore your gut reaction, when you don't follow your heart? Literally, pay attention to bodily sensations that often give valuable signals before your intellect actually kicks in.

The Journey Home—a Meditation

This meditation is wonderful anytime, but especially at points in your life when you wish to start over and clear the slate of old, outdated energy in order to bring in the fresh and new. It may serve, too, as a rite of passage, allowing you, through intention and imagination, to visualize a new reality.

Sit comfortably, cross-legged on the floor or in a straight-backed chair, feet flat on the floor, hands resting comfortably at your sides or on your knees. Close your eyes. Scan your body, beginning with your feet and moving up to your head, and notice if any particular area is tense. If it is, ask that part of your body to let go of its tension and stress.

Now, direct your attention to your breath. Take a deep breath and let it course through you. Release any tension as you exhale. Do this again—breathe in; breathe out; breathe in; breathe out.

Now imagine that you are walking on a beach. It is an absolutely beautiful day—not a cloud in the sky, warm and balmy, a calm and tranquil sea of blue and green reflecting the light of the sun. There's no one else on the beach. It stretches for miles ahead of you, seemingly endless. You're starting to feel relaxed; tension and anxiety seem to melt away. You're thinking of nothing else but this moment. See yourself. Notice and describe how you look to yourself—your body, your face, and your hair. Notice what you are wearing. Remember all of these details. How do you feel about yourself today? How do you feel about yourself generally? Take the time to really notice things.

You continue walking along the beach, feeling deeply relaxed. Now you stop to gaze out over the ocean. Your body rhythms seem to be moving in sync with the rhythms of nature. Your breath rises and falls gently in sync with the waves of the ocean.

You feel free, liberated. The water invites you, so you remove all of your clothing, leaving each piece on the sand. The warmth of the sun envelops you. You walk toward the water, then into the water, deeper and deeper. The waves buoy you; you float, embraced by the warmth of the water. You feel at one with nature. Going further, you duck beneath the water, all the way down below the surface. You trust that you are being taken care of by the natural Mother. She holds you and supports you lovingly, gently. You lift yourself out of the water, and when you are ready, you swim back to shore.

Your clothing is gone, but there is a bag lying on the beach. Open it and look inside. You remove the contents—new clothing. You dress yourself in your new garments. Notice them carefully—their color, texture, and design. How do you look? How do you feel? Notice and remember everything.

The rest of the day is yours to do with as you please. When you are ready to come back to the present, bring your conscious attention to this place and time. Become aware of your body. Become aware of your breath. Inhale; exhale. Inhale; exhale. Slowly open your eyes.

CHAPTER FOUR

Passages through Loss

Loss is nothing else but change, and change is Nature's delight.

—Marcus Aurelius

We are healed of a suffering only by experiencing it in full.

—Marcel Proust

Passages through the territory of loss are among the longest and most difficult we may encounter, underscoring the primacy of our bonds to others. The internal events that accompany loss unfold in their own time frame, often extending well beyond the external event. Ending an intimate partnership can be a devastating emotional experience; even in a seemingly amicable breakup or divorce, life is turned upside down. Aside from the many practical matters involved, issues of identity and self-esteem, feelings of having failed, and anxieties over the loss of commitment and security abound. The death of a significant other—parent, child, spouse, or close friend—churns up still further emotional traumas, since it signals not only the ending of a relation-ship, but the actual loss of the person him- or herself.

Grief can be a normal reaction, an appropriate emotional response, to anything felt to be a loss. There are many passages we encounter throughout our lives that may engender a sense of sadness, even when they are ultimately positive. On an individual level, leaving a part of ourselves behind in order to assume a new identity may be accompanied by a feeling of bittersweet sorrow, a sense of melancholia for what once was. We will miss those parts of ourselves that we enjoyed being, especially those that served us well. When we marry, move, graduate, or change financial situations, it usually represents positive growth, but nevertheless, we are still saying good-bye to the old.

Grief and loss can encompass physical changes and challenges. Menopause may represent the loss of beauty and the physicality of youth. Loss of health through illness or accident, or abuse of any kind at any time, may engender a feeling of helplessness and loss of control, and may ultimately represent a potential threat to one's self-preservation and even one's mortality. And finally, the loss of spirit, the questioning of one's faith, or doubt in the purpose and meaning of one's life, at any time in the life cycle, but most especially at the midlife point, or having suffered through a series of losses in life, may be accompanied by profound grief and a sense of despair as well.

This chapter will focus on passages through loss of relationship, since it is through our encounters with others that we most readily access significant parts of ourselves. We see ourselves mirrored back through the eyes of others. Our relationships inform us about ourselves and often shape who we are and who we are to become. So when a significant relationship ends, either because of a conscious decision to move away from it or because of circumstances beyond our control, we are left alone, often feeling as if an essential part of ourselves has been cut away. Working through this painful form of passage, drawing upon resources that can facilitate the process, and bearing in mind that one can gain even from loss is the ultimate challenge.

Grief, loss, hurt, and anger normally accompany divorce, or the ending of any significant, committed relationship. In these circumstances, someone we once loved and depended upon (and maybe even still do or want to) failed and disappointed us; they stopped being present for us. The ending of such relationships may actually feel like a death. It may take a very long time to process all of the emotions and to sever ties in as healthy a way as we are able. When someone we love dies, we may feel the accompanying grief and loss more profoundly because it is this relationship that has sustained and supported us. The person who is our "other half," who has shared experiences and intimacies with us in a way that no one else ever can, is suddenly no longer there for us.

Incomplete grief may cause "fearful choices" and "hypervigilant self-protection," and this may ultimately "(limit) the ability to be open, trusting, and loving, dooming the next relationship to failure."[1] Prolonged grief or nonclosure of a relationship can lead to the unhealthy syndrome of idealizing, memorializing, and even canonizing (especially one who is deceased), or conversely, demonizing, the one who has left us. Either way, the grieving party may remain stuck, unresolved, and unable to move forward. In *The Grief Recovery Handbook*, James and Friedman suggest that, "to complete an emotionally incomplete loss, you must complete it."[2] Rites and rituals can help contain these difficult times, structuring the often confusing feelings and emotions and bringing a sense of completeness and closure to what would otherwise be too overwhelming to endure.

For our purposes in this chapter, loss of relationship may occur as a result of *parting*, the act of leaving someone with whom we have been in a significant, committed partnership, although not a legally sanctioned relationship; *separating*, a severance of a committed relationship that implies necessary formalities and legal involvement in order to be completed; and *departing*, the ending of a deeply significant relationship as a result of death.

Parting

Beyond Ceremony: Bringing the Gifts of the Unconscious to Consciousness

New relationships may find their way into our life at any time. Normally, the quality of the relationship we choose will reflect where we are in our life, our own personal experiences adding dimensions to a partnership. Relationships established when individuals are younger may have the advantage of allowing the partners to grow and develop together. Sharing values and defining goals such as raising children, establishing careers, and creating a desired lifestyle often help cement couples in relationship. But the pressures of life, the personal demands on each individual, influences from the outside, and often a significant "parting of the ways" may ultimately determine if a relationship survives or dies.

Just as there are many different "kinds" of marriage, so there are many different ways that couples may choose to navigate their way through relationship. With the divorce rate climbing these days, it's no stretch to conclude that severing a union is a fairly common solution. But for Hilary, sustaining her marriage was essential for her children. Only when they left home to go out on their own was her marriage over. Although Hilary had worked on learning as much as she could from all of her past significant relationships, from her family of origin, and from her marriage, she was not prepared for what happened to her in the promised land of a new love. The tempting and enticing pull of feeling loved as she had never felt before provided the test for how much she had really learned and for how much she really valued herself.

Ultimately, Hilary enacted a rite of passage not only to mark the ending of a love affair, but, more poignantly, to express and release her sense of profound grief at having given away the best of herself to those supposed intimates committed to unconsciousness. Not surprisingly, her conscious rite of passage is affirmed by a dream—a rite provided by the unconscious.

It is important to note that in popular parlance, the word *unconsciousness* is used to refer to a lack of awareness. In analytic terms, the unconscious refers to that part of the mind that does not consciously perceive, or know, although its influence is almost certainly felt in conscious life. The unconscious, without rules and regulations, knows without compromise; the conscious mind often compromises the knowing with rationalizations and defenses.

"I stayed in a bad marriage for twenty-nine years. While I'd like to think that I would not do that to myself, if I had to do it again, I have no regrets about staying for my children, who are as solid as rocks. Their lives would have been greatly disrupted by a divorce when they were very young. Their father is a chaos machine, and in those years I did not trust my capacity to remain as steady as I thought I needed to for myself and for them.

"By the time I ended the marriage, there was nothing left to mourn, no need for a rite of passage, a ceremony to bring closure. The love I had once felt had been systematically mangled beyond recognition. I was greatly relieved to let it go."

After a while, Hilary had a two-year love affair in which she physically felt her heart open. She can actually remember where they were at the time and how profound her awareness was that she was receiving a kind of love that she had been a stranger to. She felt loved as never before; this man saw who she knew herself to be, something she had not been able to make happen in her family of origin or in her marriage. This was so precious to her. But, as it turned out, it was not enough.

"The love of my life, my soul mate, did treasure me, did love me dearly, but I came to understand that his life experience had left him so insecure that he could not understand or trust that I only had eyes for him." He "saw" her glancing at men that she says she could not have described if someone put a gun to her head. In essence, he needed her to behave in ways that totally took care of his anxieties. It got to the point that wherever they went, he could only be comfortable with her if she looked nowhere except at her shoes. "I was in love, and I was in jail." When he refused couples' counseling, Hilary's commitment to herself, and the rules of sanity, dictated that she end the relationship.

Her grief exceeded any pain she had felt in ending a long marriage or in breaking up a family. But this grief was profound, not only for its own reasons, but also because, attached to it, was the grief of having spent fifty years giving the best she had to offer to parents and a spouse who were committed to unconsciousness, and in that commitment could only see themselves. "My love had seen me, and I felt I had opened like a flower. Yet here I was again with someone who, at the bottom of it all, could only see himself. It felt like the biggest betrayal of all.

"For me, healing necessitated going through a process, a big part of which was a ceremony. First, I needed to wrap my brain around the truth of who he was. This took time. A full two years went by before I was ready for my ceremony."

When the time came, Hilary planned a three-day silent retreat in her own home, culminating on New Year's Eve. She spent time caring for herself, shopping and cooking sensual meals, resting, reading, meditating, and collecting her thoughts and memorabilia. On New Year's Eve, before a sumptuous meal, Hilary lit a fire in her fireplace and surrounded herself with candles. "I gave my thoughts and prayers, both oral and written, and pictures and other keepsakes, to the flames and, in my mind, to the universe. This felt like a cleansing and like true closure."

It had taken her two and a half years to get out of the quagmire by going through it. Although agonizingly painful, it became clear through the process that her perceptions about him had been correct. But there was still a final phase to the process. This man began to write to her, because she had asked him not to call. It was clear that he still loved her, saying that he wanted to share "something" of their lives. Hilary knew that if he wasn't still so insecure, he would have wanted to share everything of their lives.

"These circumstances called for more than just the closure I had achieved. He wasn't letting go. The wisdom that I needed came to me in the form of a dream. In the dream, I was driving a huge garbage truck when I became aware that it had no brakes. I pulled over to a lookout point because up ahead there was a downhill grade, and I didn't want to hurt anyone. I woke up knowing that this dream was a gift from the universe. It taught me that I needed to take a risk—to drive the garbage truck to the dump, downhill or no. I knew what I had to do."

She sent him an e-mail that was straightforward, claiming the space that she had cleared with her ceremony. Once again, her assessment was confirmed. He sent her an e-mail back that was a complete distortion of what she had said, likely because it was not what he wanted to hear. And he accused her of things that proved to Hilary that he really didn't know her at all.

"I guess the moral of the story is that if you are in a world with anyone whose underlying belief is that he or she is at the center of the universe, no amount of coaxing can get that person to move over and share the spotlight that shines on a truly loving relationship. It may be necessary to go beyond ceremony and drive to the dump."

Hilary intuitively understood the power of ritual, a fire ceremony in this situation, to carry away old energy that was no longer useful and to clear the way for new channels to be open for positive future growth. An alternative rite of passage could focus on reclaiming a part of yourself that you have given away or that you have allowed to fall by the wayside. In the shamanic tradition of soul retrieval, the shaman journeys to find "lost pieces," which are then ceremonially returned to the individual for reintegration. If your taste runs more toward the literal, identify a few pieces of yourself that you feel have gone missing. Creating a rite or ritual provides a vehicle that acknowledges and incorporates these elements, bringing them back into your conscious life.

At the end of any challenging relationship, it is often tempting to simplify and abbreviate the whole experience as "time wasted" or a "total failure." But oversimplifying the complexities of human relationship is unfair both to the individuals involved and to the process of growth. In fact, summing up the relationship in a negative way may not only leave a sour taste in your mouth about the relationship, but it may carry over into future ones as well.

The next time you find yourself talking or thinking about that old relationship, pay attention to the words you use to describe it. Make a conscious effort to remember some important features of the relationship that you've discounted. By realistically addressing the issues, you may be able to reframe the entire relationship. Just because some aspects were difficult does not mean that some positive things didn't happen. People learn and gain from almost all relationships, even troubled ones. Every part of the journey counts—all of it, not just what happens at the end of it.

Separating

Good Grief

The ending of her marriage brought about a huge status change for Kathleen, working through all she had thought to be true up until that point in her life. What she learned, most importantly, was that the grief process that an individual goes through may reflect on her prior life experience as much as on the event that triggered the loss. "I had a long history of dealing with denial; you might even say I was raised on it. Although that's a story for another time, it has everything to do with the denial I went through in my marriage and that subsequently contributed to how I processed my grief for the loss of my marriage."

Although Kathleen had kept her thoughts to herself for many years, she had had a deep concern about her marriage from the outset. Cracks she could no longer hide began to surface in the seventh year of her marriage. Each time she tried to discuss the issues with her husband, she always ended up feeling worse than before. He let her know that it was her problem and that she was wasting valuable time of his that could be better utilized at his work. After many unsuccessful attempts at working together as a couple, she suggested going to a marriage counselor. Her husband thought it was a ridiculous idea but eventually went as an alternative to separation. Aside from joint sessions with the therapist, they each had individual sessions, and during these Kathleen poured out the details of her whole life. Sometimes she thought her husband might have done the same, since he seemed very emotional when he arrived home. During the joint sessions, they each brought up their issues and tried to work through them.

For a time, Kathleen thought they were moving forward, but the cold, hard realization eventually hit her—she was deluding herself. She asked for a divorce after fifteen years of marriage. And then the conflict only got worse. Divorce wasn't a word in her vocabulary as a Catholic, not that she didn't believe in the need for it for others. But the holy sacrament of matrimony, for Kathleen, was as important as the other six sacraments. From the day she recited her marriage vows, she fully intended to abide by them for the rest of her life.

Although not wanting to break a sacred vow, and fully aware that divorce would dismantle the entire social structure of her and her children's lives, she also recognized that she was living a lie. After taking years to work through her denial and really getting in touch with her anger, Kathleen eventually got the courage to act. It was like a house of cards falling down; the once orderly family life broke into chaos. To make matters worse, the kids, her husband, the courts and the attorneys, and herself were mostly all at different stages of the process on any given day. It often seemed as if each participant was going his or her separate direction out of necessity, and sometimes out of spite. Although Kathleen firmly believed that she was doing the right thing, she was still filled with guilt, especially watching what her children were going through.

Work was the only place where she could keep a stiff upper lip. "In my daily personal time, at the supermarket, church, or cleaning the house, I'd end up in tears. I'd walk alone on country roads and along the Jersey shore trying to find answers for my life, in the materials I was reading or the professionals I was seeing. I would sit behind a family in church and bawl my eyes out, knowing I'd never again be part of a family of four in church. Depression hung over me like a wet blanket."

Through church, Kathleen started going to a group called Beginning Experience for the widowed and divorced. Although she'd read about working through the process of grief—denial, anger, bargaining, and depression—attending a real session struck her hard. "As we went around a circle telling our stories, all I could do was cry. I choked on my words. One priest jokingly said I was what was known as a 'basket case' as he handed me the Kleenex and wastepaper basket. I learned that the time needed to work through each element of the grief process is a big unknown. Because of my history of denial, it took me a very long time to come to grips with the fact that I was mourning the loss of qualities I had ascribed to my marriage that had never existed."

The process of grief reworked a lot of Kathleen's misconceptions. If she was going to stop living a life that was a lie, she had to learn to live from her inside out, taking full responsibility for her life. The words of a Protestant minister really hit home for her, "Loss must be mourned and a new contract formed." "Over the years, during and after my divorce, I formed that new contract with myself. Sometimes, now, I think that each step of my many walks was a step in a new direction, and each tear I shed was part of the cleansing process of my inner self."

Can you identify with the concept of disconnection, when the reality of a situation does not match up to what you perceive to be true? Kathleen was mourning the loss of perceived healthy, positive aspects in her marriage that had never existed. Understanding the difference can quickly help you determine what is real as opposed to what is wished or hoped for. Spend some time identifying what are imagined or fantasized aspects of your relationship—things you wish for but that aren't there. Compare this to what is actually happening in the relationship, without being too defensive or judgmental about it. Most importantly, get in touch with how this disconnect makes you feel (sad, angry, frustrated, irritated, panicked, overwhelmed, or helpless).

While breakup, divorce, and death are external manifestations of a process and the culmination of a series of events, the accompanying affective states (psychological and emotional) usually unfold in their own way. Often, the time frame for these internal affective states is different and separate from the physical enactment. In thinking about these passages, you may want to consider doing two separate rites around a specific event. One can serve as a logical, practical conclusion, a ceremony of respectful closure to an actual event or process. The other, less tangible perhaps, could focus on issues, even those still unresolved, that also need containment, delineating psychological, spiritual, and emotional changes.

Departing

Death: The Final Journey Home

I lived through again the good and bad fortune of each life,
And my death in each life, and came to life, again and again.

—Buddha

Not all deaths are alike. Death at the ending of a long, full life is sad; we miss those we loved, those intimate ones who shared and molded us by their presence. With the passing of parents, we assume the role of elder. Though this passage is bittersweet, it nonetheless is the natural, organic way that life progresses. Not so the death of a child—thousands of tomorrows, prematurely extinguished forever. How do we make sense of this? How do we move on with our lives when part of our own future is gone?

We choose our friends and spouses. The death of friends, often closer than family, may come to feel like a "death" for the living, as if a part of themselves had gone along with the deceased. Perhaps the most complex of all relationships are those individuals we choose to be with for a lifetime—those "traveling companions" who share our hopes and dreams, our sorrows and tragedies, our triumphs and joys. Sometimes these are dear friend as well as spouse; sometimes these are individuals who provoke and engage us in a tumultuous and exhausting experience that is more adversarial than loving.

Nevertheless, the death of any spouse, even an ex-spouse, marks the end of a once-shared life, and this absence forever after may create a painful void. A friend poignantly described that although her marriage had been seriously troubled for years and the divorce had provided her with much-needed peace and resolution, the continued relationship she shared with her ex-husband around their children and grandchildren came to an abrupt end when he passed away. She experienced this as a second loss, different from the divorce, but nevertheless just as dramatic. In the absence of the one person who had known her best in so many ways for years, she was suddenly left alone with only her own memories to validate her experience.

With all the technological knowledge we possess, with all the wisdom we have accumulated over the millennia, and with all the progress we've made in our evolution, we haven't in many ways progressed much closer to understanding our final transition out of the physical plane, a real crossing over into unknown realms. Death remains the eternal mystery and, as such, is honored as a rite of passage in virtually all cultures. As a communal rite of passage, the funeral releases the soul of the deceased to its final resting place and allows those who are left behind to mourn the passing of their lost loved one.

As rites evolve and shift with the times, funerals today may follow a traditional format or an unconventional one. Harkening back to the customs of old, close family and friends may choose to be involved in the preparation of the deceased for burial, helping to begin the healing process very early on. But the burial is a practical enactment of closure. Ritual should continue well after the actual event. There's a need to find ways to learn to sit with death, to accept its inevitability as part of the cycle of life. Perhaps because of their belief in reincarnation, the Eastern religions seem to do this very well, accepting death as part of a continuum. "Most people have an almost instinctual sense that there is a broader consciousness that transcends 'this skin sack we call our selves,' a consciousness not limited by the body and the ordinary mind."[3] For many, believing that they will return, albeit in some other form, ensures that sacred attention is paid to the passage of the soul.

And perhaps we, too, can learn from the traditions of cultures different from our own. Certain established rituals honor the dead, upholding the custom of annually remembering deceased loved ones, both in the context of family and within the larger community. In Mexico, All Saints' Day is set aside for families to come together to exchange gifts and bring food offerings to feed the dead. Other cultures practice similar rituals on All Saints' and All Souls' Day, and these seem to be uniquely tailored to meet the needs of each individual community.[4]

While visiting Guatemala almost forty years ago, driving up into the mountains from magnificent Lake Atitlan to the town of Solola, I was struck by the cemetery at the entrance to the town, so unlike any I had ever seen at home. The stones marking each grave were pastel colored "houses," each the home of a deceased soul of the community. In stark contrast to what I had thought all cemeteries must look like—somber places, rather monotonous landscapes of inscribed gray stones—I remember having the distinct feeling that life was still going on here. Today, when I visit the graves of my parents and grandparents, I try to remember what I felt so long ago, so far away, in a culture so different from my own. After I have placed a small rock on top of each gravestone of family members, I take the time to walk through the blocks of "my town," saying hello to those I once knew.

The Death of a Child
In the natural order of things, parents are not meant to bury their children, yet through illness or accident, a parent's worst nightmare can and does occur. Unlike illness, painful as that kind of passage is, which gives some extended, quality time with the child, death by accident offers no warning, no time to prepare. There is no time to process what is happening, no time to say good-bye. These often are more damaging to those left behind; it is as if the invisible cords that connect us to one another are abruptly and violently severed. Losing a child in any way, however, is probably the singular most devastating passage anyone could be asked to endure during a lifetime. Some women I've met over the years still have not fully resolved the deaths of their children. And when that happens, getting on with their own lives, with the care of their own souls, doesn't fully happen. Several others have made peace with their losses, having emerged perhaps more appreciative of the life they have moving forward. Although some of the women who share their stories in this book chose to focus on other life passages, still several share in common the loss of a child.

Each person's capacity to endure through difficulty, to cope through hardship, and to handle extremely adverse obstacles throughout life is dependent on many things. Some people seem to have a natural ability, whether constitutionally inherent or acquired over time, to effectively meet life's challenges. Some people heartily embrace and even thrive on situations that require drawing upon inner resources, seeing these as welcomed opportunities for growth. They may even choose to view these difficult situations as vehicles for discovering their inner strength, for learning how tough they are, and for seeing what they are really made of. On the other hand, some individuals simply "fall apart" at what appear to be the smallest changes in their lives, seeming to lack the capacity or the flexibility to rise to the occasion.

The way that each of us has learned (or not) to adapt to challenging situations and life transitions is probably the very same way that we will process whatever happens to us in the future. The individual who has learned to expect and handle adversity will be able to anticipate this and to meet the challenge. The rite of passage provides the essential structure that helps us contain every possibility that life hands us. Having successfully moved through some of these, we know we can do it again.

David's Spirit

As mothers, we think we know everything there is to know about our children. Sometimes, though, it takes a child's death to help us fully understand and acknowledge the meaning of that child's life. Through an outpouring of heartfelt expression, Carol came to realize that David's impact on those who knew him was far greater than she ever could have imagined.

Carol never set out to create a tradition. The rituals that she followed according to her religion guided her through the funeral and the required period of mourning. Having that structure certainly helped her get out of bed and move through the day, though much of the time she remembers feeling like she was in a fog. "Looking back to the days and weeks just after his death, I felt like I was caught in a rough giant wave that eventually rock-and-rolled me to shore. I know there were people around that guided me to land, but for much of that ride I was alone, caught in the turbulence of my grief. The story is simply that all the rituals and ceremony that surround someone's death are adequate enough—that is, until you lose a child. Then, at least for a while, nothing works and nothing matters."

David died one month after his tenth birthday, after nineteen months of chemotherapy, radiation, eight or nine operations, and a bone marrow transplant that put him in isolation for a month. The rare children's tumor, rhabdomyosarcoma, just couldn't be stopped.

His death and his family's terrible loss were felt by the entire community. Though temple funerals are usually reserved for important elders, the rabbi opened the doors to David and all those who mourned for him. His fourth-grade class walked en masse the five blocks to the temple as the custodians worked feverishly to provide more seating to the overflow crowd. The newspaper wrote about his battle with cancer and his love of life. Carol received hundreds of notes and cards, some from people she had never met, offering their prayers, their stories about loss, and their love. She saved every one of them in giant photo-type albums. The act of placing them in the books took up time, a mindless activity. She did it because it kept her with David.

At the funeral, the rabbi spoke of how we don't measure the beauty of a song or a book in terms of its length. So it should be with a person's life. At ten, David had in many ways lived a fuller life than many adults. "But his death shatters the myth of how life is supposed to unfold. We are not supposed to bury our children. We are supposed to watch them grow into adulthood, hopefully giving them the roots and wings they will need to succeed, and then, if we are lucky, we sit back and enjoy them and our grandkids. I believed that. I felt cheated. We all did. Michael was fourteen when David died. He lost his little buddy, the one he could complain to, or about, the one he could tease, the one who shared the backseat in the car. It wasn't until many years later that I really began to comprehend what it must have been like for Michael every time we went out somewhere. Henry and I had each other, but the twosome in the backseat had been halved. At a restaurant, it was odd to go from saying, 'Four please,' to 'three.' My brain would say, 'We had a fourth once, but he's not with us now.' Silent thoughts, but always there."

Carol promised herself that she would not continue on in her life morose and depressed as the way to honor David's life. Her sorrow would not be his legacy. David loved his life too much for her to do that in his memory. Months before his death, Carol happened to overhear a conversation that Michael and David were having in her bedroom. Michael asked, "Do you ever think about dying?" David answered, "Sure, I think about dying, but I try to live every day and have as much fun as I can." His gift to Carol was not sadness; it was courage. He was life affirming even in the face of death. "Once, near the end, when we had just found out he had another spread to his lung, indicating that the chemo hadn't worked and his need for more surgery, he noticed my expression and, taking my hand, gently said, 'You're not giving up, are you, Mom?' His passion for living would be the part of him I would come to embrace and memorialize, but first I had to mourn."

Memories of that first year: He died in February, and that spring, his school, after raising the money through bake sales and tag sales, dedicated playground equipment, a tree, and a plaque with his name in a ceremony that involved the principal, teachers, and children. In response to their love and generosity of spirit, Carol remembers that she could barely squeak out a thank-you, so overcome was she with emotion. What proved to be the most valued and cherished gift was a book made by the children and teachers who knew him. For those who wanted to participate, they were asked to write about an experience they had shared with David, or a memory they had of him, or any feelings they had about him. The result was a book of vignettes, like little snapshots, of David in his life at school, sweet little stories that Carol would never have known about, and that she still treasures.

Also, that spring, Carol got a phone call from one of Michael's teachers. She had found him standing in the opening of a very large window on the third floor at school talking about going to join David as he looked up at the sky. "My dear son, the one who was alive, was dying from a broken heart, and I needed to do something about it fast. Fortunately, our family had been in therapy with an extraordinary man who helped us through David's illness and death and well on into the healing process. His strength and integrity in the face of our family's enormous pain was life saving for all of us. How did he help? He made it possible for us to talk about all of it."

In December of that first year, during the festive Chanukah season, Carol had an experience that remains unforgettable. "I was feeling very blue, and all the holiday merrymaking wasn't helping my mood. I decided to cook a stew and needed some wine to complete the recipe. In the liquor store, I overheard a conversation between the woman behind the counter and her customer. The customer asked the woman if she had put up her tree yet, and she replied that she didn't have the heart to do it. It had only been a month or so since her son had died. She mentioned Sloan Kettering, where David had spent so much time, and I felt like I wanted to reach out to this woman and say, 'Me too, I know what you've been through.' But what I didn't know and would soon find out was that this woman had lost not one, but two sons from a rare genetic blood disease that afflicts Italian families. My heart broke for her. I remember leaving the store thinking that you never know what heartache people carry around with them and what strength they possess to carry on in spite of it."

In January, David would have been eleven years old. Carol doesn't remember if she and her husband came to this decision individually or after talking it through, but they decided not to go to work on David's birthday. Their patients were not to be a priority. Nothing would be more important than going to the cemetery and placing a flower on his grave, speaking or not; it was all about him. "We went for a long drive, most of it in silence, both of us lost in our respective memories, occasionally sharing a remembrance. We stopped for lunch and then headed back home to look at pictures of a lost life. We cried, we laughed, and somehow we knew that this was his day and would always be.

"A month later, on the 25th of February, we faced the first anniversary of his death much as we had faced his birthday—no work, no distractions, nothing but a day of quiet sadness amid the flood of memories. The day belonged to him as did his birthday, and thus began our family ritual that continues even now, twenty years later."

Seeing Claudia Again

When one of Gladys's daughters was diagnosed with myasthenia gravis, an autoimmune-driven, neuromuscular disorder, she and her husband went in search of the world's best specialists, but to no avail. Claudia passed away at the age of thirteen, two years after painful surgery. "We were all devastated.

No rite was useful. The first day after her death, my older daughter and I had a grandiose feeling of connecting with her, that she was a pure soul and that she was so ahead of us that there was a purpose in her life. But I couldn't cling to this feeling and instead felt such tremendous pain, an unbearable suffering. Talking about it and crying over it didn't seem to help resolve it.

"I returned to my college studies after a year, and I appeared to be normal, but any image of my daughter that came to mind would instantly undo me. A very dear friend who had gone through the ordeal with me brought me back from hell, forcing me to talk about my daughter while she shared her own sadness. As memories came up and were spoken out loud, I started to feel better, and the cloud seemed to lift. Letters Claudia had written that I could not bear to bring myself to read earlier became comforting companions to me. Her written words made her alive for me. When I read them, I see Claudia again, and this brings me peace."

The Death of a Friend

The bond that links your true family is not one of blood, but of respect and joy in each other's life. Rarely do members of one family grow up under the same roof.

—Richard Bach

Friends are often the family we wish we'd had. Bonds of friendship go way beyond duty and obligation. You do for friends simply because you want to, knowing that they would do the same for you. True friends show up for you, support you, tolerate your shortcomings, accept you unconditionally, and love you no matter what. Friendship is a partnership, two people coming together on equal terms. They bring out the best in each other. They give their all. Friendship demands more than love; it expects and endures through the good, the bad, and the ugly.

The inevitable twists and turns of our lives down the long and winding road that is our journey are made sweeter and far more meaningful by the "sharing and caring" in a cherished friendship. Rites of passage—marriage, babies, death of a significant other, or any number of important milestone events—are celebrated and honored together.

In friendship, the sum is greater than the parts. As friends, we are ultimately transformed into something far greater than each of us is alone. We open new doors for each other; stepping over the threshold into new worlds, we broaden each other's horizons.

When we recognize one another on a soul level, we are helped spiritually as well. John O'Donohue calls this the *anam cara*, translated from Gaelic to mean "soul friend." The *anam cara* is a person to whom you can reveal the hidden intimacies of your life. The friendship, then, is an act of recognition and belonging. "When you had an anam cara, your friendship cut across all convention and category. You were joined in an ancient and eternal way with the friend of your soul."[5]

Soul Sisters

For Rita, Deedy was just such a soul friend. Although separated by years in age and preoccupied by their very different stages of life, they shared a sensibility and a very similar worldview. Deedy was an actress with an amazing singing voice. In spite of the fact that she had been diagnosed with lupus in her mid-twenties, she was still a ball of energy nearly thirty years later. She quickly became part of Rita's family. But in her early fifties, Deedy's body started to break down from the disease. When she went for dialysis three times a week, Rita accompanied her. The last seven weeks of her life were spent in Rita's home.

"This period of my own life was extremely intense. I was thirty-five years old and had never faced anything like this before, or, for that matter, had never been asked to help make such critical medical decisions. My entire family, including my husband, sister, cousins, and even my four-and-a-half-year-old son, became involved in helping with the endless details of a progressive illness, trying to get Deedy on her feet again. She had no family of her own to be with at this difficult time, and so she became ours. Our already close relationship got closer still."

When Deedy's body and spirit could no longer make the effort to remain alive, she passed away on September 18 of that year. For Rita, it was both a relief to see her friend free from the pain and suffering, and yet so devastating to lose one of the people she had grown so close to and had loved so much in this life. Rita then experienced the roller-coaster ride that seems to be a common occurrence. Although relieved that Deedy was no longer in pain, Rita suffered guilt that maybe she could have looked into making different medical decisions, changing doctors, or researching other treatments. But, more than anything, Rita was trying to come to grips, wrestling with the huge loss of this wonderful person who had been like a sister.

"I also felt extremely grateful that I was the person who was able to spend the last seven weeks of her life with her, giving her some peace and comfort, even when circumstances were so difficult. Just knowing that was a real healing for me. 'Finishing up,' being in charge of everything after her death, was also helpful for me. I was able to distribute her possessions to others who had been special in her life, and I wrote and arranged her memorial service.

"The real rite of passage came on my birthday, two months after Deedy passed away. That morning, I suddenly felt that it was exactly the right time to spread her ashes. My husband and I walked to the park close to where she had lived and found the perfect spot. I then 'planted' a few handfuls of the ashes under a beautiful tree and scattered the rest. It was a very freeing feeling—the time was right, and I knew she would love the idea of her ashes being in the park that she had always enjoyed so much. This closure brought me great peace.

"I sensed that all was well and in place. At that point, I was free of any guilt, especially since the autopsy report clearly showed that there was nothing more that could have been done. With the spreading of her ashes, I knew that I had done everything I could have done. Feeling a sense of completion, I was able to let go of the focus of her death and get back in touch with her life—remembering the joy and loveliness that was, and will always be, Deedy."

"Finishing up" is part of the dying process for both the dying and the living. Taking care of personal property, wrapping up business and financial dealings, and giving away valued possessions may help demarcate life on the physical plane from the existence after crossing over. This is empowering to the dying person, giving her a sense of control, letting her know that she can still actively make decisions, and allowing her to determine how the remainder of her life will play out. We come in alone; we go out alone. Symbolically, letting go of material things helps the one dying to "let go."

As death approaches, it is of primary importance to keep the lines of communication open. Make sure to have "closure" conversations with the dying person while she is still lucid and aware and not too ill to integrate or comprehend the discussion. Often the greatest regrets are about the things we did not have time to say to a loved one. Although death is an uncomfortable topic and is often avoided, sometimes facing things head on helps us gain clarity and perspective and helps the person dying end her time on earth with grace and dignity and with her integrity intact—thus creating a "better" death.

Our Circle Is Broken

Having another individual bear witness to your life is a fortunate thing. Having three such people is nothing short of extraordinary. Barbara's story is about four special women sharing the experience of creating "safe space" for each other's lives, whose ongoing relationship helped to mold and shape who they would become as women. With the profound loss of a dear friend, life witness, and fellow journeyer, part of who we are dies too.

"We were four women who were bonded together from the age of twelve. We were inseparable throughout junior and senior high school, sharing our experiences and feelings about cute boys and changing bodies and learning from each other's strengths. That is where the circle starts for adolescent women. During our eighteenth year, we shared the intimacies of our first sexual experience. Then it was off to college."

When Risa lost her mother to leukemia during the first year of college, all of the women were there to provide comfort and support. This was their first experience with loss. Risa and Gail were roommates during their junior and senior years, and so their bond grew even stronger. During the college years, all four spent summers and holiday vacations together, reminiscing about high school; supporting one another during those times when there were breakups with boyfriends or family issues; and generally seeking each other's approval.

Again, after graduating from college, they took new directions in their lives. Risa, Linda, and Gail were all married in their early twenties. After a short while, Gail and Linda left their marriages. "My friends were there to help me through two long-term relationships that were painful. During my early twenties, my father was murdered on my birthday. It was surreal when I got the news from my younger sister. She told me I had to come home right away; I thought they wanted to give me my birthday present. Through it all, my friends helped me deal with this sad and tragic time."

The women continued on their own journeys. Linda moved to Los Angeles, Gail remarried and moved to San Francisco, Risa stayed in Boston, and Barbara moved to New York. They kept in constant touch with each other by phone and through visits, although these weren't as frequent as in earlier times. Although Linda and Barbara remained single, they shared in the joy of seeing Risa and Gail become mothers. They tried to be with each other during the important times of new babies, men problems, and just growing older.

"I vividly remember the day Gail told me she was having a bilateral mastectomy. I had just flown in from New York, and we immediately went to Nordstrom's in San Francisco for our girlie lunch and the usual shopping. Gail's doctor had done a biopsy (one of many she had been having over the past few years), and the cells found were atypical. With the probability of cancer in the future, there was no question in her mind what had to be done.

When I asked her if she was sure, she responded that she had her two children and that her breasts were not that important. I had never seen her that definitive. Although we couldn't be there physically with her at the time of surgery, we were all in constant communication with her and each other. We were told the surgery was a success."

Two and a half years later, in January of 2000, Barbara got the phone call from Gail's husband. Bad news. On vacation in Park City, Utah, Gail had become incoherent. The cancer was back with a vengeance. They learned that at the time of surgery, malignant cells had been found in her breasts; the cancer had metastasized to her brain, adrenals, sternum, and lung. She immediately began chemotherapy.

"Gail's illness was bringing us closer. We all went to see her that April. She was determined to be a survivor. Aside from her wearing a wig, our time together did not appear to be any different than it had always been. But it was. The three of us realized that Gail might not be growing old with us. Life was changing. We talked more than we had in the past, days became more precious, and our good health was not taken for granted." Gail underwent conventional and nonconventional treatments. No matter how bad things were, she always had a smile, never wanting her friends to know that she was getting worse. But she was getting weaker and was tiring from the chemotherapy. The women could not imagine themselves without her. Gail kept the circle together.

In February 2001, they all gathered for the bat mitzvah of Gail's daughter. Gail was in liver failure, and her friends were in shock. Through the ceremony, she showed enormous strength, posing for pictures, standing on the altar, so proud of her daughter. At the evening festivities, Gail behaved as if she was a well woman. The four friends danced together for the last time.

"That Sunday morning, the three of us wrote a good-bye letter to Gail. We gave it to her husband to give to her when he felt it was the right time. We never spoke of her dying, but she was making preparations for her death. Risa went to visit Gail on March 17, 2001. They spent thirty-six hours lying on her bed, writing letters to her children for special times in their lives in the future, reminiscing, crying, and laughing. She told Risa how each person in her family would behave after her death. She was so right. Gail died on March 28, 2001.

"My life has been different since her death. I realize the importance of always being there for those close to me. I no longer take things for granted, and I am grateful for my good health. The four of us, first together at the parties of our young lives, and Lindsey's coming-of-age celebration, the last time we would ever be together—without you, Gail, our circle is broken."

Creating a "living record" of the dying person may be enormously helpful to those who remain. Tape-recording or videotaping someone's life story keeps them alive for family and friends in the future. A way to create a moving and very powerful ritual is by helping the dying person write letters to children, grandchildren, and so on to mark future occasions, thus becoming a living reminder of the deceased. As we watch people we love go from life to death, this rich, bittersweet time can bring many gifts with it. Authors, doctors, and therapists agree that terminally ill patients seem to die better, with dignity, grace, and a sense of closure, when they are able to create and perform rituals and rites, individually and collectively.

The Death of a Spouse

The death of a spouse will inevitably occur, certainly at the end of a life cycle of many decades, but often unexpectedly, well before that time. Sometimes the commitment to be together survives even when the marriage has failed. These relationships are often codependent, dysfunctional, and even adversarial. By painfully recognizing and defining the marriage in which she found herself for what it really was, unhealthy for the couple and detrimental to herself, Linda came to understand that the only way she could survive was by saving herself. This knowledge helped her endure through her husband's premature death by suicide, and it set the stage for her own transformation into a new life on her own.

The Gift of Life

"I look at my husband's suicide as a gift. He gave me my life back.

"I married my high school sweetheart after his four years in the service and after I graduated from college. At first the marriage was good, and then it slowly deteriorated, first due to drugs, and then alcohol. I happily went to work every day as an elementary school teacher. To the outside world, my life was 'perfect.' It wasn't. I was married to a substance abuser. The drug of choice always changed, but it ended up finally being the easiest one to obtain—alcohol. At one point in our marriage, I started really taking care of myself. I began to really watch what I ate and took up jogging. I would no longer party with him. With my mind no longer cloudy, he was becoming a person I did not like."

A binge of his brought Linda to Al-Anon. Her husband was off somewhere. She knew what he was doing, but she didn't know where he was. In the twelve-step program, she was told to detach with love. What a great revelation it was for her to be told that his alcoholism was not her problem.

Linda went on living her life and trying not to be involved with her husband's destructive behavior. This proved difficult for her, but she made an attempt at it. Going to Gurney's, a spa retreat, for a union-sponsored workshop, she asked the people that she was with to not allow her to call home. She knew that if her husband answered the phone, the conversation would bring her down. She fully intended to enjoy herself.

Upon returning from the workshop, his car was not in the driveway, and the garage door opener wouldn't work. Linda figured her husband was on another binge, but the garage door had her baffled. She walked in the front door only to find a note on the door to the garage from the house that said, "Call 911." "I knew that he was in the car in the garage, dead. I called 911 and a friend. I was calmly angry. He had talked of suicide, and I had told him that I couldn't help him anymore. I had a twinge of guilt, but it didn't last. I didn't cry. I believe that I was in shock. The police came and wrote their report. Hard to believe, but the teacher in me actually read and corrected the report before signing it. I can only imagine what they thought of me."

Linda planned a funeral—her first. The man in the funeral home reached a point where he refused to talk to her. "I wanted the door to the room to say Eddie, not Eddie Grady; to everyone, he was just Eddie. The man didn't want to do it; a friend pulled off the letters of his last name. The only time I showed any anger was when I was by myself. I yelled at Eddie, called him a coward, and told him all he had to do was ask for help. I composed myself and went through one of the most draining days of my life."

The funeral was uneventful. It was the first Grady family gathering without alcohol. "I had made a decision to do things my way. I know I pissed off a lot of people. I consciously made a choice—join him or go on with my life. I wasn't ready to die. I had to go on." With a house full of people that evening, Linda left to attend an Al-Anon meeting.

Linda asked people for what she needed. Friends really wanted to help, but they didn't know what to do. Sometimes, knowing what she wanted was difficult, but once she figured it out, Linda always asked. After Eddie's death, Linda wanted to talk to others who had gone through the same experience. She tried Survivors of Suicide but couldn't stand the attitude of the members. "They were all saying, 'What could I have done?' 'If only . . .' I said, other than quitting our jobs and being with the person twenty-four hours a day, there was nothing we could have done. I had no guilt, and I knew I would be okay. I didn't return. The group leader did call and tried to convince me to continue. He said I could help the others, but it wasn't helping me.

"When people ask me if I was ever married, I say yes. When pressed for details, I say that he committed suicide, and I always follow it with, 'His death was a gift.' When I look at his death as a gift, it is easy to accept what he did and not be angry."

Couples are often challenged by a "third party" being introduced into the marriage. It is easy to understand when this "other" party is a person, but harder when it is an abused substance. If this story resonates with you, take time to identify what "third parties" exist within your relationship. For example, write down "alcohol" on the top of a page, and then categories for mind, body, and spirit. Now write down how alcohol has affected each of these areas. Next, address your role as an enabler, listing things that you do physically, mentally, and spiritually to soothe the turbulent waters. The impact of addiction is not limited to the addict; it tends to weave its negativity into virtually every relationship it touches. Individuals are often willing to look the other way when the abuse heaped upon them is only mental and spiritual, never recognizing it as abuse unless it actually turns dangerously physical.

More subtly, have you allowed other "third parties" to invade your relationship? Perhaps this third party is a career, overinvolvement with children, intrusive family members, or time-consuming physical ailments. Take a good look at your behaviors. For example, being a workaholic is a socially sanctioned way to avoid the emotional needs of family life. Chronic women's health issues can serve as a way to block intimacy. Allowing pushy family members to determine the course of a relationship can be lethal to a loving bond between two people.

What messages have you received from society or your family about being selfish, and how can you come to terms with these as you think about your own well-being and create new boundaries around yourself? As a powerful visual reminder of taking care of your own needs, draw a picture of yourself and your goals, hopes, and dreams in the middle of a page. Then put a border around it. Place all the people and things that endanger your own sacred relationship with yourself outside the border.

Here is another visual example. Imagine your "home" on a plot of land, as big as you need and want, surrounded by a white picket fence. Only invited guests may come through the gate and up to your front door. If, in your mind, unwanted guests invade your space too often, even setting up tents on your front lawn, you may need to be more vigilant about protecting your boundaries and the sanctity of your home.

Emerging Butterfly
When a marriage to a dearly beloved friend and life companion ends in sudden, unexpected death, the effects on the remaining partner can be devastating. Martha set out to review the process of her grieving after the death of her husband, Timothy Francis Daly, in 1991. Her goal was twofold: (1) to understand the process she had gone through in order to better help others going through a similar process of loss, and (2) to understand how the process and this immense event in her life had affected her ability to be a therapist. Martha's concern was that somehow she might avoid the questions that could help others find their pain. Her hope was that, by reviewing her grief process again, she would gain a different perspective on the way she approaches others in search of their grief.

In August 1991, Martha's mother had a severe stroke while house-sitting for Martha at her home in Delmar, New York. Martha and her husband were on vacation in Vermont and sped home after an emergency call from her father. Her parents stayed with them for the eight to twelve weeks of her mother's hospital recovery and subsequent physical therapy.

"The Monday before Thanksgiving, Tim and I made dinner together and then went our separate ways until we went to bed at around 10:30. He tossed and turned and said he was going to the other room to read. I fell asleep almost immediately. Tim woke me at 11:30 telling me he thought we should go to the hospital, as he had food poisoning or maybe the flu. He was experiencing pain across his chest and down his arm, but he insisted it was not a heart attack. I jumped up and started pulling on my clothes before the words had left his mouth, and called the doctor. He called back with the ambulance number. I phoned the first alert and went downstairs to turn on the outside light at Timothy's suggestion. When I returned, he was on the bed in convulsions."

Tim lived for five more weeks, waiting in hope for a heart transplant. He died at about 3 p.m. on December 31, 1991. His family had no history of heart disease. Tim himself had no history of high blood pressure, high cholesterol, or any other indicator of this lurking disaster. In fact, ten days before his heart attack, he had completed a full company physical with flying colors.

"I remember the day of his death as one of stark contrasts. Remnants of hope deteriorated as Tim's heart stopped three or four times that day. The doctor came in to the waiting room to tell us Tim had died. Tim's best friend,

Gary, and his wife arrived, and we spoke about where to send Tim's body. It was New Year's Eve, and so Gary took us out for dinner. Everyone was walking down the street blowing horns and celebrating. I wanted to shout, 'He's dead. How can you rejoice?'

"I suppose the grief process had already started earlier in the week when Tim had been reintubated. I saw the curve of his recovery plummeting. Now that he was dead, I was in shock, just like all the books tell you. I needed to 'do.' Tim's children and I busied ourselves with the funeral. My family drove and flew into Omaha, where much of Tim's family lived. The warmth and love felt welcome against my seemingly frostbitten spirit.

"After the funeral, I felt like a sail blowing in the wind with no idea of which way to point the boat. My brother seemed to hold me together; we made plans for my immediate future. Tim's younger daughter, Katie, and I went to Florida for three weeks in the interim before the memorial service back east. It was there that I started my deliberate search for the process called grief that I hoped would someday help to stop the growing circle of emptiness in my chest."

The very first book Martha picked up debunked several myths about grieving, including the following: "It takes two months to get over your grief," "When grief is resolved it never comes up again," "All bereaved people grieve in the same way," "You will have no relationship with your loved one after the death," and "Grief will affect you psychologically, but in no other way." She derived a lot of comfort and hope from this, as well as from Harold Kushner's *When Bad Things Happen to Good People*. Both authors told their personal stories of grief, and she knew that they had lived through the process. Amazingly, there was hope.

"There were piles of letters upon my return to Albany. Tim had friends all over the world, and letters and telegrams came from Argentina, Italy, Venezuela, England, and all over the U.S. and Canada. I have never been afraid to cry, and in fact tears have usually been my friends. These were different tears than I had ever experienced and a pain that I had never felt before. I read somewhere that the chemical composition of one's tears during grief is different from tears at other times. This makes sense to me. It is a time different from all that went before."

Martha joined a widow's group of mostly young widows and widowers and found a warmth of kindred spirit that she had found nowhere else. These people knew about the hard time she was giving herself, because they had been there. They told their stories, many of them heart wrenching, and gave her little gems about caring for herself. They also told her that many of them felt changed forever and that they were not sure what their relationship would be like if their spouse were alive today. "In a way, we were all the same, as we understood the pain of loss, the freshness of the wound. They told me not to worry about Tim's things. There was no rule that said they must be moved from the house. So I left everything as it was the night he died, and I joked about living with a dead man. They all understood what I meant."

Friends, family, and Tim's children were a life support. People came by to visit. They called, wrote letters, and invited Martha to visit. She learned who was helpful to speak with and who wasn't. Some friends seemed to want to tell her how she should feel. She let them know that this was not helpful, or she just didn't call them back.

"I have never thought much about the benefit of ritual. I had very small wedding ceremonies (Tim and I were married to each other twice); I didn't attend my MBA graduation ceremony. On the other hand, the funeral and memorial service rituals were very important to me. What else could I have been doing the day after Tim's death other than planning an important cere- mony of acknowledgment? The memorial service a month later was also a major milestone for me. Even now, I light candles for Timothy in church or at home."

Martha's journals are full of pain, confusion, loss, and absurdities. These writings not only recount events but, more importantly, develop underlying themes of the grieving process after death. Keeping a written record not only helps to clarify unfolding events and emotions as they occur, but it also affords a level of control at a time when feeling out of control seems to be the norm. Ultimately, writings give an overview, a history of a significant time in the life. Beyond the story, it may be the important insights that are gained, once time has passed and issues and emotions have been worked through, that prove to be most valuable.

"I found a note I had written on January 1, the day after Tim's death, on the plane to Kansas City. 'How did we ever get here? Why couldn't I stop this? Why didn't I see this coming? What am I going to do without him?'" Throughout January, her emotions seemed to ping-pong, from guilt to anger to loneliness and back. Over three hundred people attended the memorial service at the beginning of February. After that, her life changed—with the formal communal services over, Martha could finally get to her own private grieving.

Martha began having months of sleep disturbances. Starting back to work was a lifesaver for her. She needed to have to get out of bed in the morning.

People often walked the other way as she walked down the halls. They didn't know what to say.

In mid-February, she wrote to Tim's brother and his wife: "Yesterday it was seven weeks since Tim died, and it feels like months. . . . I thought my heart would start healing, but it seems to have gotten worse, not better. . . . I figure there is no sense trying to act like I am fine. . . . I told my therapist that it seemed like nine months since Tim had died, and he said, 'It is; the calendar is wrong.' So much has happened. All the hopes and dreams have vanished." His children, Martha's stepchildren, were now related to her in what way? Would she lose them, and with them, more hopes and dreams?

February 17: "Last night I dreamt that I redid our lives. I watched you like a hawk."

March 20: "Honey, I never said good-bye. I was afraid that if I gave up hope, so would you. I have felt so responsible for your death."

April 15: "Last night I spent all my dreams looking for you."

June 12: "I seem to have come out of the abyss."

July 4: "I have realized recently that I have been out in the middle of the ocean, and for the first five months after Tim's death, I was drowning, going under and coming up just long enough to spit out the water and gasp for breath. Now I am on the surface of the sea, swimming toward land, but the shore is a long, long way off. . . . I used to feel like half a person when I visited folks we had known together. Now I feel lonely but almost whole."

July 30: "I am amazingly serene about being manless. . . . I am so uninterested in men it is strange."

In August, on a trip to Minnesota and Iowa, Martha met Doug Peters.

September 3: "I have been on an emotional high for the past two and a half weeks . . . filled with such joy and laughter because of Doug. At the same time, the mourning for Timothy has come up out of nowhere."

September 15: "It seems as if the contrast between my continued sorrow and grief over Tim and my out-and-out joy about Doug clashes like a cymbal. I want to yell out that I was dead and now alive. And still the pain of the loss of Tim continues, an ever-present reminder of the joy we once had."

December 5: "Dear Timothy, I need to say good-bye in some ways. I will never really leave you, as I don't think you have left me. . . . I love you, Timothy. You were my strength, my wisdom, my love. We were a good team."

While Martha's relationship with Doug grew deeper, the grieving for Tim continued. Many thought she was joining in a new relationship too soon. Martha says that sometimes we don't have a choice about timing. Her therapist gave her a lot of space around Doug, congratulating her for giving herself the joy of Doug in the midst of her grief over Tim. "Some said I moved too fast, and others told me to let go of the past. Both of these comments were painful for me, as I was where I was."

Conversations with her minister provided enormous comfort and helped her sort out the intense confusion. A message in one of Gregg's sermons was particularly meaningful for Martha: "At the most seemingly unimportant crossroads, we make some of the most important decisions of our lives. . . . There is an unnamed crossroads in Iowa where there are no street signs because everyone knows the streets locally. But at the corner is a multilayered sign saying, 'fifty miles to Iowa City,' 'one hundred and fifty miles to Des Moines,' 'five thousand miles to Hong Kong,' and 'three thousand miles to Buenos Aires.' It is at these seemingly unimportant crossroads of our lives that we decide if we will go to Des Moines or Hong Kong."

The journaling continues. It has been good for Martha to go back and look at the craziness she felt during the first year after Tim's death and later. The initial period was one of numbness. "And then the enormous hole in my chest developed, and the angry seas engulfed me. The sea definitely calmed as time went on. I worked hard at taking the opportunities given to me to ride the storms and feel their strength and understand them. . . . And death is absurd. It is so much a part of, and yet so contrary to, life."

Martha's story holds many valuable lessons for all of us, whether we have actually experienced a death of this kind ourselves or have gone through the experience with someone close to us who has, or even if we have suffered a loss of something in our lives that is monumentally important to us personally.

Martha's healing process traveled along many avenues: the initial evening of Tim's heart attack and the five weeks in the hospital between that night and the afternoon of his death; the many cards, prayers, and letters of support that she received; the books that helped her through her grief; the widows' group called "Emerging Butterflies" run by volunteer widows and widowers; conversations with her minister; therapy sessions with her doctor; hours of phone conversations with family and friends; the funeral, the memorial service, and other important rituals of remembrance; and, very importantly, her writings. All of these proved to be valuable resources, ultimately providing places to go for discovery, places to gain insight, and places to find solace and comfort.

Loss is an inevitable part of life. All things exhibit a dualistic nature—light/ dark, good/evil—with each of the polar opposites of the duality informing us about the other. If we attempt to deny this principle as it applies to the human condition, seeking to avoid what we perceive to be negative and too painful to bear, and fearing the consequences and the challenges that loss will ultimately bring us, we may end up living an insulated, unbalanced existence devoid of the richness and fullness that experiences at both ends of the spectrum promise to give us. Learning to embrace loss and the opportunities it affords us is essential to our continuing healthy development.

Lessons of Loss

Acknowledge your loss. Acknowledging is about understanding. Before anything else, it's important to talk about your loss, recounting the details and circumstances surrounding it. If the loss is about another person, it's essential to understand your relationship as it has unfolded over time. By acknowledging, you state what has happened to you, in light of the loss you have suffered.

Mourn your loss. Mourning is the vehicle for emotionally acknowledging what was, what actually existed in the relationship. Mourning goes to the heart of expressing what the relationship means to you and how the cessation of it makes you feel.

Take the appropriate amount of time to grieve. It is essential to recognize that there is no specified time period for grieving a loss. Your loss is unique to you. Each person will find his or her own way through grief, creating his or her own time frame.

Don't succumb to stereotypes about loss. Don't allow others' opinions or experiences to influence you about what to feel, think, or do. People who claim to know what you are feeling probably don't. People who attempt to help you cope by delivering pat advice and often misguided information probably mean well but are ultimately not being sensitive to your specific situation.

Take the time to remember. Even after a loss has been successfully mourned, it is essential to set aside time to remember the person or the event. These could include annual days of remembrance such as the anniversary of a death, a deceased's birthday, the ending of a relationship, or any other significant occasion.

PART TWO

THE TOOLS

CHAPTER FIVE

Myths and Symbols

Myths are the mental supports of rites; rites, the physical enactments of myths.

—Joseph Campbell

Myths provide the most direct experience of the timeless and universal themes that define what it is to be human. These themes are just as relevant today as they were in the deep past. But the myths of the primitive world were charged with a reality that is hard to understand and experience today. In ancient times, while the natural world was directly perceived in its basic state, it was also imbued with a sense of the supernatural, a place where the sacred and the transcendent were made manifest.

To understand the myth means to know what the gods and heroes did and how they lived. In essence, it is about knowing a divine history, "a series of events that are unforeseeable, although consistent and significant."[1] The old "myths, totems, and spirits"[2] that once captured man's imagination no longer hold our interest. We are no longer engaged by the myths in a way that would inspire awe and wonder in the magic and mystery of the cosmos and of man's incredible journey within it. When that interest and excitement is missing, the passion for performing rites, and the power they have to transform us, is also missing.

The most evocative metaphor for life is the journey, both outer and inner. Although the journey through life's passages is ultimately ours to do alone, if we remain in touch with those who have gone before us, we know there is a road map illuminating the way. We don't have to "risk the adventure alone; for the heroes of all time have gone before us; the labyrinth is thoroughly known; we have only to follow the thread of the hero-path."[3] By following the mythic map, we are ensured not only completion of the journey, but transformation to a higher level of being. This is the importance of the myth; it is a "shorthand" form that tells us how to successfully navigate the human experience. When we enact the myth by performing the rite, we are living a mythological life. By consciously participating in this way, an individual can learn to live a spiritual life.

"The prime function of mythology and rite [is] to supply the symbols that carry the human spirit forward."[4] Originally, the imagery of ritual was also tied to man and his relationship to the cosmos. As man's knowledge of himself and his universe evolved, the meaning of these symbols moved from the real to the literal, and hence the magic and mystery was lost, and the value of the symbols was diminished. Even rites handed down through the ages, largely from religious traditions, have largely lost their ability to inspire, to excite, and to evoke reverence.

Campbell faults traditional religious institutions for trying to label symbols and imagery with enforced connotation rather than letting the individual find his or her own meaning and significance. Our task is to personally find ways to recapture that interest, to reimagine the stories, symbols, and sacred objects that best define ourselves and describe our place in the world today. The shift is away from searching for and engaging the mystery in the outside world. The final frontier lies within.

A Soul's Table of Contents

Beyond (the intellect) . . . there is a thinking in primordial images—in symbols that are older than historical man; which have been ingrained in him from earliest times, and eternally living, outlasting all generations, still make up the groundwork of the human psyche. It is possible to live the fullest life only when we are in harmony with these symbols; wisdom is a return to them. It is a question neither of belief nor knowledge, but of the agreement of our thinking with the primordial images of the unconscious.

—C. G. Jung

Symbols provide pictorial representations of the constellation of traits assigned to the archetype. "It is through the symbol that the archetypes become visible and the unconscious is brought to consciousness."[5] When the picture "triggers" an awareness of the archetype, something instinctively known and felt on the intuitive level is made manifest to the tangible, logical, thinking mind. Through the symbol, "the opposites are brought together, consciousness receives new life from the unconscious and we contact our essential being—our own wholeness, ourselves as both human and divine."[6] Since modern man suffers from a lack of meaningful symbols, and since society provides few communal rituals and rites, it is up to the unconscious of each individual to bring forth the archetypes that will "provide contact with the highest and most important values, that is, with God."[7]

> The moon spins time and weaves human lives.
>
> —Mircea Eliade

While the meaning and force of any particular symbol will depend in part on the individual encountering it, some symbols have widespread, nearly universal significance. They seem to speak to something primal in us all. Not surprisingly, the moon is such a symbol for women, thought to rule the tides of not only the ocean, but of the emotions themselves.

Sometimes our transformations, our passages, come to us seemingly out of the blue. Although they are not consciously enacted, these magical occurrences are clearly rites of passage as well, since our consciousness is radically shifted in the process. Katie, now in her late twenties, remembers this one experience as though it happened yesterday. Indeed, the moon that rose that night is the same moon rising tonight. This symbol serves forever as the unifying principle of her life.

"Although I could describe what everything looks like, like a moment held in a photographic image, the deepest impression lies in my senses. That moment lives as a memory, guide, partner, agent, and a veritable North Star of sensory perception of my soul's place in this life. This moment holds a connection to the past, present, and future. It is not one dimensional, like a picture or a birthday party or a coffee table in your parents' house, but rather immeasurable and essential, like the force that is our breath, our vision, and beyond our human capacity to grasp in its totality.

"I reconnected consciously to this memory when, during my first year in college, for my first education class, I was asked to write about my own first memory. Since one place in my childhood had such a significant role in my life and effect on my heart, I began to review the experiences that occurred there. I recalled bathing in the claw-foot orange-and-white tub with Lilly soap, the smell of the sea wall mixed with salt water, the distant honeysuckle flowers that lined the road, and especially the morning breakfasts consisting of honey graham oatmeal and hot chocolate that I made for myself and ate at a small table in the living room while the rest of the house was still asleep. Then, something in that flow of experiences triggered a moonlit night during my third summer. Although all of my experiences that summer seemed to encompass similar feelings of safety, trust, freedom, and nurturing, this one specific night seemed to expose something that I still hold deep in each cell of myself."

As Katie remembers it, that night, in and of itself, was not an unusual one at this beach house. "Dinner, my parents' friends, some entertainment, and then the routine jaunt out to the dock with my dad to check out the night sky. But this night, as we exited the house, we were even more delighted with what we saw. As if perched on the roof of our house sat the biggest and brightest orange moon that I have ever experienced. The color was so deep and intense—like an overripe mango—and the light from it was warm and glowing in a most inviting way. The waves turned on the beach with an exceptional flow and aroma, and the stars seemed to step back to honor the moon.

"I can clearly remember being there, next to my father, and being in utter awe of the world we had stepped into. It was as if all worldly elements had dissolved into the background, and the universe stepped forward to present itself in all its graceful and bold essence. The vision was striking, and the feeling was freeing and nurturing at the same time. But the most significant thing was the unspoken conversation that was occurring between the moon, the sea, the sand, the air, and the nameless elements around us, which in this moment shared their tones, murmurs, cries of joy, and voices with us. For whatever reason or chance, this moment was like a door into the universe in its pure and essential state. It was the first time that I was able to hear these sacred interactions, and I still feel grateful to have experienced them."

The evening itself was not one of particular distinction, but it remains the most affective experience Katie has ever known. "This moment teaches me about my truest nature and place in the universe. It has been able to educate me about who I am in the universe, to help me understand how I perceive, and to guide me on my path and deepen my awareness over and over. Since that first class assignment, I have recalled, written, painted, meditated on, and dreamed this moment. I have begun to understand that it was a rite of passage for me, in that I made an unspoken agreement with the universe about my existence and role here. In this event, I literally passed into a new phase of awareness and existence, one that continues to speak to me today.

It always manages to inform me of new teachings, feelings, and, most significantly, elements of my soul and spirit."

As Katie has progressed through other milestones on her developmental path, elements from that moment continue to reemerge. "It acts like a table of contents, index, or family photograph where the contents appear in one single, orderly image, but each section contains multitudes of information in its own singular story. Each chapter that one reads responds to and enforces the central thesis and theme while also carrying its own depth of expression and evolution. It speaks to me constantly, but always with new emphasis, new exposure, and ultimate consistence. It is a road map, in many ways, of my sensory and self-experience. In fact, it seems to function spirally, like the inside of a conch shell or a strand of DNA that revisits familiar but slightly varied curves along its natural progression. This moment stands somewhere on the map of my soul's spiral and reappears to my consciousness each time I round a similar bend.

"The moment holds keys to the elements and images that always have and still do fascinate me, but also to my personal, visual, sensory, and emotional aesthetic and to my experiences in this life. I feel as if it was my initiation into the self I am living to express in this lifetime. *This was my initiation into the participation of life's great elements, cycles, and seasons in my own capacity and form. This moment speaks for what I was, am, and can become in this everflowing bloom of life.* In some ways, in its organic nature, that moment is me in my truest and most essential self, because it was where I became distinctly aware of myself in the universe, my place, my role, and my understanding, without conscious construction about my identity."

Since Katie did not work to create this event, coming about on its own, she continues to revisit elemental experiences in her life in order to gain access to a similar awareness of other rites of passage. Rather than looking to larger, more proscribed events, she searches back for memories that evoke a youthful sense of awe, love, appreciation, and joy. In exploring these moments, Katie has learned much about her perspective, her senses, and her emotions. The most essential part of this process seems to be finding those moments that invoke distinct sensory and emotional responses that most deeply speak to her present self. These responses have collectively been the key for her to begin mapping out the history and experience of her self and may prove to be an insightful and fruitful exercise for you as well.

Symbols that intimately speak to you may come from nature, from a spiritual practice, through dreams, or from cultures that may seem foreign to your life but that somehow are familiar and comforting. How do these symbols inform you? Find those places that evoke visual and visceral responses—museums, houses of worship, places of natural beauty, or sacred sites—and allow your intuition to guide you to find those symbols that most resonate with you.

The Great Goddess: Mediator of Transformation

Although each woman will find her own unique way to express herself, all women hold within them the collective memory of certain feminine symbols, most notably those associated with the Great Mother and the Goddess. The ceremonies and rites used to worship both of these entities of the feminine manifestation were virtually the same in content—with one essential difference. Since the Great Goddess came to represent symbolically the mystical and transcendent aspects of the feminine principle as opposed to the natural and biological aspects as embodied by the Great Mother, any rite, ceremony, or myth relating to the Great Goddess came to function as a symbol, a way to be transformed, to "dissolve the self in God consciousness," as opposed to being only a mere sign, as in the case of the Great Mother.[8]

Understanding the many dimensions of these archetypes can enrich and enliven a woman's understanding of herself, for historically, the way the Goddess was treated over the course of centuries reflected the way women were treated. The plight of both can be traced from veneration, honor, and respect, to betrayal, devaluation, and subservience, to reemergence as a universal feminine life force.

Sheryl intuitively understood and felt this connection to the archetypal Feminine. "As I approached my thirty-ninth birthday, I felt an urgency to know more about myself. I knew that the myths, the classics, and the Bible all presented archetypes for our life journey. In studying the Greek myths, I had come across the story of Demeter and Persephone; that myth, with its many layers, really spoke to me.

"Through studying this myth, I felt I could find whatever it was I had come into this world with, but that remained hidden from me. What particularly struck me was the profound realization that Demeter, the Earth Goddess/Mother, and Persephone, her daughter, were really one and the same. By finding our own 'seasons,' we can descend into the underworld of our own darkness and 'return' every spring (or any other time we choose), to be reborn, to transform to a new status."

The Goddess, "mediator of transformation,"[9] is an archetype that lives inside all of us, a being that we can access and that can emerge at any time.

Universally known symbolic representations of the Great Goddess have taken diverse forms in various cultures, spanning many centuries. Isis, the Egyptian goddess, and Sophia, representing wisdom in the Old Testament, are perhaps her most recognizable expressions, but she is also known as Astarte, Ishtar, Hathor, Ningal, and Nut, among others. Only recently have we "begun to recognize the presence behind these many goddess masks of a being who is Goddess as opposed to God, a force who long preceded her male counterpart as an appropriate metaphor for the Great Metaphor of existence."[10]

The internal identification with the archetype was so compelling to Sheryl that she sought to find the essence of her own original or mythic self by traveling to a place that was synonymous with its source. We'll pick up her story, her journey to the ancient site where it all began, in the next chapter.

The Sacred Vessel: Rite from the Earth

Jungian analyst Erich Neumann's definitive and now classic text *The Great Mother* recognizes early civilization's emergence and development as largely resulting from women's work. Women contributed to all aspects of society— agriculture, ceramics, cooking, weaving, and healing. In the early cultures, women were, quite literally, responsible for survival. Each of these essential activities was ritualized, and these life-enhancing rituals were so valued that they were often passed along secretly among women. In this climate of respect and mystery, the Feminine assumed a creative, transformative role and so became the determining factor in the evolution of early human culture.

Among the most potent symbols associated with the Feminine is the vessel—a sometimes humble, sometimes beautiful container for nourishing food and drink; in addition to making such containers and providing the family with the contents that would fill them, women were also vessels themselves—containers for new life.

As a symbol of the Feminine, then, the vessel holds all that is necessary for survival. Here is a story of the sacred container—in this case, one made of earth from the motherland, and which, in its own creation, provided not only a representation of the Feminine but a rite of passage within itself.

"Walking home from an island off the shoreline of Helsinki, I found myself thinking, 'This is happiness. I have completed a circle; I feel at home.' The sun was shining, and the Baltic Sea was sparkling in the afternoon light of early autumn. In my bag, I had the five beautiful little pots and jars smelling of smoke fire and burned wood, glossy in their blackness after having been rubbed with beeswax. I welcomed this feeling, the same one I had experienced just a few weeks before, with pots I had made of red Finnish clay. I felt the breathtaking security of knowing that there was no other place in the world I wanted to be at that moment and that the vehicle for my creative flow, from now on, would be clay. It was a powerful feeling of being finally connected to myself as well as to other cultures, to the rest of the world around me, and to other women of strong intuition and creative strength."

Tuija felt fortunate to have trusted the intuition she had had while walking on another island two years before. Her family had just moved back to Finland from the United States. Explaining to her then five-year-old son what they were seeing in this outdoor museum, touching the surface of the very old wooden buildings with her fingers, she knew that what she was feeling, somehow part of the buildings and surroundings, was very special. Tuija had the strong sense that if she didn't do something about this intense intuitive knowing, she would be wasting her life, her skills, and her creativity.

It had taken her two years to find a way to express this life force, and for most of that time, she was unaware of the process that was taking place inside her. But now the recognition that she was home gave her the awareness, power, and courage to live her life from that time onward the way she wanted, and it gave her the strength to face and learn from the disappointments and mistakes she knew might happen along the way.

"This knowledge and the process itself, in its intense strength, also make me humble. When I stand in front of the products of my hands, I feel so new and so freshly ignorant with this material that it takes me by surprise to see the results. Where do the forms come from? Where are they taking me? Do others feel the connection to ancient people and places that I do when I handle them? I feel that the clay chose me to work its surface, to bring out the warmth and color that connects me to the land of my birth and the forms that connect me to other cultures and to times long past. I feel humbled by the sheer force of the creative process and welcome it with joyful suspense. Why is it that I am so at home with this feeling? And why did I follow my intuition after so many years of exile?"

Tuija's earliest memories have to do with nature and connection to the earth. Her mother told her that a few weeks after she was born, in the summer of 1963, she was wrapped in a blanket and put next to a stack of hay while the adults worked the field. "I must have been content and happy, with my belly full of milk, the sky blue above me, the smell of hay, and the sounds of the kiuru bird high in the sky. To this day, these smells and sounds awaken a happy, belonging feeling in me."

Her earliest memory of being aware of happiness as a child links her again to the earth. Next to her house, across the dirt road, was a field of tall grass and flowers sided with tall granite cliffs and pine trees. Tuija remembers lying on her back in the grass, feeling the heat of the earth beneath her, looking up at the white clouds sailing by, and naming them by shape.

Before starting school, she played in the woods a lot, sometimes with neighborhood kids, but lots of times alone. She played in the pile of sand in her yard, building cities with roads, parks, and houses. In the winter, Tuija enjoyed building snow castles and snow sculptures late into the dark cold evenings.

"I remember this happiness ending when I turned fourteen. In the woods, I no longer fit under the branches of that certain tree I had used as my hiding place. All of a sudden, I was too old to play in the sandpile; I was embarrassed. I did continue to allow myself to build snow castles and sculptures (I still do), but I missed the woods and the sand. I realized that the changes taking place in my body were sending out certain messages to the outside world, and I became aware of the fact that there wasn't much in the woods to answer those messages. I needed to be with others my age to find out whom I was to become.

"But why did I go on to spend so many years, willingly, in exile?"

Tuija did grow up, of course. Exciting things happened to her during the next twenty-five years, including a year of student exchange in the United States, a good job in Finland, a marriage to an American, and the birth of a son. During her exchange year, she was offered a chance to study in an American university, and this truly changed her life. She spent seven years in America completing her BA and MFA in graphic design, working a year in between the degrees. During the final year, Tuija met her husband. They moved to Finland for three years, where their son was born, and then spent another five years in the United States. A few years later, they moved back to Finland.

Tuija's years in the States were full of life and energy, but also very lonely. She was a stay-at-home mom to her son while her husband worked. "I felt very alone, an outsider to others, my husband included, as well as to myself. All of my creativity went into taking care of our son. Pleasant and rewarding as this was, it wasn't enough."

She eventually set up her own business in their newly remodeled base-ment, but everything was ruined when a subtropical storm flooded the base-ment. Five days into the flood, hundreds of bees suddenly began pouring through a hole in the ceiling of her son's room. A month later, she found herself running down nine flights of hotel stairs with her son in her arms after being awakened by a 7.0 earthquake. In another month and half, they were stranded in a car covered with sheer ice in the middle of the woods in Maine, unable to make a move. After that momentous fall of 1999—the flood, the bees, the earthquake, and the ice storm—they moved back to Finland in June of 2000.

"I really feel that after I got married, I began to keep who I am on hold in order to survive. It sounds like an old story, but I put my own needs aside while taking care of my family, and I lost myself in all of it. Coming home to me meant finding myself again, allowing myself to be the real me again. In some sense, I am only rediscovering myself now as I am tapping into my creativity and discovering my gift for working with pottery. With an acute sense of wonder, I work with the clay, and it seems to guide me. The clay demands patience and concentration, and when I give it (and myself) this, the clay rewards me. The clay seems to form me. I feel fortunate and blessed to have this opportunity to define myself anew."

Often, the patterns of our life become clear to us once we are able to step back and gain a broader perspective. Sometimes these patterns or "life designs" are very subtle, both in their appearance and in the way they work themselves into our lives. Along Tuija's journey, nature served as the tour guide, both informing her early life and later creating patterns and designs, natural mishaps, that, when looked at retrospectively, served to jolt her world and get her attention. Have the events in the external world mirrored or foreshadowed what was happening, or was about to happen, to you internally? Have aspects of the external world influenced you, perhaps providing a heightened awareness or even shifting a course, as they did for Tuija and Katie?

Jung suggested another way to access valuable aspects of ourselves that we may have lost sight of along the way. He understood that our "life mythos, or dream," may be reflected in those things that attracted us as children, the activities and projects that occupied us for much of our alone time. He asked his patients to remember what it was that fascinated them as children, what held their interest for hours, especially from ages four to twelve. By reconnecting to ourselves in this way, and by identifying and engaging our own special gifts and talents, we can once again create excitement and enthusiasm for our lives.[11] Here are some questions to help you reclaim those unique parts of yourself:

1. What were the things you loved to do as a child?
2. What did you enjoy doing when you were alone?
3. Who were your favorite people? Those you felt closest to? Those who encouraged and/or mentored you?
4. What were the themes of your favorite stories (books, shows, films)?
5. What were your fantasies? What did you dream about, in the daytime as well as the night?
6. What exciting characters, actually existing or made up, did you engage or play with?
7. What did you do really well? What made you feel especially good when you did it?

Sometimes, when we are out of sync with ourselves, being "out of our element" makes us feel as if we are in exile. Recall times when you may have felt "exiled" on an external level—in a new job, place, or relationship, or what have you. For example, if you felt exiled starting a new job, was it because the place was new and unfamiliar, or did you feel unsure and insecure in your abilities? For each external factor, note what was happening to you internally. Track any patterns you may notice and seek the theme of your exile.

The Labyrinth

The labyrinth has appeared as a powerful enhancer and engager of our consciousness from ancient times. Perhaps the story that best illustrates this is the myth of Theseus and the Minotaur, in which the labyrinth symbolizes the initiatory ordeal. Ariadne gives Theseus a ball of thread to carry with him into the maze as a way to mark his path so that once he has slain the dreaded Minotaur he can retrace his steps out of the labyrinth. The hero faces death at the center of the labyrinth, overcomes it, and returns to life reborn. The myths reflect a belief system at a level of consciousness representative of the times from which the stories emanate. In these old stories, the initiatory ordeal is really risky business; one's life is really in jeopardy. In more physical ways than today, initiations were potentially dangerous, the adversarial forces unknown, the trials formidable, and the return uncertain.

The labyrinth not only twists and turns around itself; it takes us on a journey through the twists and turns of our spirits, the winding roads of our psyches. It is a spiral form that represents "the cosmos, the world, the individual life, the temple, the town, man, the womb—or intestines—of the Mother (earth), the convolutions of the brain, the consciousness, the heart, the pilgrimage, the journey, and the Way."[12]

As a spiritual meditative tool, the labyrinth is emblematic of one's individual journey or rite of passage. The pilgrim symbolically leaves his or her own world by entering the labyrinth, walking its path, and returning to life, spiritually purified and energized. Here, a shift in consciousness clearly exists, for in this model, all one need do is follow the path, the way, placing one foot in front of the other and moving forward. There are no tricks or traps, only a path toward wholeness. Higher consciousness promises spiritual renewal, found simply one step at a time in the very act of participating.

With the passing of her son, Patricia felt as if part of herself had died too. But life goes on. Her recovery from the depths of despair signaled not only her return to the world of the living but to a renewed faith in the world of the spirit. The memorial labyrinth she constructed is a powerful tool that connects her every day to the eternal mystery.

"When my twenty-two-year-old son took his own life, no one could understand why, especially me. What had driven him to want to end his life? Many years after, I understand his death in a very different way. For him, it was a leap of faith to something better—a burst into eternity, I call it. He gave himself over to become a gift into the mystery."

Patricia immediately recognized the symbol of the labyrinth; she didn't have to research it. It resonated so deeply within her because she was in it; there was a conscious awareness of the mysteries inherent in life. Zen Buddhism taught her early on in life that we are part of the mystery and must try to learn from it. There is no life or death; there are no openings or closings, no beginnings or endings. The symbol is universal; the labyrinth is a journey.

Patricia created a labyrinth on the grounds of her home as a tribute to her three children. Forty-four feet in diameter, it is comprised of a center, or core, the heart of everything. Emanating from the center is a series of loops, the spiral form, which represent the way our life evolves. The core is constructed of bricks made of burnt magma; the spiral, of blocks of tile and white gravel. She created islands in between, places of respite, as well as holes that represent those dark places waiting for all of us on the journey of life. Two hundred and eighty stepping-stones circumscribe the spiral.

"My daughters and I do walking meditations. It is a time for questions, for inquiries. Communally, the mystery of the labyrinth is open to a wide circle of friends, the 'spiritual midwives' as I call them. There, we may gather together to celebrate a wedding or to remember 9-11, or Hiroshima.

"For myself, I practice the labyrinth to access and express the various aspects of my loss. It serves as an affirmation, a sense of belonging to something universal. Nothing is disconnected or arbitrary. I am a part of the mystery. For me, there is still darkness and a pain that is raw, like a stabbing wound. The sense of being in the trauma is still there. Sometimes there is the pain and the tears; sometimes there is the joy and the laughter. It is all part of the healing process.

"A friend once told me that a pearl begins with a piece of dirt. The oyster tries to get rid of this irritation and so excretes a substance to form layers around the dirt. But dirt is still at the core. Pain is still at the core. With trauma, there is a whole different set of questions and inquiries. The mystery takes you. Each time I practice the labyrinth, another layer is added. Eventually, the pearl will emerge."

Perhaps the most recognized labyrinthine configuration exists on the stone floor of the medieval Chartres Cathedral in France. A recent resurgence in interest in this meditative form has been initiated by Dr. Lauren Artress of Grace Cathedral in San Francisco, where both indoor and outdoor labyrinths welcome anyone seeking spiritual renewal.

Each journey along the winding path is unique; at times, there are fellow pilgrims, at other times, one travels alone. "The very act of walking the labyrinth is a ritual. . . . You experience the power of walking a sacred pattern. . . . You need to go all the way to the edge in order to reach the innermost point."[13] The real growth often happens when we risk taking ourselves to the very edge.

Thresholds

The secret heart of time is change and growth. Each new experience that awakens in you adds to your soul and deepens your memory. The person is always a nomad, journeying from threshold to threshold, into ever-different experiences. In each new experience, another dimension of the soul unfolds.

—John O'Donohue

Symbolic passageways—bridges, doors, gates, and arches—mark the movement from one world to another, from before to after, from the profane to the sacred. Rites of passage actually move us from one status to another. As we pass to the next stage in life, there is an actual "opening of the door," a wonderful metaphor for the sense of real spatial movement that symbolizes our shift in consciousness. It is as if we've entered a new room in our inner house: a new identity emerges, another part of ourselves is revealed. When that movement to the next phase is harrowing, we speak of a narrow gate or a bridge eliciting dangerous passage. Standing on the precipice can feel dangerous. Ordeal, trial and tribulation, darkness, demons, and dragons—this is the work of the threshold. What we know to be true and right for ourselves seeks to move us forward.

Threshold imagery must surely be part of the collective unconscious, for, without conscious knowledge, many of the women who share their stories here chose this symbolism to describe their experience. Katie described her moment of profound revelation as "a door into the universe." We witnessed Patti's crossing back over thresholds in search of a son she has not seen for forty years. Sheryl's pilgrimage to the temple of Demeter will lead us, gate after gate, to a moment of heightened recognition, a spiritual crossing over. For Maggie, conquering a deeply ingrained fear is a rite of passage, serving as a vehicle for opening the door to a world much bigger than she ever could have imagined. For Christine, bearing witness to another's pain, opening the way into another's psyche, is a sacred obligation, and a privilege. When Dunya goes through one doorway, there's always another waiting to be entered. As she teaches movement and dance to other women, she watches a familiar scene unfold over and over again—each woman seeming to walk through a doorway into an unknown place.

Over the course of many years, I have had the good fortune to travel to many wonderful places throughout the world. Visiting ancient sites in particular, I am always struck by how, amid the ruins, the post and lintel of a doorway often remains standing, helping to define spaces that once existed. Stepping over a threshold, I can almost sense the life that once was.

The Wizard of Oz: A Young Woman's Mythic Journey

A new mythology of our culture, relevant and applicable to this time in history, may be emanating from stories where a young person is the hero or heroine. The widespread popularity and overwhelming success in reaching vast audiences of *Harry Potter*, *The Lord of the Rings*, and *Star Wars* attest to this phenomenon. All of these depict rites of passage and seem to address a collective unconscious need for their expression, especially at this point in time. Writers and filmmakers today, like their ancient scribe ancestors, understand that in order to shift the way that people engage socially, the information must be mysterious and inspiring, activating the archetypal, mythic aspects of ourselves. While the core content of myth, based on the themes of our existence, may remain the same, the form that these myths take in order to be effective teachers and touchstones for us has to change.

The universal appeal of L. Frank Baum's *The Wizard of Oz* for audiences of the past as well for those today may very well be attributed to the mythic thread that runs just beneath the surface. Unlike so many other spiritual journeys or quests made popular in literature and film, this pilgrim's journey is about a young girl coming of age and coming into her own. It is an initiation, a rite of passage, in every sense of the word—the departure, the threshold with its trials and ordeals, and finally the return home transformed.

For the very young, it is simply a great story with mostly likable characters that can be enjoyed at face value. For those a bit older, the unconscious can begin to conceptualize about the dual nature of all things, about conflict and resolution, and about decision making and risk taking. The story is replete with rich symbols and layers of meaning; it is literal and metaphorical, fanciful and mystical. It is about exploring the real, practical world, as well as the worlds of the psyche and the imagination. It teaches valuable lessons about friendship and loyalty, it celebrates joining in community for a common purpose, and it embraces the sentiments of love and appreciation of family and home. The message: when we trust ourselves, we honor our individual spirits.

The story of how Oz got its name may be merely apocryphal, but I like it anyway. The author, L. Frank Baum, purportedly created it from looking at this file cabinet, A–N and O–Z. Dorothy, meaning a "gift from God," is counterbalanced by her surname, Gale, which indicates that a storm is brewing; this is the pair of opposites, the dynamic duality which creates a whole. The Good Witch and the Bad Witch are archetypal extremes of a whole as well. Dorothy's best friend and companion in her otherwise dreary life—her little dog, Toto, meaning "the all, the everything"—instinctively understands all there is to know. But Toto is far more than this to Dorothy; he provides the container of instinctive knowing until Dorothy grows into owning it herself.

As the movie opens, we see Dorothy and Toto running down a road that is simply and starkly marked by horizontal fences and vertical poles. On a tree in the foreground hang a triangle and a circular rubber tire. The house itself is "all right angles and triangles,"[14] while the bridge that Dorothy later crosses to get to Professor Marvel is decidedly triangular. These geometric elements symbolize home and safety.

Life is dull and drab in Kansas, barely lifting itself beyond shades of gray. Dorothy's unconscious awareness of all things, as they appear to her in black-and-white, is decidedly being challenged. The film's "driving force is the inadequacy of adults, even of good adults, and how the weakness of grown-ups forces children to take control of their own destinies, and so, ironically, grow up themselves."[15] This speaks directly to the lack of containing walls for young people. If the adults have not been initiated themselves, there is little empathic understanding and recognition of the needs of young people who are attempting to come into their own, with the result that so much potential stands in danger of being misdirected or even lost.

Dorothy's anthem of release from this monolithic, washed-out landscape, "Over the Rainbow," is set against a horizontal and vertical backdrop, with the added circular form of the wheels of the farm equipment. It might very well be that the only thing of color Dorothy has ever seen is a rainbow. We see her gazing longingly heavenward, to a break in the skies, from which emanate soft rays of light. This child of imagination is caught in a world of practicality. The adults are too busy counting chickens to pay attention to her and too submissive to protect her with as much as a reasonable protest when Ms. Gulch comes to take Toto away. Dorothy's inner world, the emerging of her intuitive knowing, links her to the memory of the land she's "heard of once in a lullaby." Who sang this to her? We are told that Dorothy is an orphan. Does she remember her own mother, or is her journey of self-discovery also about the search for the archetypal Good Mother?

As these powerful themes emerge, Dorothy passes into the unknown: "Danger and evil are invariably twisty, irregular and misshapen"[16]; her inner turmoil is mirrored in nature itself. Since running away is no solution for her problems, nature provides her with the vehicle for escape. The order of her simple life, with its clear, habitual, and logical routine ordinariness, is threatened by a tornado. Yet, far from evil, the events set in motion describe the heroine's journey—leaving the ordinary, embarking down a road to lands unknown and mysterious, and enduring through ordeals meant to shake one's beliefs and attitudes to the core. Surrendering to the process, both inner and outer, rather than to the threat of sinister forces which demand that you give up the fight and meekly submit *is* the mythic journey of transformation.

And if that were not enough, the film is symbolically filled with threshold imagery. The sequence leading up to stepping foot into the "land beyond" is rich with the symbols of the threshold, where the initiate enters that liminal, transitional space and place in order to be transformed and healed. As the increasingly violent winds threaten to blow everything apart, Dorothy tries to push through a narrow gate. As she struggles to reach the door to her house, the screen door violently flies off its hinges. Finally, opening the door, and then a series of doors within the house, she searches for Auntie Em and Uncle Henry. Unable to find them, Dorothy runs out of the house and tries but can't open the cellar door, so she runs back into the house. In her room, the window breaks free from its frame, knocking Dorothy unconscious. She wakes up to view a surrealistic parade, a series of people in apparently unrelated events, floating by her window, and it is here that Miss Gulch becomes the Wicked Witch. The house, once a safe haven, twists and turns wildly out of control, and suddenly all is still. Dorothy opens her bedroom door, stepping into a world vibrant and alive with color and nuance.

Her fellow travelers to the wizard are the scarecrow, the tin man, and the cowardly lion. Each of them joins Dorothy with a personal request for what he most hopes to receive—the brains, the heart, and the nerve. The spiritual journey balances the capacity to be mentally alert and flexible with the ability to feel, to be emotionally open to whatever comes along, and cultivates the courage to live life fully, with total awareness, so as to best express one's truth.

When the foursome embarks on their journey, Dorothy is given the ruby slippers. Estes notes that "feet represent mobility and freedom. . . . Without psychic shoes a woman is unable to negotiate inner or outer environs that require acuity, sense, caution and toughness."[17] Throughout the journey, the Wicked Witch tries to snatch the slippers. "Red is the color of life and sacrifice. To live a vibrant life, we must make sacrifices of various sorts."[18] Red, too, is the color of the first chakra, the grounding chakra. As long as Dorothy stays grounded, keeping her feet firmly on the path, proceeding on her journey one step after the other, she is able to continue moving forward.

The ruby slippers serve as a transitional object, affording her continued protection. As Dorothy travels further along on her path, she claims more of herself and ultimately gains true ownership of her own unconscious, made conscious in her integration of courage, feeling, and mental strength. After a while, Toto ceases to be the object of pursuit. Instead, it shifts to Dorothy, whose life and vitality present a real threat to the Wicked Witch. The realization hits her hard that the slippers will never come off as long as Dorothy is alive.

The yellow brick road is depicted as a spiral, the form here contained and symmetrical, unlike the out-of-control, wildly spinning cyclone. Glinda, the Good Witch, makes her appearance emerging from a perfect ball or bubble, the geometry changing to indicate the circle of wholeness and unity. The spiral form depicts not only life's journey but is a descriptive symbol of the basic organization within the natural world, including the development of consciousness. Yellow represents the third, or solar plexus, chakra, the seat of feelings. Dorothy and her companions are asked to "follow their feelings" as they go in search of the wizard, to the Emerald City (green representing the heart chakra), to the place where they hope to find their heart's delight.

All of the elements of the natural world come to Dorothy's aid: wood and metal (tin woodsman), the plant world (scarecrow), and the animal kingdom (lion). When only humans (Dorothy) and animals (the lion and Toto) fall asleep, succumbing to the poison of the poppy field, the scarecrow and the tin man come to their rescue, waking them in order to escape.

Fire heralds the appearance of the Great Oz, but its most prominent display is when the Wicked Witch attempts to destroy the scarecrow. Using her broomstick to set the scarecrow on fire, she cannot anticipate Dorothy's quick action in response. The water meant to put the fire out instead douses the Wicked Witch, dampening her power and causing her to melt away into oblivion. Rain rusts the tin man, threatening to put him out of commission, and tears of emotion tell us that the tin man has no reason to fear that he has no heart. As it snows, the spell of the poppies is broken, helping to awaken Dorothy, the lion, and Toto. The element of air demonstrates its force in the cyclonic funnel destroying everything in its wake. But air is most associated with the wizard, a kind but befuddled and flighty man, who just makes it up as he goes along, as full of hot air when he is the wizard as he is as a balloonist. At the end, as the balloon takes off leaving Dorothy behind, he exclaims, "I can't come back. I don't know how it works."

Having finally gained access to her own unconscious, Dorothy learns to fully trust her innate intelligence and instinctual wisdom. Over the course of her journey, she comes to embody her whole feminine self and all that is identified with it—intuitive knowing, imagination, love of nature, family, friends, and home. "The power center of the film is a triangle at whose points are Glinda, Dorothy, and the Witch; the fourth point, at which the Wizard is thought for most of the film to stand, turns out to be an illusion. The power of men, it is suggested, is illusory; the power of women is real."[19]

In his simple, direct way, the scarecrow states the obvious concerning the ordeal: "I think it'll get darker before it gets lighter." And he's right. Through the forest, through the poppies, they finally arrive at the gateway to the Emerald City. Getting an audience with the wizard takes time and persistence. Once in his presence, Dorothy and her friends are filled with fear and trembling at the sound of the great man's name, his booming voice, and his huge presence.

Having placed their fate in the hands of this self-proclaimed "head" of state, they have incorrectly assumed that someone to whom they have assigned unrealistic powers can actually grant their wishes. But Toto is not fooled. In touch with his primal instincts, he unmasks the trickery of the wizard, reducing him to just a man, "a good man, but a terrible wizard," with no special abilities to make things happen for anyone.

What to do now? When Dorothy and her friends realize that they have taken responsibility for themselves all along, having acquired the brains, the heart, and the nerve through their trials and tribulations, they know that they are able to complete their journey successfully on their own. The wizard, combining a little hot air with a lot of wisdom, understands that conferring the gift of a "symbolic seal of approval" upon each traveler is the necessary finishing touch. And so, the scarecrow becomes a "doctor of thinkology," the tin man is given a "ticking testimonial," and the lion is given a "medal of courage." As for Dorothy, she comes to know that she always had the power to return home—not just to Kansas, but home to herself.

Lessons from Oz

Heed the call to adventure. This call is the internal impulse that alerts us to move beyond the circle of what is most familiar and intimate to us personally. By doing so, we gain access to aspects of ourselves that we might otherwise never know. Adventure broadens our capacity to explore and experience.

Choose traveling companions wisely. Our journeys are made easier and our experiences are greatly enhanced when we choose to surround ourselves with individuals who share similar values and who have learned to put aside personal goals for the good and welfare of the collective group.

Press on. No matter what happens to you on the journey, you must promise yourself that you will not stop until your desired goal is reached. *But, if it becomes necessary . . .*

Know when it's time to change course. Be flexible. Learn to adapt to changing conditions. Become aware of shifts in your environment as well as shifts in your perceptions about what is going on around you.

Develop your instincts. Cultivate your intuition. This is a distinctly different capability from what you understand through accessing information. It is totally separate and apart from what you logically perceive and can reason intellectually. Heightened instinctual knowing promotes survival.

Surrender to the mystery. Surrender does not mean giving up. It means *giving over* that which you don't know or understand to a higher power, trusting that what will ultimately happen is for the greater good.

Strive to live big. The heroes of the past have shown us that the mythic life is one lived on a grand scale. The landscape of the mythic journey offers wide-open vistas and challenging terrain.

Meditation: Gifts of the Darkness

Sit comfortably in your chair, feet flat on the floor, hands resting comfortably next to you or on your knees. Close your eyes. Scan your body from your feet to your head for any tension. If there is stress anywhere, ask that part of your body to let go of its tension.

Now, direct your attention to your breath. Take in a deep breath and let it course through you. Release any tension as you exhale. Do this again. Breathe in; breathe out. And breathe in and breathe out once again.

Now imagine that you are on a road designed to help you find your way on your own personal journey. You are walking down this road without any expectation. All that is being asked of you is to continue moving forward. You do this for a time, enjoying the scenery around you, the sounds, just enjoying the moment.

Suddenly you see something very far in the distance. As you get closer to it, you can see that it is a building. In fact, as you get even closer, you see that it is a castle. Closer yet, you see that it is massive, made of stone, seemingly impenetrable, and guarded by several soldiers.

A moat surrounds the castle, but the bridge over the moat is down, so you hurry across it. An armed guard stands in front of the gate. It is your job to get inside the castle. Imagine how you would do this, and remember it.

Once inside the castle amid the labyrinth of rooms and the meandering corridors, it is your job to find the dungeon. Imagine how you would do this, and remember it.

There is someone waiting for you in the dungeon. Imagine who this is, and remember it. You have a question to ask this person. It is a question you have thought much about. Imagine what this question is, and remember it.

This person has a gift especially for you and has been waiting for you to come to receive it. Imagine what this gift is, and remember it.

Now it is your job to find a way out of the dungeon. You must take this person with you as well. Imagine this, and remember it. Out of the dungeon, you and your companion need to find a way out of the castle so that you can continue on your journey. Imagine this way, and remember it.

Once out of the castle, you and your companion (if he or she so chooses to accompany you) are free to continue walking down your path. You feel wonderful. You have achieved your goal. You have a deep sense of personal accomplishment.

When you are ready to come back to the present, bring your conscious awareness here, to this place in time. Become aware of your body, become aware of your breath. Slowly open your eyes.

CHAPTER SIX

Exploring the World

If we are always arriving and departing, it is also true that we are eternally anchored. One destination is never a place, but rather, a new way of looking at things.

—Henry Miller

Journeys are one of the most powerful and literal tools for making passages because they manifest our internal drives and desires in the outside world. The journey is a deliberate effort to move beyond ourselves. We venture into unfamiliar territory to seek challenge and change, to find new answers and dimensions. Journeys free us from the bounds of our own space, allowing us to experience things in a way that is not possible in our home environment. They open us up to the unexpected and the magical. Such experiences can be consciously recognized as markers of past growth and impetus to further growth, as steps beyond limitations and into freedom, and as leaps into new aspects of one's identity.

Journeys also help us connect with the universal sense of what it means to be human. When we journey among others beyond the familiar, we have the opportunity to see what is common among all people: how we love, how we work, how we relate in family and community, what our basic needs are, and how we meet them. Journeys connect us with the pathos of the human experience, and through this teach us compassion for others. They broaden our understanding, heighten our experience of who we are, and challenge us to express our true nature more fully.

The journey may be a trip to just get away for a while, or a move to a place that becomes our new home. It could be a "call to adventure"—the hero's journey—following a deeply felt desire, an instinctive pull to a place for some purpose. Our journey may be to overcome a specific obstacle or to connect with a spiritual or historical source. Or perhaps the impetus simply resides in the knowledge that going someplace new will bring new opportunities for change. We may not know what we're looking for, but we know we're looking, and the journey helps us find it.

There is a long history of renowned rite-of-passage journeys. In literature, the protagonists of works such as The Odyssey and Pilgrim's Progress were transformed by epic journeys that moved them through several phases of their lives. The enlightened religious masters tested their faith, strength, and resiliency, or strove toward a higher level of understanding, in solitary journeys. The Buddha left his cloistered world of privilege to witness poverty, disease, and death. Jesus journeyed into the wilderness for forty days and nights to test himself against temptations and evils. Moses climbed Mount Sinai to receive the Ten Commandments. Pilgrimages are another classic form of the rite-of-passage journey. According to anthropologist Victor Turner, the pilgrim hopes to have "direct experience of the sacred, invisible, or supernatural order, either in the material aspect of miraculous healing or in the immaterial aspect of inward transformation of spirit or personality."[1] In addition to being an obligation for the devout, more and more individuals are visiting sacred sites like the Vatican, the Ka'aba in Mecca, and those in Jerusalem, Lourdes, Santiago de Compostela, and Machu Picchu, to access and enrich their spiritual lives.

In contemporary culture, the hero's journey is a widely used rite of passage. Its appeal is evident in the enormous interest in reality TV shows like Survivor and its countless spin-offs, which depict all kinds of challenges and transformations. The key ritual elements—separation, the ordeal, and return—are present, yet instead of being positive journeys to the soulful place within, these journeys are typically about outdoing fellow travelers, with competition obliterating compassion. Nonetheless, this phenomenon is evidently tapping into the collective unconscious: exploration and pioneering are, once again, exciting to the human psyche. Something stirs inside us when we see human beings entering forsaken lands, carrying nothing to ensure their survival but their personal baggage. We encourage them from our living rooms. We root for someone with whom we identify. We plan strategies, fantasizing how we would behave, what we would do, if we were there. Remarkably, the medium of television, which all too often dulls our awareness, seems to be activating an ancient consciousness within us. This same enthusiasm can serve us immensely if it moves us beyond spectatorship, spurring us off our couches and into the adventure of our own lives.

I've found journeys to be a great tool for making passages in my own life, and I recommend them to my patients when feasible. Journeys may serve to give them a boost, to remove them from a difficult situation, or to help them experience new things without daily life excuses; for instance, they can gain new perspectives on their psychological life by wandering alone or speaking with strangers, they can acquire enrichment through embracing other cultures and traditions, and generally they can do things they would never do and be someone they would never be at home. The journey is often the key to moving them into new phases of their lives.

These same benefits are among those described by the women who share their journeys of passage here. Their stories, while distinctively contemporary, mirror the age-old drive to journey beyond oneself. While airplanes and divorce did not figure in the lives of our distant ancestors, the forms of journeys they used as rites of passage, as well as their motivations and outcomes, are all echoed in the journeys of women today. In thinking about these stories, bear in mind that the journeys are not so much about going to a certain place but about bringing the world inside oneself, and in doing so, broadening one's self-knowledge.

Envisioning a New Life

The hero's journey always begins with the call. . . . The call is to leave a certain social situation, move into your own loneliness and find the jewel, the center, that is impossible to find when you're socially engaged. . . . You are to cross the threshold into new life. It is a dangerous adventure because you are moving out of the sphere of the knowledge of you and your community.

—Joseph Campbell

A powerful way to mark a passage is to create one based on the classical model of the hero's journey: intentional separation from the familiar, the transition, entering into a no-man's land with potential dangers to contemplate and overcome, and the return home, transformed and victorious. The test is both external (being in the wild, amid the unpredictable elements) and internal (an extended period of solitude and contemplation). As difficult as the external trials may seem, the internal test is the ultimate challenge. You are being asked to sit with yourself with no distractions and to allow whatever comes up to simply do so, without censoring or judging or being critical of yourself or of the fear that may arise. It is about coming to know yourself, your fears and your strengths.

This is the work of the vision quest, a type of hero's journey in which the journeyer traditionally goes out to gather spiritual knowledge and then comes back with a vision to feed the tribe. Previously only open to men in tribal cultures, the quest marks the passage to adulthood. Elise, one of the bolder journeyers interviewed for this book, chose to make this dramatic rite of passage at a pivotal time in her life. But why? What would make a fifty-four-year-old woman carry a thirty-pound pack for five hours up a two-thousand-foot elevation and then stay alone on a mountain for four nights and days?

Divorced, with her grown sons heading off on their own, Elise found herself alone for the first time in thirty years. The experience was both liberating and frightening. As much as we may look forward to having more time to ourselves, when we do, we may suddenly find that we are required to look within. Elise knew that she needed a formal process to help her successfully make her transition. As a shaman accustomed to exploring the natural world, the vision quest suited her ideally. In many ways, it is an accelerated form of psychotherapy—one for the hearty. Instead of your weekly appointment with the therapist, you have an appointment with yourself—all day, for several days.

But not even nine months of preparation with a facilitator fully prepared Elise for what to expect. What she did know was that there was a very real element of danger. You might die out there. Hypothermia was a possibility. You could break a leg or get sick. But that is a part of it: the risk, and the accompanying fears. At a sweat lodge on the night before she ascended the mountain, other questers prayed for her vision.

"The hike in was the hardest physical thing I had ever done. Birthing babies, your body takes over the job. Here, every step was by choice. If I looked to see what I had to do in the next ten feet, I'd get demoralized. It became a meditation. Nothing but one foot, next foot. Everything else dropped away.

"Finally, the top! Escorted to my site. The job of setting up the tent. Then the dark—no moon. All the sounds at night are so loud. The first night, I got scared. There was something out there big enough to break twigs when it walked, sniffing at the door of my tent. I froze. I prayed. It helped. Whatever it was moved off. I heard a wolf or coyote howl nearby. It sounded like a woman. I hoped it wasn't calling for others to join it."

Elise's protection against the night was a tent—a very thin piece of material. What is the metaphor here? For Elise, it was the acknowledgement that she feared things in her own darkness that she had not identified and did not know how to work with. But one doesn't have to go into the wilderness to identify the very fine membrane that separates each of us from everyone and everything else. This self-protective barrier invisibly shields us from what we perceive to be potentially dangerous, the challenges to our integrity coming from external sources. How thin or thick-skinned are we? How well will our suit of armor protect us from fatal strikes? How many defensive walls protect our tender inner core? Can we break down these walls and confront our demons to stand in our own authenticity, gaining, once and for all, ownership of ourselves? This was one of Elise's great tasks.

Confined by a site in dense underbrush with steep drop-offs on three sides, Elise could only sit, with nothing to distract her from the process of observing her mind and her surroundings. For the next days and nights, she experienced the beauty of a star-spotted night sky, relentless rain and a leaky tent, a wind sounding like a freight train, cold nights and layers of clothing, and sporadic sleep filled with dreams of animals pushing on the tent.

"All the while, something subtle and extraordinary was going on. I'd watch the wind in the trees for hours. I watched every bird hunting the bugs that tortured me. I saw the mice in the fern jungle. Each day, I got quieter and more attuned to the vibration of the place I was in. The animals came closer. As I dozed in the sun, a chipmunk jumped into my lap, startling us both. The birds perched two feet from me, eating worms on the pine tree.

"My brain would shut down; then the most vivid realizations would come. I loved it there—the expanse of time, the slowing down of everything. I wanted to stay. I was holding on to the last day. I tried to think of how I could get food up there and never come back. But that last night was uncomfortable—no soft place. By morning, I was ready for all the soft things: warm food, hot baths, deep beds, shampooed hair.

"The interior change in me is the real story. Things that hurt me terribly just do not anymore. The hurt is gone. I have accepted my humanity as a beautiful thing and have acquired a kind of self-respect that can't be described. I see all the fruit of the hard labor that my life has produced. I have the singing of the stars and the teachings of the stones, and I am grateful to my bones. I am breathing new air, in a new life. I am still being informed by what I learned . . . and will be for the rest of my life."

Elise chose a particularly challenging journey—with dramatic results. Having to confront whatever external and internal challenges presented themselves to her taught her acceptance, independence, and strength. She was able to put certain feelings and relationships behind her and came away with a greater appreciation of herself, a deeper connection with nature, and a new sense of time. She came down from the mountain a very different person than when she had gone up. It was a true rebirth.

For Elise and for others who make the hero's journey, old beliefs and identities fall away, allowing a fuller expression of the person, their essence, and what is most essential to them. But climbing a mountain to find your truth may not be for everyone. Outward Bound trips, retreats, sweat lodges, and even vacations devoted to being by yourself in one place with no set agenda are alternate ways to discover or rediscover parts of yourself. Choosing to sit with yourself in a remote place with no distractions is a very effective way to access your inner knowing. To make the most of the experience, track your feelings by journaling, drawing, or through any other medium that appeals to you. This can help bring greater awareness of what is happening to you during the experience itself, and later it offers a record to reflect upon that may be more reliable and direct than memory.

Flying beyond Fear

Working with obstacles is life's journey. The warrior is always up against dragons. Of course the warrior gets scared, particularly before the battle. . . . He or she is just about to step into the unknown, and then goes forth to meet the dragon. The warrior realizes that the dragon is nothing but unfinished business presenting itself. . . . Basically what we work with is our fear and our holding back, which are not necessarily obstacles. The only obstacle is ignorance, this refusal to look at our unfinished business.

—Pema Chodron

Obstacles may be physical impediments to forward movement, or they may be mental blocks, and thinking and talking about them will not necessarily allow you to overcome them. Sometimes an action is what is required to make a shift. Journeys can be the ideal action for overcoming obstacles. They can provide the vehicle for taking you outside of your head, shaking up your perceptions, forcing new behavior, and fostering growth. Journeys can help individuals conquer fears, allay anxiety and depression, gain valuable self-insights, and acquire additional tools needed to work with future emotional, psychological, and spiritual transitions. In the end, overcoming a mental or emotional obstacle is a true rite of passage, for our inner journeys are every bit as real as those we embark upon externally.

A lot of what we're all going through is something called life. We often need to work with what's there rather than try to eliminate it. When we reframe issues such as depression and anxiety as points along a natural continuum of life passages, we broaden their definition beyond the medical and pathological. Psychological conflict and psychic pain are part of our internal wisdom's positive alert system. They are red flags signaling that there's something we need to address. The best approach may not be to find a quick fix to recovery, but rather to offer a clear path for individuals to reap the benefits of their own fertile darkness and grow from all of their experiences, light and dark, good and bad. Any attempt to interfere with or short-circuit the natural cycling of a conflict may cut off the necessary ordeal on the way to emotional growth.

As a therapist, I have encountered many patients who exhibited heightened anxiety and even panic, most specifically in the liminal or threshold phase of a physical passage from one place to another. For Maggie, whose story follows, and for many others, the idea of being up in the air for hours is terribly frightening. But even movement over bridges or through tunnels can manifest the same feeling of being out of control, in the betwixt and the between. It is that unknown place between here and there that is the most uncomfortable. How do people overcome such feelings? Some address the symptoms, which often *feel* like the problem, but aren't, so relieving them does not tackle the problem at its source. People's willingness to face personal obstacles at their root, and how they go about it, depends on a number of factors. How uncomfortable are they with the problem? Is it merely a nuisance, or is it critical to make the change? To see how such issues play themselves out in the real world, let's take a look at how one woman went about making her most feared passage and how this action affected her life.

Maggie wanted desperately to move beyond the narrow parameters of the small town she had grown up in, but she felt paralyzed by her fear, especially her terror of flying. "Fear—and the anxiety it engenders—is a really big theme in my life. I've been afraid of a lot of things, but my worst fear has always been of flying. It was intense enough, for example, to make me take a train (followed by a rental car) to travel the seven hundred miles to my sister's wedding in Ohio. This trip took far more time and energy than flying would have, and cost four times as much! So the next time I went to Ohio, I resolved to fly, and I did. But the experience wasn't a pleasant one. Miserably afraid and uncomfortable, sick to my stomach, and clutching the seat, I told myself, 'I not only want to fly; I want to be comfortable.'"

Maggie took a weekend seminar on the fear of flying given by American

Airlines. Boarding a plane, the pilot talked about the mechanics of flying and explained the controls on a tour of the cockpit. Maggie and her classmates were taught relaxation techniques and a way to contain anxiety by consciously restricting one's worrying to a limited period of time. At home, Maggie stood in front of a mirror and articulated everything she was afraid would happen to her. After a while, she found it difficult to keep coming up with new things that scared her. At the end of the weekend, the group took an actual flight to Raleigh-Durham with the pilot, attendants, and the two psychologists who were on their "team." Everyone was amazed at how little fear they really had. When Maggie became frightened in the middle of the flight, her team buddy had her draw a picture of her fear: a black cloud with snarling eyes. Then together they "overcame" the picture by ripping it up and throwing it away. At the successful completion of the course, everyone was elated and proud.

Continuing to build on her success by taking other flights—one through a hailstorm and another through a snowstorm—gave Maggie the ability and the courage to make her own decisions about where she wanted to go. The culmination of all her effort and intention was a trip to Paris. That had always been her "icon," her long-term goal, and she finally achieved it.

"I remember getting out of the cab in front of my friend's apartment in Paris, thinking, 'This is me, standing in Paris. This was not supposed to happen, and yet it did.' When I look at pictures of myself from this trip, I see an ear-to-ear grin. I was beyond anywhere I had imagined I could go in my life."

Maggie relates that there's an element in her that says, "Your life is not supposed to get this much bigger." Having grown up in a small town amid a tightly knit community, she believes that the fear of flying had something to do with a self-imposed sense of "How far away from your source can you get?" Funny as it may sound, as a child she often felt as if she was in the wrong family. Once she moved to New York City and accepted that she was actually there, she came to an understanding that there was no point in trying to unknow things that she knew she knew. She accepts, without guilt, that there is a certain part of her that her family and friends back home will never know, just as there is a part of them that she'll never know.

Another great benefit that Maggie derived was being better able to distinguish between the real and the imagined. "I think that doing something such as conquering a fear, working with it, has done a lot to bring clarity into my life. I realize I have to define whether something is *really* dangerous or just *feels* dangerous. It helps me to evaluate situations, to balance the physical situation with my reaction to it. This process has given me a tool for examining other situations in my life, appreciating what is imagined and what is real. I've recognized that I go back and forth between living in my very fertile imagination and living in the 'real' world. This is not an entirely bad thing; as a creative person, my imagination is extremely important to me and to my work as a designer. Other people need to move the curtain to get to their imagination; for me, it's about moving the curtain to get to reality."

Having done a fair amount of worrying about her health throughout her life, Maggie can now apply the same principle to that. As a child, she used to fantasize that she had a spare set of organs in case one failed. "Overcoming my fears has given me a metaphor for enabling myself to see things differently. It's as if there has been a shift in me—from seeing life as dangerous with pockets of safety to seeing life as safe with pockets of danger. This has created a place of greater trust in me. The fact that other people are doing something I am afraid of also helps me trust. Now I gather evidence and trust that it is accurate."

Maggie has utilized what she's learned to do more and more, gaining confidence and continuing to stretch and grow. She advises that when something works, build on it. Apply its principles and use it to move even further. "I used to be 'afraid afraid,' having panicky feelings for a lot of my life. But you don't have to not do something just because you're afraid. Fear and joy are both valuable; how would you know either if you didn't have the experience of the other? Learning the techniques to deal with my fear of flying helped me deal with all of my fears. Instead of employing 'homemade ways of coping,' which I made up as I went along, I learned to bring people in to help me, which removed the sense of isolation I'd always had. It allowed me to learn from others who were as fearful as, or more fearful than, me. It all came down to this: one day I realized I'd rather die in an airplane accident than live my life hemmed in by fear."

I shared Maggie's story with a patient of mine, Lucille, who had not flown for over thirty years. When she and her husband were first married, she had experienced extreme anxiety on one difficult flight, and that was that. Off and on, for years, she'd attempted to tackle this issue, which had acquired a substantial life of its own. In fact, the problem was a symptom of a much larger issue: taking risks. When Lucille's son announced his plans for a destination wedding in Costa Rica, a resolution to this issue became necessary. Maggie's story inspired Lucille, giving her the courage to pursue whatever modality was necessary to accomplish the task at hand. She began working with a therapist specializing in hypnosis, she listened to meditation tapes, and she practiced relaxation and behavioral modification techniques she had been taught. On a beautiful sunny morning in August, Lucille boarded a plane to Costa Rica along with her husband and some friends and successfully overcame her most dreaded fear.

Journeys can be used to overcome any number of obstacles. Consider the obstacles in your life and how journeying may help you overcome them. A journey can take you

- beyond the fear of traveling alone or being alone
- away from a difficult situation you need to gain perspective on
- beyond the rut you are stuck in, or the overly familiar
- beyond the narrow boundaries of your life
- beyond your fear of any environment that seems alien or foreign
- beyond your aversion to taking risks
- away from conditioned thinking and reinforced belief systems

Leaving Home to Find Home . . . Again

A good traveler has no fixed plans, and is not intent on arriving.

—Lao-tzu

Leaving home is a necessary rite of passage for everyone. The departure signals that individuals are ready to strike out on their own, to care for their own well-being, to exercise good judgment, and to make appropriate choices and decisions. Changing statuses and identities from one who is immature, dependent, and uninitiated to one who is able to take responsibility for him- or herself in a reasonably capable way is the work of the passage. It is the job of society in general, and the family or community in particular, to ensure proper and safe passage.

Leaving one's parental home is the first great leap, but one can also leave one's own home, and can do so any number of times over the course of a lifetime. This may come in the form of a move out of town, an extended stay abroad, or the departure from a household following a change in relationship status, to name but a few examples. Choosing this form of journeying means having the courage to say good-bye, sometimes permanently, to an established base and transplant oneself to new ground. Leaving home repeatedly, and repeated journey making in general, can become a valuable tool for personal growth. Using it over and over again, people learn to expect that certain changes will emerge. Journeys may satisfy a physical, spiritual, or emotional yearning that needs attention at a particular time. The more experienced you become at journeying, the more adept you become at choosing what sort of trip you need at a given point in your life. The purpose becomes more important than the form.

This is very much the case with Alice, a seasoned journeyer who feels totally at ease with separating herself from one home and venturing to another one. Her moves are not impulsive or escapist but are driven by the knowledge that in leaving her present base she will discover new aspects of herself, new places with their own rhythms and themes, and new definitions of home. Alice's journeys from home to home, each a rite of passage, have become the key points on the map of her life's journey.

Growing up in Texas in a conservative religious environment, Alice was expected to accept traditional roles, with limited choices of careers, and was not encouraged to travel or move more than a few hours from home. Even going to college was suspect, due to the possibility of "negative" outside influences. Little did her grandparents know that a trip to California that she made with them when she was fifteen would be, as Alice describes it, "the beginning of a love affair with California that continues to this day—an instant recognition of the place in this country where I feel most at home."

We all tend to think of home as a place: a house, a state, or a community, with familiar people and settings. But home may really be more a state of mind, a state of being comfortable in your own skin. Connecting to something vital, something that feels authentic to you and that you are passionate about—this may be the true home. This is what Alice seemed to sense during her first trip to California.

Knowing that Texas had ceased to be "home," she waited until the time was right for her to leave. She chose to go to college in California. This first big break from her place of birth taught her that leaving home was a necessary rite of passage for enabling her to inhabit the places that were nurturing of who she was and who she wanted to become. "I learned that I had the power to break out of the mold, the power to make things happen, and that there were environments other than the one in which I had been raised that more fully supported my personal values and belief systems."

Over and over again, leaving home became Alice's rite of passage. Going abroad to study during her junior year of college marked the beginning of her identity as a world citizen, as a sexual adult, and as a partner in an intimate relationship—the prelude to a marriage that lasted thirty-four years. Moving to Germany when her first baby was six weeks old marked the passage to motherhood. A five-week trip to Europe many years later was an attempt for

Alice and her husband to stave off a midlife crisis, to renew a commitment to each other following a separation, and to strengthen family ties.

After her second child left for college, Alice began to explore her personal dreams. Fortunately, she had examples on her matrilineal side of strong, independent women who thought out of the box. Emboldened by this, and by a grandfather who encouraged her to be all she could be ("To whom much is given, much is expected," he would say), she opened a small import business. Her work took her to Asia, an exotic but strangely familiar place that also felt like home. She also traveled within the States to see friends and take workshops. "My need to express my independence and individuality, along with my desire to make changes for a 'new home,' was ultimately one of the catalysts for ending my marriage."

While leaving home was a major life theme for Alice, returning home to her extended family of origin several states away for six months provided other rewards. This revisiting afforded her the opportunity to develop a different perspective on her life and relationships from the one she had had growing up. In other words, she was able to fill in the blanks and reframe her thinking based on what she had learned over the many years she had been away. The experience allowed her to transition, gaining closure on her childhood relationships and on her parents' marriage, and preparing her for the coming changes after her separation.

A recent solo trip to Asia, one of Alice's most significant journeys, was a conscious rite of passage to mark the end of her couplehood. Once again, she was leaving home—this time, the home of her marriage. Unlike many of her other journeys, this one was a very moment-by-moment trip, with only herself to consider for the first time in her life. Arriving in Bangkok with a vague itinerary, making arrangements as she went along, Alice eventually visited Burma, Laos, and Cambodia, arriving in certain cities without even a hotel reservation. Since traveling alone is a rarity for a middle-aged woman in Asia, she was repeatedly asked, "You are only one?" It became a joke, to which she would typically respond, "Do I look like two?" Many times a day, she was able to ask herself, "What do I want in this moment?" Through it all, through the heat and the fatigue and the loneliness, the experience was precious to her because it belonged totally to her. It reminded her over and over that she could make the rest of her life whatever she wanted it to be. "I learned more about who I am, who I am not, and who I want to become. With deep gratitude, I've come to understand that, ultimately, *we* are the journey."

Presuming that, as adults, we have all experienced this rite of passage at least once, there is no need to pull up roots to bring the lessons of leaving home into our own lives. Instead, set aside some time to remember and reconnect with past moves you have made. Note whether the physical move was accompanied by an equivalent internal move. Did you become a different person in the process of moving from here to there? Did you literally leave old things behind for a new way of being? Did the new way fit you better or worse? Is there a thread or pattern to the moves beyond practical necessity? Consider the important moves you have made as markers on the road map of your life. How do they stack up in terms of frequency and significance against your other important life passages?

Meeting the Goddess, Meeting Myself

While all journeys have in common the motivation of an internal longing, a search for some kind of missing piece, for women, there is a real missing piece: the integrated woman as embodied by the prepatriarchal concepts of the Great Mother and the Goddess. As with all archetypes, the integrated woman is one in which the dualities of male and female, bad and good, and light and dark peacefully coexist. A number of women today are journeying in search of this source. They intuit that by journeying to the sites where these stories were born—to where the Goddess lived—they will gain access to the original integrated archetype of the Feminine and will find a wholeness within themselves.

In the ancient Sumerian myth of Inanna, the goddess descends into the earth (the underworld) to confront her sister, Ereshkigal, the dark side of herself, and emerges whole. Rebirth requires integration, a letting go of an old identity in order to acquire a new and higher one. Not only do we move from one status to another, but, as individuals, we move through ourselves. We bid farewell to those parts of the self that are no longer useful to us so that we can find and incorporate parts that are necessary but that are as yet unknown to us. Such spiritual rebirth is at the heart of the original concept of the rite of passage.

Sheryl's journey was motivated by the kinship she felt with the many-layered myth of Demeter and Persephone. The outer layer of this tale speaks of the changing seasons and how these were integrally connected to the Eleusinian mysteries. The inner layer addresses the mother-daughter relationship and the dark and light sides that we all carry within us.

Sheryl longed to make a direct connection with the historical and spiritual source of the Demeter-Persephone story, so she traveled to the land where it originated. Here is her story.

"I chose to spend two weeks in Greece and Magna Grecia, which is now Sicily, carefully planning significant places to visit once there. Although I was almost dissuaded by an unexpectedly strong snowstorm in New York just as I was getting ready to leave, a strong voice within me urged me onward, and I managed to find a taxi driver willing to risk the drive to the airport.

"Once there, happy in the sunshine, I took local buses to get around, seeing much of the land and meeting many people. I vividly remember the gorgeous orange blossoms and, oh, the fragrance! The earth was terra-cotta colored, and the sea was the most incredible blue: turquoise, cerulean, vibrant and alive. There was a sense of pride in the land; people were proud to be Sicilian. I visited an archeological park that featured many temples of the gods. Although in ruins, they seemed remarkably intact. Wandering through this park, I looked for the temple to Demeter, but it was nowhere to be found.

"High noon, and it was hot. Finally I asked for directions and was directed up a hill. At the top, I found a gate that looked closed but was in fact open a crack. The gate creaked open. Suddenly, as if from nowhere, a man with a tanned-leather apple-doll face and piercing blue eyes appeared. No one else was around. He welcomed me, remarking that no one today ever remembered how great Demeter was. He had been there since the war, he said, caring for the grounds. He led me along a dirt path perched on a cliff, overhanging the ocean. Descending six small steps, the man produced a key with which he opened the next gate. We made a horseshoe turn to the left, and I had my first view of what appeared to be large stone tubs, behind which were several caves.

"Something within me recognized this place. I could not contain the extraordinary, deep, almost primal sobbing that swept over me. Comforting me, the man began to show me around the caves. On the grounds was a small, low "brick" building—a sacred spot—that featured a pit where, purportedly, human sacrifices had once been performed. The hair on my neck stood up. Part of me felt that I had been there for those events. Being on that sacred ground, I was tapping into something strangely familiar. Instinctively it hit me: the rocks speak; they have a history. Awakening within myself was a remembrance of another time, a sense of mythic proportions. I was *living* the myth, in a time that was at once present and ancient. I felt as though I was beyond time, experiencing a moment of eternal time."

Crossing over into new territory, each new frontier an act of becoming, helped Sheryl realize that being the Goddess was not only about becoming. By descending into the underworld, she learned the value of letting go of who she thought she was. She was struck by the realization that Demeter, the Earth Goddess/Mother, and Persephone, the daughter, were really one and the same. She recognized that finding and befriending an unknown part of herself was an essential step toward wholeness. And, as with others who journey to historical and spiritual sources, in making a deep connection with the entire history of a place, its people, and its stories, she was transported into a realm beyond time.

Perhaps you can remember a specific time in your life when you knew you had to leave your present circumstances and go in search of something. How did you choose where to go—or did you let the destination choose you? Maybe you clearly understood what this something was, or perhaps it just presented itself as a vague feeling, a sketchy sense of something that had not taken form and shape as yet. Before you embark on your next journey, begin to access what you hope to find by creating your intention from the start. Using whatever creative methods resonate with you (journaling, art, music, or whatever), make a statement about what you wish to happen. If possible, before your journey begins, tangibly plan out places to go and things to do that can bring your intention to fruition. Make an effort to imagine not just the destination, but every step along the way, being cognizant of what you hope to find, preparing yourself physically as well as emotionally and spiritually for the shifts you'd like to experience along the way.

Perhaps there is a place in the world to which you've always felt pulled. Following this feeling is listening to your intuition. Identify what is most compelling about this place—the scenery, the people, the customs, the traditions, the arts, or what have you. Try to recall your earliest associations and memories of this place. Attuning yourself to accept instinctual insights can help you bypass the preconceived notions, judgments, and anxieties that often muddy the waters of your unconscious wisdom.

Pilgrim's Progress

Ideally, a human life should be a constant pilgrimage of discovery. The most exciting discoveries happen at the frontiers. When you come to know something new, you come closer to yourself and the world.

—John O'Donohue

As we've seen in this chapter thus far, the journeys that women have described are largely those of self-discovery. Whether a vision quest, a journey beyond obstacles, a journey of leaving home, or a journey to connect with a mythological source, the individual endeavors to access essential pieces of herself in chosen yet unfamiliar territory. The pilgrimage offers yet another way to do this.

When we embark on a pilgrimage, the aim is very much the same as that of a traditional rite of passage. Van Gennep's classic model for rites of passage applies just as well to the ritual and initiatory nature of the pilgrimage. Through encountering specific sacred sites, pilgrims are hoping to tap into an oasis of spiritual energy. The desired outcome is twofold: the individual not only offers him- or herself up, surrendering to the experience in absolute faith, but also attempts to gain entry to the place where the sacred and the profane meet, accessing the Divine in original, eternal time and space.

On many pilgrimages, the journeyer may also experience what anthropologist Victor Turner calls "communitas." The concept of communitas describes a state of an individual on a journey, but it is uniquely different from any other ritual or rite of passage. Communitas is more than just about leaving one place to go to another. It is specifically about honoring the movement through the unknown. In communitas, an individual is on his or her own journey and yet is also in community with others walking the same path. Separated from their own society, the social structure and rules of conduct within it radically change. Turner refers to this as "social anti-structure" and defines relationships in communitas as "undifferentiated, egalitarian, direct, non-rational (though not irrational), I-Thou, or Essential 'We relationships.' "[2] In his *Autobiography*, Malcolm X describes a communitas experience during his pilgrimage to Mecca. Most notable for him was the dissolving away of numerous stereotypes as a result of experiencing the "love, humility, and true brotherhood that was almost a physical feeling wherever I turned."[3]

One can locate communitas most readily in the liminal or transitional phase of a rite of passage. In its purest form, the journey creates a way of relating, first individually, then as part of community. Everyone is on equal footing because they are all outside their comfort zone, outside the realm of their usual social and political status. It is a sacred time when each person assumes the role of pilgrim on a journey, with no hierarchical structure, and with all seeking meaning from the embarkation upon and completion of the journey.

The two stories that follow speak about the transformative power of journeys to sacred sites. While the first journey was deliberately undertaken as a pilgrimage, the second evolved into one out of the journeyer's open spirit and the sheer power of place.

Mount Kailash, the sacred home of Shiva, lies at the western end of the Himalayas in Tibet. When Els discovered that she could join a small group of pilgrims who had gained access by permit to travel to Tibet, she signed on immediately. The journey to the mountain—the altitude, the elements, and the austerity and severity of conditions along the way—is intense. Once there, pilgrims walk around the mountain, circling for a distance of about thirty miles over approximately three days. For followers, the mountain symbolizes the Axis Mundi, the Heart of the World. The faithful circumambulate the sacred center in respect and devotion. There is no beginning and no ending. The completion of the journey corresponds to a literal and symbolic union with the Source.

Before the actual pilgrimage began, Els purchased a fur-lined coat for about a hundred dollars, which is considered quite costly in that region. She knew the coat was not for herself, but she felt compelled to buy it anyway. Although yaks were employed to carry most of the group's baggage during the pilgrimage, Els carefully packed the coat in her backpack. Along the way, a friendly dog led her to a man who, in turn, invited her to his tent. For reasons having nothing to do with logic, Els reached into her backpack and gave the man the coat. Something told her that this was the right person and the right time.

When we first talked about her trip years ago, Els told me that she felt extremely humbled by the very devout pilgrims, those who came as a sacred commitment of devotion and faith. For these journeyers, the trip around the mountain could take weeks, since they not only walked but meditated along the way, often prostrating themselves in an act of surrender. It opened her eyes to witness how profound this rite was to the devout. What Els recalled most vividly was the energy of the site, a constantly vibrating force field that was everywhere. This energy permeated everything; every gesture, event, and interaction seemed to resonate and attune itself with this vibratory field. Els remembered, with deep satisfaction, being proud and grateful that she had permitted her psyche to freely enter into this experience. She knew that being present and tuning in to the environment and the events around her would give her the best experience. When I asked her if and how she had been changed by this journey of the spirit, she replied, "It was not so much going to the mountain that transformed me. It was, rather, letting the mountain come into me."

I had a similar experience more than ten years ago. My tour of India was not intended to be a pilgrimage. I was certainly hoping to have some spiritual adventures along the way, but I hadn't personally designed or sought group events for that specific purpose. It just seemed to me that letting things unfold in their own time was the way to go.

The night before a predawn visit to the Ganges River left me restless. I couldn't sleep; I was excited and anxious at the same time. India has a lot of people, and I was fully expecting to find the ghats—the stone steps lining the river—to be teeming with people pushing their way to the sacred waters. I had seen just such a picture in a book, where the crowds had gathered at some festival to celebrate and pay homage.

Once up, I was ready to go. A small group of us boarded the bus in the still-dark hours of the early morning. A short while later, we disembarked to walk the rest of the way through the quiet streets. Vague light colored everything blue gray. There were no crowds, only some folks starting their day before the rest of the world woke up. Sacred cows walked freely, getting the respect and attention that is their birthright.

Suddenly we are at the steps. The light is softening toward dawn. For a little while, anyway, the river belongs to us. We board what can best be described as an oversized rowboat. Our pilots are three generations: a grandfather, a father, and a young son. The sight of them together moves me. I feel my heart ache, opening in recognition of that which is precious in relationships. We are each given a large leaf that holds a small candle and flower petals. "Send this down the river as an offering to its goodness," we are told. "Send this down the river asking for its blessings."

Slowly, the dawn reveals a brilliant sunrise. The light permeates the life on the river, giving it vitality, enhancing detail and highlighting color, making everything vibrate with its intensity. It is the om made visible.

For the next several hours, we move up and down the river. The Ganges shows me the holiness of every day, every minute. People wave from the steps. They smile at us while taking a dip in the healing waters. Bright clothing newly washed in the river hangs to dry in the sun. People meditate. They pray. They eat. They honor their dead.

I had feared the scene of the dead waiting haphazardly along the banks of the river, waiting in their last moments as physical beings on earth, waiting their turn for the fire to take them. But this final rite of passage unfolded in a very different way than I had expected. With great ceremony and profound respect, at specifically designated sites, individuals on pyres are set on fire. They take their leave, a life completed—until the next.

There was a calm, a peace, something I had not known for a very long time. As is often the case on pilgrimages, I was operating outside of ordinary time and space. In times long ago, when rites of passage were key to people's lives, their experience with them, as well as the effects upon the people, were more profound. The power of the rite was to bring you back to an original time and to a first enactment. Being in this timeless place transported me into "original time." On this river, I witnessed the beauty and sanctity of everyday (any day, day after day) life. The river flows in its eternal rhythm, and I, upon it, move toward eternity.

> Were I possessed of the least knowledge,
> I would, when walking on the great way,
> Fear only paths that lead astray,
> The great way is easy,
> Yet people prefer bypaths.
>
> —Lao-tzu

As different as these women and their journeys are—and as different as we all are—the themes within them are ones we all experience. At certain times in our lives, we all experience the fear of being alone. Or, once in a relationship, we may fear being left alone. Or, in a new place, we may discover a new home or a link to other peoples and times. Each journey carries us forward on our journey of a lifetime, which is to come to know ourselves and to become our own best friend. In mastering our lives, our task is to be open to all the possibilities of who and what we are and to accept what is without making judgment. Humans are complex creatures: the good, the bad, the ugly, and the Divine reside together within us. If we can honor and work with all aspects of ourselves, we move toward completeness.

Rules of the Road

The journeys of passage that we make, both external and internal, involve physical, intellectual, emotional, and spiritual challenges. In preparing ourselves to meet these challenges, we should begin with a level head and an eye toward the practical. Here are some general principles to bear in mind before setting out to lands unknown:

1. Don't run away *from* something; run *to* something. Although journeys take you away from the familiar, the intention is not to escape from something unpleasant. New territory may actually provide a better,

more fertile environment for finding new solutions or new ways of viewing a situation.

2. Travel light. Take as little baggage along as possible, literally and figuratively. Too much baggage is hard to keep track of. Too much energy and time is expended packing and unpacking and packing again. Essential items may get lost. If you need something bad enough, you will find a way to acquire it. (On my trip to India, I met a businessman who could well afford to take as much as he wanted with him and spend as much as he wanted once there, but he chose instead to travel with a single small bag. In addition, he took clothing ready to be given away, and that is just what he did all along the way.)

3. Don't assume anything. And especially don't assume that what you do at home is the way people do it elsewhere. Observe and appreciate differences.

4. Don't expect anything. Setting yourself up with expectations limits your experience. Thinking in a limited way will give you a limited experience. Be open to new ways of experiencing and doing things. *However* . . .

5. *Do* expect the unexpected. Being present without your usual routines, habitual behaviors, and attitudes creates room for new impressions in all realms and allows for new discoveries by all of your senses.

6. Be prepared to meet the stranger. Strangers you meet are mirrors of yourself. Conversations with strangers may provoke a dialogue with parts of yourself that seem unfamiliar and foreign.

7. Remember that the way you choose to view the world will be the way the world reveals itself to you.

CHAPTER SEVEN

Ritual and Creativity

Creativity is God's gift to us. Using our creativity is our gift back to God.

—Julia Cameron

In the realm of women's rites of passages, creativity and ritual are intrinsically linked. The upside of the historical fact that women have been largely excluded from the tradition of public ritual is that they have used their creativity to design their own rituals. Creativity and ritual can work together in a number of different ways. Sometimes creativity is brought to bear on a traditional rite. Sometimes creativity leads to the birth of a new rite. And sometimes a creative exercise is *itself* the rite of passage. Because the creative process is the consummate expression of one's individuality, the essence of a person made manifest in the external world, rituals that involve it are all the more meaningful and personal.

Some people are born endowed with natural talents. Knowing that these abilities exist early on in life is a gift in itself, for it informs and affirms that we are unique in a special way. Sometimes, finding our own creative expression is difficult because it is not something that comes naturally, it hasn't been encouraged, or perhaps it has even been stifled. Sometimes it doesn't occur to us that we could or should step outside the box or draw out of the lines. But often, when we take a fresh approach to some endeavor, we wonder what took us so long.

The necessary focus is to get beyond criticism or judgment of our own process, to forget about what the final product should end up looking like, and to stop thinking of creativity only in terms of what we imagine perfection to be. Every creative endeavor is perfect as is. Creativity is a feature of all rites of passage; they are creative projects.

The Ritual Process

The ritual process always contains several essential parts, whether we are performing a deeply personal ritual alone or one communally in the company of others. The same key elements described in the classic rite of passage can be used as a model when creating rituals. These include the following:

Setting the intention. Get as clear about the meaning and purpose of the ritual that you want to perform as possible. What do you hope to gain by enacting it? What change do you wish to bring about in your life?

Separating from and severing ties with the familiar. Set aside the time to remove yourself from the habitual and everyday routine. When you perform ritual, nothing else exists; nothing should ever intervene or disrupt you.

Creating the optimal threshold experience. Incorporate the appropriate ritual "tools" necessary for the ceremony at hand. Remember, stepping over the threshold takes you from here to there, changing your status or identity. What elements will help you do this in the best possible way? If there are specific symbols that appeal to you, these should be utilized as well.

Reincorporating or reintegrating. At the completion of the ritual, leave sacred time and space behind, hopefully for future ritual enactments, returning to ordinary life transformed and filled with a new sense of purpose.

For example, lighting a candle without thinking about what it means may be a nice thing to do, but it's just simply lighting a candle. Lighting a candle with intention, however, can represent that this specific time is being set aside from the rest of the day, from the activities of daily life. We are allowing ourselves to slow down, giving ourselves permission to create space where quiet and reflection can enter in. The act of doing this symbolically puts us in a flow with a different kind of rhythm than the one we usually experience most of the time.

There are specific universal tools used by many cultures for traditional ritual making. These are powerful alone or in combination. For those who are familiar with the ritual process, this summary (the categories are adapted from Cahill and Halpern) will serve as a review of what you already know. For those who are just getting started, this will give a brief idea of how to utilize important elements when creating your own ritual.

Purification. Many diverse traditions use cleansing with water, such as ceremonies of baptism, conversion, and being "born again." The washing of hands and feet figures prominently in many religious traditions as well. Native American tradition uses smudging; the smoke of burning sage cleanses individual and spatial energy. From ancient times, anointing with oil has been used to purify, making one ready to assume a new status or identity. It is used today in ordination and healing ceremonies.

Calling on Spirit. Verbally stating our intention sets the tone for the ritual actions to follow. This can include prayer, invoking divine help for the task at hand, or seeking the blessings of ancestors. Dancing and singing are other ways to access spirit.

Calling in the Light. Lighting candles to mark holidays and holy days, or to sanctify any event, is part of most cultural traditions. The lighting of candles is probably the most commonly performed ritual, often done as part of a daily routine. Building fires or creating a fire ceremony is frequently used to consume the old, casting aside that which is no longer useful.

Making Sacrifice. This may imply some form of sensory deprivation, such as keeping vigil, fasting, or practicing a period of silence. Ordeals designed to test one's strength, endurance, resolve, or resilience may be undertaken. Periods of meditation may help us to focus our awareness inwardly.

Gathering in Community. Conversely, giving or exchanging gifts, feasting, and sharing ritual foods are done in many cultures and traditions. Embracing and joining hands often connote celebration of transitions communally. Women's inclusive, compassionate social patterns often allow for the spontaneous enactment of rituals, since one woman's experience may trigger the expression of those around her.

Worshipping. This can include praying, making offerings, and creating altars that contain items of individual significance, including power objects. Personally adapting elements used in traditional ceremonies may be more comfortable for those who wish to follow familiar, prescribed rituals, especially from religious tradition.

Communing. Expressing one's self through music and song, dancing, and symbolic gesture are ways to commune with spirit as is using the smoke of a burnt offering (incense, herbs, etc.) to carry prayer.

Exorcizing. Ridding oneself of something unwanted or deemed to be of negative value can be symbolically accomplished by breaking or severing, as in cutting a cord or ripping a piece of fabric or an article of clothing. Burning, burying, or scattering can accomplish this task as well. More simply, verbal pronouncements can be utilized to eradicate a negative force.

Symbolically Dying. Crossing thresholds is the hallmark of the classic rite of passage. This may be accomplished by moving in and out of a circle or by creating any act that implies spatial movement.

Rebirth. The creation, wearing, or exchange of masks, as well as dressing oneself in symbolic clothing, are ways to celebrate rebirth. Taking or receiving a new name signifies a change in status or identity and imparts protection.

Catherine Bell, associate professor of religious studies, whose work focuses on the changing face of ritual and the emergence of new ritual forms, especially for women, notes, "We are seeing a new paradigm for ritualization. Belief in ritual as a central dynamic in human affairs . . . gives ritualists the authority to ritualize creatively, and even idiosyncratically. Ritual is approached as a means to create and renew community, transform human identity, and remake our most existential sense of being in the cosmos."[1]

Ritualizing today, especially for women, whose spiritual lives and ritual practices had been largely dictated and prescribed by religious and sociopolitical systems in the past, allows for and offers new ways to reengage and reimagine ideologies so that they, once again, become alive, deeply relevant, and personal. In *Ritualizing Women*, Lesley Northup offers these categories of valuable, insightful raw material to use in developing new rituals:

- the Western liturgical tradition
- the rediscovery of Eastern religions
- ancient ritual traditions
- the rituals of other cultures
- natural patterns, symbols, and objects
- personal experience
- the women's movement and feminist consciousness
- women's creativity[2]

Not surprisingly, without prior study or a formal understanding, most of the contributors chose one or more of these categories to contain and describe their own experience. These themes, then, are ever present and alive within the collective unconscious of women and can be called up and expressed at any time.

Just as there are common themes that make up a ritual, there are also, according to Northup, several categories of emerging features in women's ritual practice, namely ritual images, ritual elements, and ritual characteristics. Ritual images, which are "recurrent metaphors and symbols" that strike a familiar chord with the Feminine, can include the circle, the horizontal plane, Mother Nature in all her mystery, the workings of the body, the miracles of birth and mothering, finding the sacred in the ordinary, communal memory, "telling our stories," the work of the shaman, and the empowerment of the human spirit.[3]

Ritual elements offer a sense of "reflection on the ritual as part of the ritual process itself." These elements can include healing, naming, smudging, purification, dancing, chanting, retelling the handed-down stories, understanding that "women tend to construct their communal history orally," and revering the wisdom of our elders. In essence, anything that women do with clear intention and focus can take on the quality of a ritual element.[4]

Finally, as a reflection of the feminine nature of ritual itself, ritual characteristics take on spontaneous and informal qualities, tending to de-emphasize formal leadership in favor of nonhierarchical, inclusive models, offering enhanced roles and reverence for the astuteness of older women, an encompassing embrace of ecumenicity, and, in its manner of consistently redefining itself, a nonreliance on conventional texts.[5]

Much has been said about the way that rituals take us from a before to an after, from the profane to the sacred. But rituals take us out of the realm of the ordinary in another very significant way. They appeal to the nonverbal part of us, which de-emphasizes the words and the language and instead allows us to perform through action. When words are not enough or cannot adequately describe and express how we feel, we can intuitively access, understand, process, and translate through ritual enactment.

Intuitive, hypnotherapist, and life coach Sheilaa Hite teaches clients how to design rituals that symbolically mirror their life issues, thus empowering them to effect significant and meaningful change. The ritual process has always made sense to Sheilaa, who believes that if you work with purpose, something positive is bound to result. When working with a client, she intuits where an individual feels powerless, or powerful, and fashions the appropriate ritual accordingly. Feeling powerless requires changing a perspective. Creating a ritual takes a person's mind off the negative, focuses her attention on what she wants to happen, and gives her a chance to affect the outcome.

In designing rituals, Sheilaa stays as close as possible to natural elements, since these are things that satisfy and stimulate the senses, even on an unconscious level. "Part of spirituality is about being practical. Living on a physical plane means having to be practical, and being practical means having to take action. In creating rituals, we have an opportunity to really see what we are doing. Then we can see the practical results, how things change.

"Ritual helps us get in touch with ourselves, in touch with the rhythms of life. When you throw a pebble into a pond, each ripple affects the next. Ritual allows for a far more conscious way of living. When individuals are in touch with their own internal rhythm, life takes on more power."

The emerging ritual process, then, is about rituals that provoke change and healing. Since rites of passage have reflected how society organizes and prioritizes the roles, and ultimately the lives, of its members, it has been suggested that this very same vehicle can be utilized to provoke change. "Thus it is possible—and sometimes salutary—to disrupt existing rituals and convert them into sites of resistance. . . . One can also attempt to construct novel rituals through which existing social patterns and structures might be reconstructed along alternative lines."[6]

If there is one principle guiding all of the rites and rituals shared in these pages, it is creativity. Even when following a more traditional ceremonial form, the women personalized these with their own unique twist. Designing and performing nontraditional rites inspired women to reach deeply into their own internal resources and ultimately helped them to create a thoroughly satisfying experience, personally meaningful and empowering.

This chapter includes variation rites for birth and marriage, two of the most universally traditional passages; a retroactive rite of passage for abortion, which is an event not traditionally marked; and, less traditional but no less essential, rites of identity such as naming a child and consecrating one's personal space in a house-blessing ritual. Finally, rites of passage that signify profound shifts in consciousness and that transform us over time are included as a new rite-of-passage form.

Showered with Love

As we've already seen, birth is a rite of passage—not just symbolically, but as a very real event. The woman undergoes physical and emotional changes for several months before giving birth. The actual birth is a literal threshold event; the potential for complications really exists. The woman is transformed; her status changes to mother, and now there is a new being as well to care for and nurture.

When Sue, a documentary filmmaker and author, was pregnant for the first time, she realized just how much she didn't know about pregnancy, childbirth, and motherhood. So, as a new creative rite of passage that she chose to celebrate with the special women in her life, she filmed a documentary about her baby shower.

Sue wanted to get some hints from women who had gone through the experience themselves about how to manage such a life-changing shift. She was ready to learn, and the women were ready to tell, and the "real stories" behind the mystique became the focus of the film. As much as a woman can learn about the topic, nowhere else is there to be found the authentic wisdom communicated in the human sharing of real-life experience. The film became a valuable opportunity for women to share their stories about pregnancy, childbirth, and motherhood. "I saw then, and continue to see, the common elements of all women's birth experiences and how much honest discussion of these commonalities is missing in our culture."

In making *The Baby Shower*, Sue wanted to create a vehicle to pass along the wisdom of birth and motherhood beyond "Are you having a girl or a boy?" The film follows Sue through her pregnancy, from an early sonogram to musings about the changing landscape of a woman's body, to doctor's visits in the last weeks of her pregnancy, to the birth of her child, with scenes of the baby shower woven throughout. The narratives of women describe their own personal experiences and perceptions, poignant and painful, funny and sad. From the difficulty of labor, to seeing the baby for the first time, to the heartbreak of miscarriage, to the devastation of not getting pregnant—these are all presented as part of the feminine experience.

"We have done this." An overriding sense of inclusion and acceptance on a gender, family, and cultural level was expressed by many of the women who felt that they were validating and fulfilling their biological destiny through pregnancy and birth. As art imitates life, and as pregnancy and childbirth are rites of passage into a sisterhood, so was this baby shower a designed ritual, and the film about it a rite of passage, not only to celebrate and to welcome a new member, but to serve as a time of reflection, honoring the sacredness of the event.

"When it is time for the actual birth, I asked, how is a woman treated? Is she respected and honored for what it takes to bring a baby into the world? One thing I learned, thankfully in advance, is that women must be their own strongest advocate in the birthing process, unafraid to voice their wishes. Another essential thing I learned is that things are not always one way or the other—that in childbirth, as in so many other things, life consists of varying shades of gray." In labor, Sue experienced terror of the unknown birth process, sadness at having to be induced, and worry about her baby's well-being. At birth, we hear Sue speak. "Hello, sweetheart," she says to her new daughter, who turns and opens her eyes wide to the camera, a new being now in the world.

The process of giving birth doesn't have to be literal or biological, though. The creative process in general—be it writing a book, making art, or forming an organization or group—follows a similar structure: conception, incubation, and birth. If there is a creative endeavor that you feel passionately about but are not sure how to go about doing it, or even beginning it, you may want to think about creating a rite for the conception of a project. A good way to do this is to start with a letter of intention stating what you will accomplish. Write as if it were already happening. Don't leave room for doubt with phrases like "someday in the future" or "I'm trying to accomplish." Rather, say, "I will," or, "I am," or, best yet, "I am achieving my goals."

If you're feeling stuck on a project or in your life, try "giving birth" to a completely new or long-buried aspect of yourself. List ways that you express yourself now. Are they representative of your fullest, richest potential? If not, list ways that you can develop your creative and artistic self that will nurture and support your growth. Often people jokingly express a desire to be a stand-up comic, or they harbor a secret wish to be a diva. While this may not be a feasible career for this lifetime, it doesn't mean that you shouldn't have fun with it anyway.

A Grandmother's Story: Your Name Shall Be

A few rituals that welcome a new baby or child into a community, including baptism, circumcision, and naming ceremonies, are still widely practiced, mostly within a religious context. But when people don't fit into traditional categories—for example, when people of different faiths marry—these rituals can be exclusionary. Here is one woman's creative solution to that problem. By taking certain liberties with the old ways, Doris arrived at a ceremony that honored both her faith and herself.

"In Orthodox and sometimes even in Conservative Judaism, women cannot do very much. As a bubbie (grandmother), I have had to take things into my own hands. As each new child of mine was born, my father went to synagogue for a naming ceremony. When I wanted to do the same for my grandchildren, I was told by my female Conservative rabbi to forget it. But I didn't forget it. I had already said kaddish (the Jewish prayer for the dead) for both of my parents and had celebrated the bat and bar mitzvahs and confirmations of my children as a full participant within the context of the religious community.

"When I discovered that a friend had become an ordained interfaith minister, I asked her to name my grandchildren in a private ceremony at her home. With my children, my grandchildren, and a very dear childhood friend, we all took part in an ancient tradition with the independence to create our own minyan (the quorum needed for prayer). Each child was named for an ancestor, and the names were extolled and symbolized. There was no doubt that we had all been blessed. We have gone back to the beliefs of my beloved grandparents as they practiced them in 'the old country.' We've possibly skipped a generation, but we go back to what has meaning as we continue to look to the future."

The Power of Names

Your name is your identity. Of all your belongings, it is the one thing you carry with you your whole life. Traditionally, naming is a sacred and solemn occasion that many cultures celebrate ritually. The Yoruba of Nigeria have a birth rite called "stepping into the world." A sacred practitioner, using palm nuts, divines a baby's name at seven days old.[7] The child receives three names: the *oruko*, or personal name, refers to the birth itself or the family circumstances at the time of birth; the *oriki*, or "praise" name, states the parents' wishes for their child's successful future; and the *orile* name refers to the kinship group to which the child belongs.[8]

In Hawaiian culture, a name was traditionally chosen in several ways. The "night" or "dream" name could find its way into the dreams of family members, it could be heard uttered by the ancestor god, or it could be given in a sign. As long as the ancestor god chose the name, it was absolutely necessary to use it, or an ill fate might befall the baby. Other secret names were considered too sacred to be uttered out loud.[9]

In the West, there is much less formal ritual around this rite of identity. We often take our names for granted, but they surely have meaning locked within them. If you don't know how you got your name, ask about it or research its meaning. Is your name, or the name of a child in your family, carrying a family tradition forward? For a child named for a particular ancestor, what stories or facts about the person would be of special interest for the child to know? Does your name resonate with you and fit who you are? If it does not, or if you are still using a nickname from childhood that you feel you've outgrown, experiment with changing it to see how that feels.

Stories and lore about the special significance of a name abound in Scripture as well. The changing of a name after a revelatory experience symbolized a radical shift in identity. Abram to Abraham, "for I have made you the father of a multitude of nations" (Gen. 17:5); Jacob to Israel, "for you have striven with God and with men, and have prevailed" (Gen. 32:28), and the conversion of Saul of Tarsus on the road to Damascus, assuming the name of Paul, are but a few examples.

The great seer, Edgar Cayce, believed that each soul is unique and so has its own individual name. As you develop spiritually, you are "writing" your name, so to speak, by virtue of the choices you make. In the Revelation of John (2:17), an angel promises, "To him who conquers . . . I will give a white stone and on the white stone is written a new name that no one knows except the one who receives it."[10] Just as your journey is uniquely yours, so too is your soul name.

Everything Old Is New Again

Probably the greatest amount of ceremonial creativity is found in the marriage rite. The many elements of a wedding ceremony make for as many variations on the theme. Interfaith minister Deborah Roth, whose New York–based practice, Spirited Living, provides life coaching and ritual creation for life passages, draws upon various cultures and traditions specifically to help couples design their wedding and commitment ceremonies.

A ceremonial element that couples seem to enjoy is called "taking their measure," a ritual "tradition" created by Deborah for two people who are about to set off down a new road together. Various measurements are taken around the couples' bodies, with each measurement holding a different meaning. For example, the couple measures each of their heights to symbolize the length of their lifelong commitment. Taken together, all of these measurements represent the elements for a happy and fulfilling union.

After performing a ceremony within this sacred circle of combined measured lengths, Deborah turns to the guests and says, "Our newly married couple would like to invite all of you to extend your wishes and dreams for their marriage by tying a ribbon onto the cord, in effect adding or 'binding' to their commitment your own wish for them or your promise to support and love them."

Another ritual element widely used today is the unity candle. As the couple is united in marriage, two candles ultimately unite into one flame. Deborah has placed her own spin on the unity candle ceremony by inviting the couple to create their own unique candle. Personally significant and meaningful words and symbols carved into the candle by the wedding couple symbolize their greatest wishes and hopes for a long future together.

An ancient tradition consists of wrapping a scarf around the clasped hands of the couple. The creation of the infinity symbol in this ritual joining of hands harkens back to Celtic tradition and is known as "handfasting." Binding themselves together in this way, the couple pledges everlasting commitment and love to one another.

Beyond a traditional religious ceremony, couples often choose specific music or significant songs to be performed throughout the service. Readings from the Bible and other sacred traditions, or specific poems and passages, may be spoken by family members and friends. Utilizing family heirlooms and articles in the ceremony, such as wine cups, prayer shawls, and even rings, links couples to their past and to ancestors. Often guests participate in turn, extending wise thoughts and good wishes to the couple.

In Living Memory

A rite of passage not traditionally marked is abortion. For many women, an abortion marks a loss that needs to be remembered. But since it is an event that our culture has trouble acknowledging, there are no accompanying ceremonies or rituals. Perhaps one place to look for guidance on how to respond to the emotionally charged issue of abortion is Japan, where abortion is legal and culturally accepted and where a ritual called *mizuko kuyo* (water-children rite) was instituted in the 1970s to address it. Although this rite was originally intended as a therapeutic response, religious institutions insinuated themselves into the process, usurping what had been personal and folk rites.[11]

A Japanese cemetery honors these children that never were with row upon row of statues, or *jizos*, each commemorating an unborn child, some dressed in beautifully hand-knitted baby clothes, and others surrounded by toys and other offerings. This is a place where feelings of loss are truly honored, where what was never to be is acknowledged and remembered. Having visited such a place in Kamakura, Japan, some years ago, I found it to be an incredibly moving experience, one that I will never forget. If, culturally, we are not yet ready for cemeteries of this kind, then perhaps another way to remember is to create living memorials in the form of private gardens and dedicated parks.

"Having gone through the experience of an illegal abortion in the early

1960s (since the only way to have a legal abortion at that time was to leave the country), I decided, nearly four decades later, to create a rite of passage to contain the experience. I wanted to find a way to give both outer and inner expression to the loss, to define and finally put closure on this life-altering event."

For Beth, the trauma of having an abortion was made worse many times over by the illicit handling of the procedure. Local medical practitioners referred patients in need of help to a kind-hearted doctor who was willing to perform abortions during regular office hours. Secrecy, shame, guilt, the terror of dying, and the fear of punishment only made the procedure more painful, both at the time and even in the years that followed. Therapy helped, but Beth still felt a profound sense of grief and loss. It seemed that no amount of talking about it could adequately address the experience.

"I created and performed a rite of passage to give closure retroactively to this experience that had so deeply affected so many aspects of my life, even over the course of many years. The rite consisted of planting two small trees in my garden—one to mark the abortion, and the other to mark a miscarriage many years later. Writing a letter to these souls, I thanked them for their presence in my life, expressing gratitude for their gifts to me, while acknowledging the sadness of what was never to be. After burning the letter, I sent its ashes, comingled with rose petals, down a nearby river. Now there is a special place of sanctity and beauty to commemorate this pivotal event which so profoundly touched my life."

Grief can accompany any form of loss, not only those through the loss of a relationship, as we've previously seen. Our personal losses sometimes hit us much harder than other kinds because we are only in relationship with ourselves, with no one else to answer to. We can choose to talk with others about our thoughts and feelings, but the experience itself is solely our own. And that, at times, is very lonely.

For healing to occur, as with any loss and its accompanying grief, there must be closure. Sometimes, the passage of time takes care of this, but old emotions often linger, and the difficult passage may still feel like an open wound years later. Retroactive rites of passage are powerful tools to contain and process old, unfinished business. It is never too late to create and perform these.

The House Blessing

Consecrating the space we live in is an important rite of passage, but one often not even considered. If we would only stop and think about what our home really means to us, we might realize that our own vital energy is contained within it; the space around us is a direct reflection of the life within us. Visiting someone's personal space can give many clues and shed a lot of light on the person's inner self. For some, home is a sanctuary from the rest of the world; for others, it is merely a place to park their baggage. Choosing to respect your personal environment shows respect for yourself.

When Sylvia decided to end her marriage, she knew exactly what she had to do. Borrowing from the traditions of her ancestors, she performed a rite designed to mark a new beginning and to set the course of her future life. But blessing the house was more than just about consecrating her new home; it was about cleansing and purifying the home of her inner being as well.

"I was alone again after deciding to end a ten-year marriage. The fact that it was my decision to leave didn't make me feel any better. I felt vulnerable and deeply afraid. What lay ahead for me? My thoughts brought me back to my childhood and how good I felt as a little girl. My parents and extended family always managed to help me understand what was happening, and no matter what was happening, they always managed to make me feel better. It was a mix of tradition, prayer, and support. If the family could not provide the answers, prayer most certainly would."

Sylvia's family, originally from India, goes back three generations in her native Trinidad. Her Indian heritage stressed tight family bonds, a sense of protection, and an emphasis on education. Sylvia's parents practiced what they remembered from the old country, but she held on to their religion mostly for their sake. The Caribbean culture in which she was raised, however, had a far greater influence on her upbringing. Although Trinidad is about 35 percent Indian, the culture is profoundly influenced by an African population that makes up about 60 percent of the island's inhabitants. European influences round out the culture of the islands.

"I intuitively understood that I needed to do something that would set my future on a positive course. My instinct was to go back to the comfort, to the feeling of bliss that I had experienced growing up. In essence, I felt that if I could reconnect to my ancestors, my life moving forward would be fine." After many phone calls and inquiries, Sylvia got in touch with a Hindu priest with whom she arranged a ceremony to be performed at her newly found apartment. But the house blessing, as she called it, turned out to be much more than that.

Prior to the ceremony, she was instructed to eat no meat for twenty-one days, and on the actual day of the ceremony, to fast. The rite consisted of a series of rituals, each carefully designed for a specific purpose. Performed together, they were meant to maximize the desired effect: to help her begin this new phase of her life in the best possible way. "All of the ritual elements were created and performed with one thing in mind—to invite the gods into my home in order to help me carry out my highest purpose."

Washing the hands signified the intention to cleanse, to purify, not only her home but her sacred space within. As instructed, there were flowers everywhere, and eventually some of these made their way into the fire as an offering. The trumpeting sound emanating from the conch shell the priest blew into, accompanied by the small gong her son was sounding, seemed to announce the arrival of the gods.

Fire received prescribed offerings meant to cleanse any negativity: sandalwood, the leaf of a special plant, coconut, sugar, and raisins, and a special cooking ingredient (ghee). Camphor was added to the fire to keep it going. Since the windows were sealed tightly shut until the fire was extinguished, thick smoke enveloped the house. A fruit offering of apples and bananas was added to the fire, providing a beautiful smell, almost hypnotic, that seemed to enhance the clarity of mind.

"The first act I performed in my new home after the ceremony had been completed was to cook something sweet (rice pudding) to symbolize the sweetness of the new life. I was exhausted that evening. I was surprised to find how physically affected I was; what I had experienced felt like a huge drain on my body. Emotionally, I felt clear; the anxiety and fear that had filled my days and nights was gone. I knew I had done the right thing. I felt validated. I had put my best foot forward and knew that my actions would continue to guide me. For the first time in my life, I felt I had complete control over my life. For sure, I knew the gods were smiling down on me."

If you check back a few pages to the tools of ritual making, you will see that Sylvia utilized almost all of them in her house-blessing ceremony. Every small ritual element gave her the opportunity to create an experience that allowed her to access all of her senses, and by so doing, she was fully engaged. In creating your own rites, select only those elements that are meaningful to you, ones that will provide the optimal experience, honoring your desired result.

Life Imitating Art

Sometimes rites of passage take a long time in coming. You may have done all of the preliminary work and may not even be aware that you are about to make a monumental passage, but somehow, when the time is right for you, the opportunity presents itself. Of course, you always have the free will not to move forward, but chances are, once everything is in place and circum-stances have been set in motion, it's just too simple not to take the final leap. Lorraine's perception of herself as only someone "who made art" was radi-cally challenged in a brief period of special time in 1985, her creativity serv-ing as the vehicle to see herself in a whole new light.

During this period of time, Lorraine had a wonderful museum job. "I had always made art; as a child, I spent years taking art classes at the Brooklyn Museum, and as an adult, I had always taken classes in painting, drawing, and sculpture, all in my 'spare' time." Her boss, also an artist, showed Lorraine a brochure of art workshops offered in Vermont—one-, two-, and three-week residencies. This was a fabulous idea, but of course she couldn't do it, for the usual reasons—her family, job, and so on.

"This reminded me of an opportunity I had had years before at Sarah Law-rence to attend an art seminar in Florence for two weeks. Although it sounded like heaven to me, I immediately dismissed it. Somehow this idea stayed with me, and at the encouragement of my wonderful boss, I signed up for two weeks. One of the most surprising things I discovered at this work-shop were the many other women artists, some of whom were there for a month or six weeks, who had families but took this time for themselves as a necessity; somehow their families survived.

"These two weeks were revelatory for me in terms of my artistic process and my identity as an artist. I remember driving home, a seven hour trip, in a state of euphoria, rolling down the windows and shouting out into the countryside, 'I'm a f—king artist!' My family survived; they still do. The first thing I did when I got home—my 'ritual'—was to convert my attic into a studio."

Rites of passage, then, can help us claim another kind of space for our-selves. They are an invaluable resource not only for navigating through what our life and external circumstances offer up to us, but equally important as a way to access and claim new elements of our identity as we move forward.

Unearthing Grandmother's Wisdom:
Healing from the Source

Your daily life is your temple and your religion.
Whenever you enter into it take with you your all.

—Kahlil Gibran

One important source of meaningful ritual can be found in the often-dis-carded traditions of our own families. Customs, ceremonies, family rituals and stories, and individual life histories not only connect us to one another over generations but may provide a rich creative source of symbols and practices on which to draw as we design rites for our own lives.

Els offered this story about her grandmother's ritual practice and beliefs. Beyond describing a nontraditional annual pagan "renewal" ritual, which is certainly a throwback to another time and sensibility, this story poignantly tracks the profound impact and influence that these rituals and beliefs had on Els' personal evolution. Through a lineage of creativity, Els lays claim to a bond that connects her own healing work to her grandmother's.

"Throughout her life, my father's mother maintained a most peculiar tradition—one that she believed to be the source of her own health and the source of her power to heal others. Every spring, after the last snowfall, which was always announced by the call of a particular bird, my grandma, whom we called Moe-Moe, would commence pacing up and down the path along her garden, staring intently at the barren soil. She was in search of any movement made by a mole. Moles are blind, and they do not come above ground, but when they awaken from their hibernating sleep, they start making tunnels and looking for food near the soil's surface. Moe-Moe, with her big bare hands and her sleeves rolled up, would trail up and down the garden as if in deep meditation. This could go on for days. Finally, when she noticed any activity, she would drop to her knees and, with her hands, begin digging away at the cold, wet earth."

Very often, her first attempt would be rewarded with a soft, small, dark brown creature. She would carry the mole into the house, holding it delicately in both hands. In the kitchen, she would take a sharp little knife from above the sink and carefully slice the mole's throat so its blood would pour into her palms. She then would rub her hands together vigorously.

Over the course of Els' childhood, she was invited to witness this sacred act many times. It was a sacrificial ritual performed with an immense respect for life. Moe-Moe believed that the blood of the mole gave her the strength to heal herself and others. When Els would fall off her bike or had a toothache, she would go see Moe-Moe, who would once again rub her hands together and hold Els where she hurt. "This laying on of hands had deep social and emotional value for me. I had no doubt about her ability to make me well."

Moe-Moe believed that over the course of the year her healing strength would diminish. She therefore repeated the sacrifice each spring, renewing her strength and faith.

"Since I was in Catholic school, I went to Mass seven days a week, but was my pagan grandmother, not the church, who taught me the difference between the sacred and the profane. In hindsight, these experiences were a rite of passage for me. I never knew whether anyone else practiced mole sacrifices in the community, but I would not be surprised if my father was pacing along the garden path at this very moment."

The value that this springtime ritual had for people who lived off the land is obvious—their hands and their health were their most valued tools. Els' grandmother's generation was extremely self-reliant and resourceful. Their connection to nature was of primary importance for their physical and mental well-being. "I do not remember doctor visits or drugs as a child. What I do remember are bubbly brews on the woodstove made from items found in the forest. Did this supernatural tradition have any lasting impact on my life? Considering that I have worked as a massage therapist for almost two decades, I do think something might have 'rubbed off' on me."

Consider what rituals or traditions are practiced in your family. Some may be linked to specific holidays or times of the year, but others may be uniquely significant to your own family. Ask older relatives to describe traditions handed down from generation to generation and ask to be included the next time these traditional rituals are practiced. Pay attention to all traditions and rituals, not only those that seem obvious.

Begin to include the heritage of previous generations by incorporating these ancestral traditions, or any variation of them, into your own life and with your children and grandchildren. Research your family's country of origin. What traditions from the old country can you incorporate into your own life and the lives of your children?

Here are some ideas to help you get reacquainted with, or perhaps learn for the first time, interesting traditions from your family of origin. These are ways, too, to create a legacy for future generations.

- Create a family tree.
- Record (audio or video) your grandmother and other elders, eliciting family history and family stories.
- Collect family recipes.
- Learn unique skills handed down through the generations.
- Collect "old wives' tales."
- Find out natural methods of healing handed down from generation to generation.
- Collect and catalog documents (birth certificates, naturalization papers,

wedding invitations, marriage certificates, passports, birth announce-
ments, bibles, and the like).
- Gather family photos and memorabilia and make a video.
- Create videos with photos and music to celebrate milestones.
- Write a loved one's biography and publish it for family members.
- Incorporate all of these into a young person's rite of passage into adult-
  hood.

Whenever we engage in ritual behavior, we are signaling a shift in consciousness. Taking us out of the flow of the mundane, rites of passage, as a
highly specific ritual form, has the ability to transport us beyond a literal
understanding of our lives, helping us to gain access to the symbolic. For rites
to be effective tools for transformation, they must inspire, evoke awe and
excitement, feel alive, demonstrate a fluidity and organicity, and be revelatory to us personally.

Re-riteing Passages

Reconnecting. Before you can even create rites, you have to reconnect
with a source of understanding that is relevant and resonant with your
own beliefs. Since many of us have experienced the ritual process solely
as a result of our religious upbringing, if and when we move away from
traditional practices, we may also leave accompanying ritual behind.
When you are disconnected from whatever you consider your source,
life may feel like a series of random acts with no organizing mechanism,
such as that which rites provide. Reconnecting helps to reclaim ownership of your own spiritual life.

Reimagining. Existing rites often lack the magical ingredients necessary
to spark excitement and invite passionate participation. Personally creating rites that do this ensures continued interest and involvement in
their performance. Intuitively sensing what feels right for you, give your
imagination free rein to create rites that embrace and express who you
are.

Reinventing. Sometimes existing rites just need your own small personal
touch for them to carry the power necessary to be meaningful. But
sometimes it is necessary to totally reframe and rescript an established
ritual, providing a fresh perspective to existing ritual elements or adding new components that feel more spontaneous and alive.

Reintegrating. As with any creative endeavor, once you have successfully mastered it, you can always do it again. By reintroducing meaningful ritual into your life and by continuing to design and perform them regularly, you are creating a solid framework around which to organize your life. The ability to design rites for any and every life passage not only provides a satisfactory creative experience but a potent tool to empower you in the creation of your own life.

CHAPTER EIGHT

Religion and Spirituality

We all dance to a mysterious tune, intoned in the distance by an invisible piper.

—Albert Einstein

I hear and behold God in every object,
　　yet I understand God not in the least,
　　Nor do I understand who there can be
more wonderful than myself.

—Walt Whitman

Religion and spirituality are so often linked together that we tend to think that they cover much of the same territory. Although the worlds intersect, sharing elements in common, there are essential differences. The root of the word *religion* is "to tie together." Since humans are social beings first and foremost, it should not be surprising that religion, functioning originally as an arm of the sociopolitical system, supplied the rules by which societies were organized, tying people's lives together for the highest good of the community.

Some of these rules sought to distinguish between the profane—the mundane, the secular, and everyday life—and the sacred, or the holy. "The [religious] beliefs, myths, dogmas and legends are either representations or systems of representations which express the nature of sacred things, the virtues and powers which are attributed to them, or their relations with each other and with profane things."[1] Rituals and rites are the ceremonial vehicles that actively express these religious beliefs. The word *ritual* means "to fit together," its origin similar in nature to words such as *order, art, skill, weaving,* and *arithmetic*, which all have to do with creating an order to things, making a cohesive whole by fitting together individual pieces or parts.[2]

And so, as individuals sought to tie their lives together, to bond with others, they also attempted to fit their lives together in a way that would best serve and support the society. As "rules of conduct," then, telling people how to behave in the presence of sacred symbols, rituals in general, and more specifically rites of passage, are movements from the profane to the sacred, progressively moving each individual through successive status changes throughout the course of a lifetime, while ensuring the continuity of the community.

But what has dramatically changed over the course of millennia is the evolution of the sacred. In times past, what once belonged to the realm of the Divine was determined and defined, sanctioned and proscribed, by the society, and was assumed to directly reflect the needs of the individuals within it. While community may remain the key structure around which all human relationships are organized, the essential dependency upon the tribe or group for survival is no longer as necessary for the individual. The greater emphasis now seems to be upon an individual evolutionary imperative, for each of us to determine for ourselves what is sacred. And, as such, it may be that the sacred is to be found anywhere, in anything that provokes change and transforms us in a personally meaningful way. Ultimately, this may be the true meaning of religion.

Spirit "has its most abstract symbol in the form that leads from mouth to breath, and from breath to word."[3] The origins of spirit, as we best know it historically, can be traced to the mythological/cosmological recounting of the story of Creation in the Old Testament. In the beginning, "the spirit of God hovered over the face of the waters. And God said: 'Let there be light.'" Here, the spirit translates literally into the breath, or the wind, of God, and so it is that according to Genesis, God breathed life into all of creation. But it is in the prologue of his gospel in the New Testament that John transforms the organizing creative principle of the universe into the Word, the Logos.

The spirit, the Word, describes a rational principle of Creation that utilizes an innate intelligence and an uncanny wisdom to bring about a perfectly ordered universe. Spirituality, then, is the belief in the interconnection of all things within creation. When we see ourselves as fundamentally linked and inextricably bound to all other things within creation, our individual journey assumes a quality of belonging to something greater than ourselves, perhaps to a higher meaning and purpose.

Today, people are finding new ways to engage their own spirituality.

Sometimes spirit is best expressed within the context of the religious experience. Many individuals are returning with a strengthened commitment and resolve to a richer expression of their own divinity within the framework of their religion of origin. Those who have had no affinity for Eastern culture and religion may find themselves reaching out to these teachings to express a spiritual longing unaddressed by their own traditional backgrounds. They may not necessarily forsake the teachings and tenets of the religions into which they were born for something new, but they often utilize the teachings and practices of other traditions to enhance and enliven their own. Some individuals, however, do leave their religion of origin, replacing it with a tradition that feels more resonant and true. Women are even reaching back to ancient prepatriarchal traditions of women's mysteries.

But there are many other ways to engage our spirits outside of the formal religious experience. The women in this chapter demonstrate that searching for and finding spirit may take many unique forms: from love of nature to love of solitude and reflection; from connecting in community with like-minded women of spirit to reconnecting with our ancestors, our link to the past; and from a direct experience with the Divine provoked by external forces to one that comes from within. Spirituality is a transcendent movement beyond ourselves into the realm of the interconnected world.

We Are All Equal in the Eyes of God

Virtually every organized religion offers an array of ceremonies and ritual passages to mark the various stages of a person's life. Roman and Eastern Orthodox Catholicism mark the transitions of an individual's life with seven sacraments, while Judaism's ritual passages, aside from marriage and death, include circumcision and bar/bat mitzvahs (coming-of-age ceremonies performed at about age thirteen). The rituals in Islam focus less on the life cycle and life transitions and more on how one lives life in its totality, day to day. Ritual obligations for the faithful include the call to prayer five times a day, fasting for the holy month of Ramadan, and the hajj, the pilgrimage required to Mecca, at least once in a lifetime. In Hinduism, there are several rites called *samskaras*, or purifications, their purpose being to transform the individual so that rebirth, and eventually release from the cycle of life and death, is attained.

While coming-of-age rites have long been practiced in essentially all cultures, the participation of women in them is relatively new. In the Jewish religion, the privilege and right to become a bar mitzvah, an active member of the adult Jewish community, was traditionally reserved for boys. Susan was the first girl in her family to participate in the rite, and since the congregation she belonged to was Reform, she was able to take part in, and even lead, some of the ceremony. Susan's father placed her tallith, the prayer shawl traditionally only worn by men, over her shoulders. She remembers feeling a shared happiness, a real joy with her father during this ceremonial act. This had become somewhat of a family tradition since Susan's grandfathers had placed her brothers' prayer shawls on them.

"After I read from the actual Torah (some people use a transliteration), we added something else that was really special. The Torah was passed from my mom's father to my dad's father, to my dad, to my brother Jay, to my brother Marc, and finally to me. I was thrilled, since the Torah is the most sacred object in the Jewish religion. Here I was holding it after it had been passed down from some of the most influential people in my life.

"I had looked forward to this day since I was nine years old, when my oldest brother, Jay, was a bar mitzvah; it seemed like such a significant event. It never really occurred to me that it was just recently that girls were allowed to participate in such an important part of growing up. I saw it as my birthright and as a privilege of being Jewish. I remember looking at my parents when I was done with my Torah portion, and I could tell by their faces how proud they were of me.

"My parents' friend made a little speech and presented me with Sabbath candlesticks, a gift from our temple sisterhood. She said it was a thrilling moment, yet a little strange for her to see me fulfilling this rite. She had three boys, so in a way she was living vicariously through me. My mom never had any doubts that I would fulfill my desire for equal treatment. I do not consider myself a rebel. I just do not let things like gender get in the way of something that I feel I am fully capable of and deserve to have equally."

Women of past generations have been traditionally excluded entirely from, or have only been permitted diminished or peripheral participation in, key rites of passage within their religions. Today, women, starting from a relatively young age, are taking active roles within their religious communities. Many women are making up for lost time by retroactively performing sacred ceremonies, most particularly those signifying coming of age. What is most significant about rituals of this kind is that they symbolically enable women to assume a full adult role in the society when this had been traditionally denied to them.

Resurrection

Entering a religious order is a life-altering decision, for all that is familiar is volitionally left behind. As such, it is a unique rite of passage. For Sister Joan, taking the required steps and making the necessary shifts to separate from the world in which she had lived in order to enter into an entirely different one took many years to accomplish. After deciding to fully embrace a life dedicated to becoming a true servant of God in service to humanity, formal vows were undertaken in a series of passage rites designed to sever ties to the old while allowing her to assume a new identity. While the aim of most rites of passage is to be reborn spiritually, from a theological perspective, rebirth to a new identity in the religious life is a real resurrection, a rising from the dead, a bringing back to life.

"Understanding that rites of passage are signposts that mark the journeys of our lives takes me back to the time when I was just five and in kindergarten. Being the child of a Catholic mother and a Jewish father had never posed a problem for me until one day, during a religious lesson, the teacher explained the crucifixion of Jesus. Afterward, in the playground, I was persecuted by my classmates: 'Your father nailed Jesus to the cross. He's a Jew. What a horrible thing to do to poor Jesus.'"

Terribly upset and crying, Sister Joan was taken aside and comforted by her teacher. She remembers feeling sad and lonely, but she didn't want to say anything to her parents because she didn't want her father to know what had happened. What a revelation when, a few days later, the same teacher explained to the pupils how lucky they were to have someone in their class who had the same blood as Jesus and Mary. This time, Sister Joan felt proud and grateful. The scenario was quite different at playtime; some children came to touch her skin and put their arms around her. "For me, it was certainly a birth-to-death-to-rebirth experience, and from that early age it has helped me to be much more inclusive and understanding in my outlook.

"From that early age, I developed a certain pride within myself of belonging to the race of the specially chosen. But at the same time, I knew how difficult it was to unite the two religions. I often went to the synagogue and attended most of the Jewish festivals and always responded to the question 'What religion are you?' with the answer 'I am a Catholic Jewess.'"

During several periods of her youth, Sister Joan had a calling from within to follow God in the religious life, and at the age of twenty-two, she entered a religious community. The novitiate is an invitation into the religious life, and as such it is an extreme reorientation of one's life. She was preparing to live the radical demands of the gospel as lived by the charisma of the founders of the church.

The first stage of the initiation process was the separation from family, friends, work, and the interests and distractions of daily life—the detachment from everything in order to fulfill the desire to be consecrated to God. She realized that this separation gave her space and a quiet time where she was more disposed to hear the voice of God speaking to her. Tribal initiation rites point to the importance of experiencing values, not just learning about them. In the novitiate, Sister Joan experienced the value of silence and prayer.

The Scriptures are opened to the novices, not as books to be studied and analyzed, but as books to be felt, as ways to experience the power, gentleness, mercy, and compassion of God. "All initiation rites necessarily involve suffering in one form or another—the pain of separation from one's immediate family, the dramatic rupture with one's past style of life, the restrictions of community living, and so on: death to one's self, to one's own selfishness, in order to rise to serve others. This is never done alone but in mutual relationship with the one that the novice gives her life to—the faithful God of Israel."

The religious life within the church exists to follow God and for service in the name of God. This not only evokes joy, love, and community, but also pain; this is the novitiate paradigm, as all of life lived to the fullest is death and resurrection.

"Religious life has helped me to understand the true center of my life; it has given meaning to all I do. As the song says, 'Just to be is a blessing.' It is in being that we fully embrace our deepest longing, realize our most blessed dream, and recognize and celebrate our fullest potential."

Growing up, what was your concept of God? From a traditional perspective, was God a benevolent, loving presence, or a shaming, guilt-provoking entity? Or were you guided more by the mystical and transcendent aspects of the spirit? How have the experiences you've had through your life, both good and bad, impacted your religious or spiritual beliefs? What, if anything, has shifted in your faith over the years?

Do you practice rituals that comfort, support, sustain, and inspire your spirit, or are they done by rote and out of a sense of responsibility? If the rote of your spiritual or religious life leaves you feeling dissatisfied, what can you do to revitalize it? Recalling a few favorite things from your religious or spiritual experiences as a child may help spark your imagination, giving you some ideas about how to capture again what once appealed to you.

Ancestors Live Inside

Although the religion in which we are raised may serve as a strong founda- tion for a good moral and spiritual life, it may still seem as if something fun- damental is missing. Going in search of our own source, we may need to access our roots through past generations. Dalila's story is about finding her spiritual self in a place often overlooked and even discarded—the lives and histories of her ancestors.

"I grew up as a Muslim, a member of the Nation of Islam. Although not Orthodox in our practice, my family's beliefs were certainly not steeped in traditional Western religion. In fact, my home was strict in the sense that we never read Scripture or the Bible." As the Nation of Islam began to undergo change many years ago, her parents became less actively involved. For Dalila, this created a void, a feeling of being empty spiritually, as she describes it.

"I still saw Allah as my God, this remaining my source of religion for a long time. Last year, I attended a Kwanzaa event at a pan-African-based min- istry, which is still in the process of evolving. After hearing a speaker, whose words really meant something to me, I started attending regularly. The min- istry celebrates and performs various rituals from different African cultures— for example, libations to the ancestors. My eyes have been opened. Although the founding members are mostly Caribbean, I've learned about all things African from the ministry. This was never taught to me before in any school experience. I learned that no matter where you are on this earth, all blacks have a similar heritage."

Why did people switch religions from their religion of origin? Dalila came to understand that a lot of religions carry similar, or even the same, themes within them, and these themes are elucidated through the perspective of elders, not from Scripture. History made her aware of the vital importance of ancestors. Dalila didn't know either set of grandparents, but when she vis- its her great-aunt now, they talk about history.

"We were forced to forget what we were in Africa. Recently I heard a speaker talk about the 'sickness' of not knowing your ancestry and of there- fore not feeling complete. Growing up, I know my parents loved me, but there was hardly any show of affection from my mother—no hugs or kisses. Someone explained that on slave plantations, black women fought the urge to hug their children and husbands or to get too close to them because they never knew when they might be sold off.

"I feel fortunate to have gotten to where I am today. I'm hoping to have children in the near future, and so I'm looking with optimism to the traditions of my ancestors for support and sustenance. Borrowing from the rituals of my heritage, I've placed an *akua'ba* doll, a symbol of fertility, on top of my bedpost, and I'm wearing earrings of cowrie shells that are worn in certain parts of Africa to encourage fertility. In reestablishing the connection to my heritage, I've learned that Africans who practice traditional religion call upon ancestors in the same way that they call upon God, and for a good reason—they are inside of you."

Meditation: Accessing the Source

Sometimes there is a need, a yearning, to access the source in a way that goes beyond what is traditionally prescribed by religious practices, something that is deeply felt and acutely personal to the seeker. Finding her path in a move away from the Catholicism in which she was raised has been a great rite of passage for Pam.

"I came to meditation over ten years ago, and it has been a life-altering experience for me in countless ways. It has allowed me to view the physical world I live in as one that constantly brings lessons that, when viewed as such, are always for my greater good spiritually. The basic awareness of my spirit as self versus body was itself enough, but the inner contentment found in meditation has slowly but surely changed me at all levels—down to the cellular, I think.

"There is enormous relief in knowing that I don't have to look for things outside myself anymore—what a gift! Many people's days are plagued by that 'never-quite-full' feeling. I feel very fortunate. Meditation, simply sitting in silence, has enabled me to begin to see all of us as 'one'—something that is simple with friends who are loveable and loving, yet not quite so easy with those whose behavior feels hurtful, those for whom sensitivity doesn't come naturally. By getting quiet in such a basic way, I have been able to find one of the greatest gifts I have ever given myself—a sense of compassion, the present of being present, every moment, every day."

Many of the women in this book have spiritual practices that include meditation of one kind or another. Although we may think of meditation as a form of solitary practice where we are asked to sit in silence, quieting our minds as best we can, following the rhythm of the breath and focusing inwardly, there are many other effective ways, many other forms of meditation, to help us access the source.

Earlier, Patricia described walking the labyrinth as a spiritual meditative tool. Meredith, Dunya, and Robin find their spiritual expressions in the meditation of dance movements, most specifically in the ritualistic elements of Sufi, belly dancing, and Lomi Lomi. In fact, artistic endeavors of any kind can be expressive of deep spiritual practice, often becoming meditative as our total attention is focused on creating from our own source.

It's a good idea and a good practice to juxtapose a mental, intellectual form of expression with an active, often creative one. Here we have the optimum opportunity to utilize many modalities in an effort to reach a fuller expression of what we are searching for. I often suggest to patients that, in addition to traditional "talk" therapy, they explore some form of bodywork such as massage, Reiki, craniosacral therapy, and chiropractic. This may help to access nonverbal material, thereby bypassing mental constructs that often get in the way or may even hinder or inhibit our understanding. Different modalities add to and complement each other. The same is true for creative activities that require our active involvement. As we learn more about ourselves by doing them, we ultimately add more to the mix.

Many years ago, I had one of those internal pushes that prompted me to take up sculpting. I have always loved artistic projects of any kind, but I found myself wanting, and almost needing, to work in a medium that would provide depth and volume. So off I went to a basic sculpting course where I was instructed how to select the stone just right for me, where to buy it, what tools and other equipment were necessary to have, and, finally, where to go to learn the basics of sculpting.

What I learned went far beyond making a pretty work of art. I learned respect for what the stone had to offer. If you try to carve something that the properties of the stone simply won't allow you to do, you risk the possibility of cleaving the stone, ultimately destroying what you've created. You learn to work with what you have—no more, no less. You don't try to impose your will or attempt to manipulate or control a situation. If you work in harmony with what appears to be an inanimate object but really is an organic, living thing, then you are bound to reap the rewards of your mutual respect and cooperation.

Elemental Alchemy

Sometimes we don't know where to turn for inspiration. Our life just seems to be going along of its own accord, no better and no worse than it's been so far along the path we're traveling. Inevitably, though, we're bound to run across unmarked places and unexpected rough patches. There may be stretches where the terrain seems foreign and alien, or where we have to decide which road to go down, or where we suddenly discover that we're not where we thought we were.

Looking back, most of us can point to at least one place, but more likely several along the way, where we experienced what was thought to be a wrong turn in the road, or perhaps there was a chance meeting or an unexpected turn of events that changed our life forever. These unfamiliar diversions from our daily lives are like the separation phase of the classic rite of passage. Something engages us and pulls us away from what we know, and suddenly we are in unknown territory, about to embark on a journey into a strange new world. If we allow them to touch us, these seemingly random but often serendipitous events can alchemize our personal transformations.

Interfaith minister and ritual creator Deborah Roth grew up as the only girl among three brothers. Given that, and having had only sons and nephews, she likes to say that she's been surrounded by testosterone her whole life. The catalyst for her change in consciousness came in December 1992 in the form of a tarot card reading, her very first. She had gone with a close friend to a reader/astrologer who took a mystical/alchemical approach to her reading. The key cards that came up in the reading were the Ten of Swords, often perceived as a scary card since it deals with death and rebirth, and the High Priestess card, perhaps a harbinger of Deborah's future vocation. The eighth house, which deals with the occult, also figured prominently in the reading. "Little did I know just how quickly my life would change. Within six months of that reading, I attended my first women's ritual at the Fourth Universalist Society in Manhattan, took my first astrology class, and found myself drawn to reading Carl Jung's writing again."

The minister at the Fourth Universalist Society gave Deborah *The Chalice and the Blade* and *Bury My Heart at Wounded Knee*, and these proved to be so pivotal for Deborah as to provide an initiation through the written word. She started attending several women's circles, including one at the Women's Rites Center; she began studying tarot and astrology; and she read all the women's spirituality material she could get her hands on. In 1996, Deborah saw an ad about a counseling training program utilizing astrology. Upon acceptance at Lesley College (now University) she found a way to incorporate these elements into her master's program in psychological counseling. "I felt a distinct sense of opening up, realizing that I was finally getting in touch with something I had been missing."

Finally, Deborah created her own women's circle based on the elemental connection of astrology, tarot, Jung's wisdom, and palmistry—a circle that has continued to grow and strengthen over the years. As she describes it, "This growth has been an organic growth, starting with Full Moon Circles open only to Fourth Universalist members and then blossoming into New Moon Circles open to all women, incorporating all of the elements of the earth holidays—equinox; solstice; and cross-quarter days such as Halloween, Groundhog Day (originally the feast of St. Bridget) and May Day (Beltane)."

At a circle in December of 1999, with a new moon in Sagittarius that honored their spiritual journeys, three women spoke of a desire to strengthen their connection to Mother Earth. As it goes when women place their intention on something, by January this had evolved into a group of seven women taking part in a special program, now several years running, called the Sister Circle Weavers program, which takes women on a thirteen-moon journey. The premise, developed from the method in which Deborah herself was trained, revolves around women taking turns facilitating circles themselves and sharing their journeys and knowledge together.

"For me, this has been an amazing journey, especially important because I am very left brain, and honoring these events helps to bring the grounding element of Earth into my astrology chart. At first, I was so self-conscious about dancing and moving. One of the biggest things to come out of the circle for me is the experience of being in my body, honoring and celebrating every aspect of it. During the teaching part of my women's circle, I speak of being empowered and nurtured by the process of reclaiming and honoring the areas of women's lives that have been devalued—emotions, intuition, our bodies, and our connection to nature because we are cyclical creatures."

In the first year or two of doing this work, Deborah was given the gift of a vision of herself facing a far shore, suspended in midair between stepping-stones that disappeared into the fog. This image would bubble up in her mind every so often. In the fall of 1999, while leading a meditation in a workshop that came out of her master's thesis about the elements, she actually found herself in the meditation as well. "I remember feeling like I was on the far shore during the meditation, seeing the path continuing off the beach, definitely a milestone reached."

As an interesting aside, the thirteen-moon journey has a fascinating origin. Robert Graves, chronicler of the Greek myths, notes, "Time was first reckoned by lunations, and every important ceremony took place at a certain phase of the moon."[4] After astronomical calculations showed the year to comprise 364 days plus a few hours, it was necessary to divide it into months, or moon cycles. These "common law months," as they were referred to, each contained twenty-eight days. This sacred number allowed for the moon to be worshipped as a woman, whose menstrual cycle was also usually the same number of days. Dividing 364 days by 28 gives us 13. Since thirteen refers to the sun's death month, it "has never lost its evil reputation among the superstitious."[5]

Like Deborah, several of the women in this book intuited a strong need to reconnect with the long-missing feminine, but in a form that is healthy and balanced. We can only assume that there is a collective unconscious memory that has resurfaced, reemerging as an appropriate expression of something inherent and instinctual in women. The moon reminds Katie of this principle nightly. Karlin designed a marriage ceremony that equally honors the divinity of masculine and feminine. This same theme stood at the core of Elise's fiftieth-birthday fire ceremony rite and celebration. For Meredith, the joy of being in her body is a manifestation of her own spirituality, a sense of connecting to something divine. Sheryl's need to go to the "source" defines what many women are seeking: reconnecting and relating to a being that recognizes and honors them.

There may be many times in your life when you find yourself on the verge of a growth opportunity or challenge. For most of us, these opportunities are happening around us much of the time, but we don't bother to recognize them, or we choose to ignore them. We get caught up in the complexity of our own lives and can't, or won't, make the time to explore new avenues. Perhaps we are afraid to let the unfamiliar and unknown in, fearing the outcome, fearing that once we have opened a new door, stepping over the threshold, there may be no going back.

- Has a person or event been a catalyst in your life, propelling you forward, perhaps unexpectedly, on your journey? Who have been your mentors and role models? What external sources—books, groups, and disciplines—have influenced and encouraged your growth?
- What changes in your life preceded this happening or opportunity? What finally got your attention? Was there something different about you at that time that allowed you to open yourself up to new challenges?
- Recollect previous sudden twists and abrupt turns in your life to help you predict what might happen in the future, or to help you be on the lookout for more such twists and turns that might be coming your way. Tracking feelings, hunches, and reflections will help you confirm the

validity of your intuition. Was there some preliminary feeling or sense about a shift that you were about to experience?

- In what ways did you embrace and incorporate this new and unexpected way of being into your life? Has your mastery of this new way changed the way you express yourself?
- How have you shared this energy with the world? How have you influenced or changed others as a result of your own transformation? What gifts has this sharing brought you in return?

Nature: Reflection of Life

The natural world gives us countless and priceless opportunities to contemplate our spiritual lives. Being in nature allows for an opening into realms that we otherwise could not access. The sheer beauty and wonder of the natural order is mirrored in our own desire for the same in our lives. When we are attuned to the world around us, the vibratory energies that surround us merge with our own, and harmony prevails.

Katie offers this reflection on the moon she saw one summer night that profoundly impacted the rest of her life. "This experience flowed from a place of childish curiosity and universal pull. I played no conscious role in designing or creating it. But that is one of the most essential things about it. It displayed to me an awakening of my role in the direction and soul of the greater universe. It taught me very early on that just by being, I would be held, nurtured, and guided in ultimate grace and purpose. This is a lesson that I am reminded of countless times in my daily life.

"My living spaces have always been adorned with images of the night sky, moons, and the sea. I often communicate with my loved ones about the moon and have celebrated the elements of the sky, moon, and sea through image, vision, art, imagination, and voice. Spiritually, in the most organic sense, on that night of initiation, I became connected to the guides of the night sky, moon, stars, sea, and different energies of the world that seemed unquestionably tangible. This moment acted as a gateway to my life and spirit where a distinct sense of guidance and being was instilled and awakened in me."

Barbara recalls a similar event in her fourteenth year that changed her forever. She was picking fruit for the war (WWII) effort and retired one night to a gym made into a dormitory. "One night I pulled my sleeping bag onto the playing field. A couple of minutes of viewing the magnificent night sky, with stars like I had never seen, being a city gal, I felt myself floating up into the starry heavens. It was the loveliest, sweetest experience of my young life. I knew there was something else for me to explore and hadn't the vaguest notion of how to find it. I continued reading everything I could get my hands on that had philosophical and spiritual messages."

Pam's love of nature began early, thanks to having no computer and to having parents who loved the countryside. She and her friend Dottie discovered a mutual love in this and began calling each other "Nature Buddy." They still do to this day. Dottie sends Pam autumn leaves every year, as does her mother. "This makes me think about the seasons. Since moving to California several years ago, my life is a bit void without these ever-repeating passages. The change of the air, the light, the silhouettes, the scents, and the emotions that come with them are priceless." She gets noticeably excited in September when she goes to Maine, her yearly ritual since about age eight.

In Maine, there are many favorite places that she returns to over and over like an old friend when she is alone. "Sitting way out on our rock outcropping overlooking the immense and swelling sea, watching the waves crashing on the rocks is hypnotic. Filtered light passing through quaking aspens that seem to wave hello, the first jog up the hill to the spectacular scene of coastline out to the Otter Cliffs, wild roses all along the gravel path, pink granite, salt air, and sweet pine everywhere—no matter how many times I go there, I am always filled with great joy and exhilaration, trying to drink it in with all the senses." These are the places and the moments that seem to evoke original time. Each time we go there, we are rewarded with a sense of awe and wonder that is energizing and assuring.

For Tuija, nature's enormous influence not only impacted her early years, figuring prominently in her daily activities, but later supplied valuable clues that helped her navigate through some rough spots in her life. Elise's journey into the wilderness afforded her a rare and precious time to go questing for her own soul, ultimately returning with a vision for the rest of her life. Attuning ourselves to the rhythms of the natural world not only provides grounding and stability but helps bring us into accord with the perfection of creation.

Flying Home to Final Rest

Sometimes the mystical mingling of the Divine and the ordinary creates ready-made rites, when messengers of spirit from nature find their way into our lives to help us complete passages and find closure. There was one such time in my own life; without question or doubt, all those present had been touched by the Divine.

From ancient times and through the lore of all traditions, birds are the intermediaries between humans and the Divine, between Heaven and Earth. They symbolize transcendence and signify the movement from one sphere of existence to a higher one.

In the fall of 1995, just around Thanksgiving, my husband and I flew back to New York from San Francisco to celebrate the holiday with our children. My son had remained living in our old apartment in the city, and my daughter was coming from L.A. to be with us. My husband had arranged to see his mother, Elly, who was living in a senior residence complex in Maryland, for dinner a few days before the holiday. We received a phone call from my brother-in-law telling us that Elly had had a heart attack and was in the hospital in stable condition. My husband immediately left to be with his mother. Tests revealed several blocked arteries, so it was decided that she should undergo open-heart surgery to correct the problem. As the proverbial expression goes, "the operation was a success, but the patient died." Thanksgiving became a funeral.

Going back in time a few years to 1992 sets the stage for what happened at Elly's funeral. My husband and I had moved to San Francisco for a wonderful job opportunity. Renting an apartment, we were perched atop Russian Hill with a gorgeous sweeping view of the bay. On many days, I heard loud, raucous screeching. Going to the window, I witnessed something extraordinary—a flock of lime green birds, parrots, with bright red markings. Flying circularly around and around, they lighted on a nearby rooftop. My eyes were not deceiving me. But what were they doing there? Several residents of the area confirmed that, indeed, I had seen what I thought. The story goes that some tropical birds had "escaped" some time ago and had now created their own colony atop Russian Hill. People I told the story to were skeptical, even disbelieving, until they saw the bright green flock themselves.

The funeral took place on a beautiful, sunny fall day. Friends and people who knew Elly, as well as people paying respect to her two sons, filled the chapel. Only one car followed the hearse—her sons, her daughter-in-law, their two children, and the rabbi. The cemetery was very old and was haunting in its overgrown beauty. This sacred place was "full"—no more plots, and so the trees and foliage grew wildly without perpetual care. I imagined that so many of the souls interred there had passed on so long ago that no one was left to visit them. My father-in-law, having passed almost a quarter of a century before, had bought an adjoining plot for his beloved Elly, who was, on that day, coming to her final resting place.

Leaving the car, we watched as the coffin was carefully lifted out of the hearse. At the gates of this holy ground, breaking the serenity of the day, was a strangely familiar sound—loud, raucous screeching. Looking up, a flock of lime green birds with red markings made several circular passes over the cemetery and flew off. Smiling, I knew it was a moment of the Divine. My husband, joyfully crying, said, "They've come; our birds have come." I could not have imagined why, or how, these friends had made the journey of a few thousand miles. Trying to make sense of this phenomenon, I offered this as a compromise—maybe they were the "East Coast cousins," still not explaining what parrots would be doing in the Northeast, especially in Ozone Park, New York.

For those left scratching their heads, the answer comes in this postscript. On the Sunday after the funeral, we were all sitting around the living room of our apartment with sections of the Sunday *New York Times* everywhere. Perusing the real estate section for some inexplicable reason, my son came across a very curious article on the first page. In a highlighted box was a small piece titled "For the Birds," which gave a thumbnail sketch of a town in Connecticut called Black Rock. The birds they spoke of were, as you can imagine, ancestors of the very same parrots from Ozone Park—their "forebirds," also escapees from captivity, this time flying to freedom from JFK International Airport and now winging their way all along the East Coast. There is an explanation for everyone, even the skeptics. Personally, it was a flight of faith that took me from "here to there."

A Crisis of the Spirit

Sometimes we may reach a place in life where we feel stuck. Intuitively, we may understand that we have reached a critical juncture. The road we have been traveling down holds nothing else for us or has just simply disappeared into the forest. The way we have navigated through life up until that point no longer seems to work, or it just doesn't feel right anymore. We may have a gnawing sense that something's got to change, but we just don't know what to do or how to do it. Spiritually, we are being asked to rise to the occasion, to confront and challenge ourselves to dig deeper, to find the strength and resilience to move on to a new path for the next stretch of the journey.

Several years ago, Sheilaa realized that she was in just such a place. The notion that she was stuck in life was accompanied by a similar visceral one, a feeling of heaviness and slowness, as if she were walking through sludge. Eventually she received an intuitive hit—to release, to let go of everything that she felt sorry about in her life. For the next three or four days, she spent minutes and even hours writing formal statements about her regrets, things that she wished had never happened. She regretted even having to write this list, but having finally completed it, she carried out the next ritual in her greater rite of spiritual passage. She burned the list, placed the ashes in a little box, and buried it.

But the passage rite was only beginning. Sheilaa knew she needed to cleanse herself of something old and finished as well. "As I washed myself off, I felt the power leave my body. Somehow I managed to crawl out of the bathroom to the living room, and lying there I recall thinking, 'I'm dying.' I knew I wasn't literally dying, but the experience felt real to me nevertheless. I understood that I was to 'lie there and die.' It was a wondrous realization—my body was being transformed."

Settling back into herself, Sheilaa's thoughts turned to all those she loved and all who loved her. She resolved to call everyone to let them know that her heart would always love them no matter what had transpired between them. Some people understood what she was doing; others didn't. Some hung up on her, but that didn't matter to Sheilaa. She knew what *she* had to do and was unattached to the responses she got. Some people cried with her. Although this was an exercise for herself, she knew that there might be benefit for others. "If it's the 'right time,' others can be transformed when they choose to take the opportunity provided by another.

"In ancient times, the initiation was the vehicle for 'dying to the old self.' My initiation was the point at which I became an adult, that place where I came to understand who I am and what I'm doing."

Things Change

"In the myths as in life, the traveler needs to keep on moving, to keep on functioning, to do what has to be done, to stay in touch with her companions, or manage alone, to not stop and give up, even when she feels lost, to maintain hope in darkness."[6] Psychotherapists often see the pain of people suffering through depression, hopelessness, and helplessness, ready to "give up trying" because one "just can't anymore." All of these symptoms bear a great resemblance to what one may encounter in the threshold phase.

Although genetics and biology drive and determine some depressions, many depressive episodes are more situational, a result of changes and challenges that we all face in life. The wisdom of the voice within, the unconscious, is at work here, moving to alert the individual that it is now time to confront a situation that is no longer useful and that in fact may be damaging to the soul's growth. As so often occurs in response to positive change, the conscious mind fights the process, preferring instead the comfort of the past, regardless of how difficult and painful it may have been. A tug of war ensues, defenses don't hold, and symptoms may appear. If we are willing to enter into that pain, we come to acknowledge the gifts and wisdom of the unconscious, even if they come in challenging forms.

Recognizing the mythic roadmap of the journey, rife with ups and downs, twists and turns, and bends in the road, we gain a sense of structure and purpose that helps reassure and organize a life. Following a spiritual path and actively engaging everything that comes along the way ensures a safe return, healed and whole.

The emphasis in the classic rite of passage is on the rebirth; one dies to an old identity to be reborn spiritually. This is the story of a real-life rebirth that began physically, with Leslie literally choosing to stay alive when she had technically died. The spiritual rebirth, as so often happens, came later, when the full impact of these dramatic events settled into her psyche, finally guiding her toward a life of unconditional love and total acceptance.

"I was 'killed,' our car hit by a drunk driver in a pick-up truck, the impact sending me hurling through the windshield." Sailing into the sky, flying into space with enormous speed, Leslie was suddenly surrounded by stars. Having lost consciousness, she still knew that there was no damage to her brain. Everything else dropped away; all that was left was a heightened awareness of the motion of soaring into space. Then Leslie heard her companion standing over her body screaming her name. "I seemed to 'reverse motion,' coming back through space, light moving past me, elongating in streams. I came to rest, suspended, over my body, hovering about three hundred feet above the ground. A man walked over to my body and said, 'Her neck is broken.' I seemed to lurch forward, craning my neck to view myself. My neck was not broken. Blue lights hovered on either side of me, wordlessly and lovingly saying, 'Let's go.' I was an observer of my own death, yet I was not afraid."

Suddenly, she had a visual image of her baby, her just-two-year-old son. Her neck wasn't broken, her baby needed her, and so she made a decision to come back. If all this wasn't strange enough, she had to actively jump back into her own body.

Leslie awoke during surgery at Georgetown University Hospital to the Eagles singing "Hotel California." She remembers feeling that the OR was a very happy place, awakening to the comfort of the surgeon saying, "She'll be fine."

"I know this to be true: we are immortal, and there are spirits to guide and help us.

"Although a very different person 'before and after' the time I was killed, I returned to my everyday life, taking care of my son, my husband, and my home. The real changes did not occur until many years later, when I went through hard times. I experienced several life passages all at once, only to find that although the passages happened, the process of moving through them was ongoing for me. But after enduring many trials and tribulations, I finally 'crossed over.'"

On a path up until the accident, Leslie seemed to derail, finding herself alone in the wilderness, married to a man in a loveless marriage. It seemed to take her forever to recognize that he was an evil man, abusive to her spirit and totally lacking consciousness. Having lost herself in the name of peace, Leslie had disappeared. "Coming back to me was jolting. A horrible divorce many years later jarred me back onto my path. About three years ago, the man I truly loved was killed in an airplane crash. We had so much connecting us, emotionally and spiritually, that even his death took on the power of a serendipitous event."

The spring prior to her boyfriend's death, Leslie had suffered another terrible loss, a devastating betrayal that pushed her further toward the edge. Then, in June 2001, during a baseball game, with her son on the mound, his dear friend Bobby died in a traumatic accident on the field. Bobby's parents, who rarely attended games, were both there. Somehow, all of the kids thought they were each guilty of killing Bobby, with each boy scrutinizing his own actions, wondering whether the outcome might have been different if he had only taken some other action. But in a very healing process, the whole community came together, raising money to redo the ball field and participating in many ceremonies in Bobby's honor.

Leslie's Aunt Lila died in July 2001, the same year that she lost three friends and her beloved ten-year-old dog to cancer. "I did not think I had consciously performed any rituals or rites around these events, except for Bobby's death, but I had. For each passage, I had written a poem to encapsulate the event, mark it, make some sense of it, and ultimately honor it."

All of these devastating losses, these soulful passages, seemed to be pushing her to her limit. Seeking some relief, any relief, Leslie entered into therapy with a very nice, well-trained psychiatrist. She came looking for answers, but there weren't any. She had symptoms of depression, but she doesn't think she was truly depressed. Her therapist took a very linear approach, giving her what he thought were helpful directives, none of which helped at all. She was given a trial of an antidepressant but found it to be worthless. Seeing her problem in a flat, one-dimensional way, her therapist was unable to see all the layers. The psychic pain remained; Leslie was in spiritual crisis.

"Today, I live in a spiritual world, seeing things as more symbolic than real, seeing things as just something to move through. I have come to instantly accept whatever happens. No more struggles—I just move through whatever happens without making judgments."

Her search led her around the world to ultimately find that her true home was inside herself all along. She read countless spiritual books, from the Bible to Bill Moyers to *Conversations with God*. At one point, she lived with monks on a pilgrimage to temples in Southeast Asia. These experiences opened her up even more to another chapter in her spiritual life—the psychic world.

"On one particular freezing-cold day in New York, on my way to an appointment with a highly recommended palm reader, I, feeling adrift and wondering about the direction I was on, stopped and said to the powers that be, 'Just show me a sign.' I wanted a really substantial sign, not just some small connection. Finding my way to her apartment, I comfortably settled in. Ellen, the palm reader, was standing in front of a large picture window. Suddenly, the image of a woman with white hair and something blue around her neck appeared above Ellen's head. The message she uttered was the sign I was looking for: 'Things change.' I was filled with sheer, unadulterated bliss, a feeling I'd never felt before, or since.

"Spirit guides surround me all the time. I hear them speak to me. They inspire me. What is communicated feels like genius—the answers I'm seeking. I got a 'hit' that my father would die, and six weeks later, he was gone from a heart attack. I believe this intuition was actually a message from my dad, who I think is around me, as is my Aunt Lila.

"So how am I a different person than I was? For one thing, I've become very loving toward myself, which I'd never been before. I take care of myself the way a mother takes care of her child—something mothers don't often do for themselves. For a person who used to be very hard on herself, learning forgiveness is a huge thing—I forgive myself. Having almost lost myself, I no longer have time for the wrong kind of people. Above all else, I've come to know that *everything is precious*."

Although a near-death experience may force the issue, one needn't have one to recognize that one road has come to a dead end while another presents itself around the next bend. Here are a few creative exercises that hopefully will give you some new insights. Literally designing a road map for your own life allows you to visually see where you've been and where you're bound to go. Where have there been detours, dead ends, or territories unknown? These roads might represent the totality of your life or singular aspects such as family, career, spirituality, or the like. If you process concepts better visually, you can draw these road maps.

Reading obituaries fascinates me. Many people skip this page in the local newspaper because it provokes anxiety or just seems too morbid. But if you can be open-minded about reading obituaries, and about eventually writing your own, it may prove to be eye-opening and a very powerful exercise. How would you want to be remembered by others? What would you want people to know about you? How do you want others to feel about you? How would you want people to describe you? What would you like to accomplish during your lifetime? What is the meaning and purpose that you wish your life to convey? Are you in the process of accomplishing it now? If not, list a few things you can begin to do now to change that, concentrating on making it a priority to take steps toward your goals every day.

Finding a guiding principle by which to live is perhaps the one essential element necessary for us in order to aspire to and ultimately attain a life full of meaning and purpose. Our individual beliefs and faith in an elemental force or essence that determines everything and that harmonizes all things in existence serves as the matrix holding each of us together, sustaining each of us in this vast incomprehensible universe.

Spiritual Principles to Live By

We are all one. In spirituality, you are attuned to the rhythm of life. As Lao-tzu says, "Ordinary men hate solitude, but the master makes use of it, embracing his aloneness, realizing he is one with the whole universe."

Choose your God. The way you see the world around you is the way you'll choose what you wish to worship. Knowing God comes from knowing yourself. When you are comfortable with yourself from the inside out, everything around you reflects this.

Be present, here and now. No moment is more wonderful or more divine than this one. The past is done. The future awaits you. Only the present is alive in the act of creating itself.

Live an open life. Everything you need for your journey is already with you. But don't assume how life will or should unfold. When you interfere with the natural cycling of things, you may close yourself off from the rich possibilities that are there for the taking.

Be faithful to yourself. Hold a deep respect for who you are apart from anyone else. Honor your individuality. Embrace what makes you different.

Be the best you can be. Your best effort reflects what is best for you. Don't judge yourself based on what others are or do. Your relationship with the Divine, God, or spirit is not a competitive affair.

CHAPTER NINE

Community and Family

Unless someone like you cares a whole awful lot, nothing is going to get better. It's not.

—Dr. Seuss

Act as if what you do makes a difference. It does.

—William James

These days it seems that being human can be a pretty lonely thing. Ironically, with all the technological advances we've made, we no longer seem to have as much time for ourselves, for we are certain that if we don't stay abreast of all that is happening to us, we will surely miss something. But when the increased ability to gather more information from the external world is coupled with an increased amount of time processing and synthesizing this information, we may be missing something far more precious; we may be losing touch with ourselves, with what is essential to us at a very core level.

Not surprisingly, our connections to one another are also deeply affected. Some of us think we are "talking" to and "seeing" someone else when we e-mail or hear each other's voice on recorded messages, but are we really? Some people actually believe they can have intimate relationships this way. Whatever happened to face-to-face communication, looking into the eyes of another for recognition, understanding, and real connection? When we diminish this contact, we lose our mirrors, those intimate reflections back to us that, more than anything else, tell us who we are and how we fit into the bigger picture of things.

The seductive force that promises progress, now overtaking our culture, entices us daily with the "new and better," pulls us away from spending essential time with ourselves, and ultimately threatens to separate us further from each other. We are spending more time with technology and with machines and less time with people. Aside from the immediate gratification we derive from receiving more faster, we as a species have no idea what long-term consequences this constant informational bombardment and the necessity of processing it, intellectually and emotionally, will have upon our evolution.

Connecting in community is a powerful way to counter this movement. The support of family and friends, the unity attained through gathering with others who share similar experiences and interests, and the performance of public rituals help ground and stabilize us. Even if the conditions of our lives dictate that we spend much of our time alone in solitary pursuit, it is when we are able to join together with others that we satisfy a basic desire inherent within humans. Community not only strengthens the group's focus and purpose; it ensures that the individual stays rooted in relationship and provides a solid, grounding structure to nurture healthy human development. Bearing witness creates a sacred space and establishes a foundation for healing to occur, for when we witness each other's stories, we are no longer isolated and alone. Therapeutically, simply being present to the thoughts and feelings of another, to the revealing of intimate details of the intrapsychic life, invites a monumental movement toward healing. It is this marking of a life, shared with and heard by another, that bridges our differences and emphasizes how much alike we all really are. By allowing the experiences of another to wash over us, we may find that someone else's story has resonance for us, touching an old familiar chord, or awakening something brand new and inspirational.

Perhaps some of our society's woes stem from "stories of the soul," our own personal myths that are never revealed. From my own experience, I've noted that whenever I've shared my own stories with others of a difficult decision or a choice I've had to make; whenever I've described a new way of thinking about things, perhaps providing a different perspective; or whenever I've revealed a new road I've chosen to go down, a curious thing has happened. Aside from the interest and support that my stories have engendered in others, an unspoken challenge is often evoked: If you can do it, I can too.

This chapter focuses on giving and receiving in the context of the larger group. For most of us, community signifies individuals joining together for a common goal. Our community could be the town we live in, or a religious, political, or professional group to which we belong, or it can be defined by common ethnicity, racial background, ideology, cause, or interest. Ultimately, it is a place where our identity, or even a small part of it, is affirmed and we feel we belong.

Community is the continuum of family, from generations past to those extending into the future. Ancestors and elders are the generational bridge helping us to navigate the way toward safe passage. Community consists of those intimates, our family and friends, who are always with us, sharing in the defining events of our life. Community can be a place of healing and recognition, even when we start out as strangers. Community may define the one-time coming together for a special purpose that exists in the communitas experience—the pilgrimage, retreat, or reunion. Community can be two individuals meeting in the act of giving and receiving through the mirroring of souls—the sacred "I-Thou." The stories here reflect these themes.

Wisdom Gained and Shared: The Role of the Elder

One generation plants the trees; another gets the shade.

—Chinese proverb

When people have no guidance and face transitions alone, "There are no containing walls within which the process can happen. . . . The individual suffers the mysteries of life as meaningless mayhem—alone."[1] The symbols and ceremonies of generations before us helped the individual to navigate his or her way through not only the actual physical journey (enacting the myth) but, just as importantly, through the psychological dangers implied in the ordeal. There is actually a great shortcut through life—honoring and applying the wisdom of the elders and the wise guides who bring their own experiences and "know the way."

"In contemporary American culture, the role of elder is essentially non-existent, let alone socially valued, with little social or emotional support available."[2] This phenomenon is relatively new. Elders throughout history and in many societies, especially in Asian, African, Native American, and Hispanic cultures, were highly valued and "essential to the continuity and identity of the community."[3] Within the community, elders held several roles: repository of wisdom (especially intuitive knowing, called "mother wit" in African cultures); celebrators of rituals; transmitters of sacred knowledge, especially to the young, including Scripture, myth, and prayer; and conduits of the past.[4]

For our modern times, proposed roles for elders might well include storytellers and historians, gatherers of family or community, mentors or role models, and beacons of hope. There is no doubt that if we could reestablish the role of elder in our culture, we would not only enhance the lives of older members but that of the society as a whole.[5]

A Journey Back to One's Roots

How does one pass on what hasn't been nurtured in one's own life? Doris tells of learning not only how to elder the generations that followed her, but of her experience in claiming her own roots, of "eldering" herself. Roots have to be watered, pruned, and tended. For Doris, the flowering came late; the blossoms seemed to have skipped a generation, and it took her most of a lifetime to trace the roots. Joyfully, she found out that they are much stronger and deeper than she had expected.

Grandparents carry on the family traditions. In the Jewish tradition, they make chicken soup and chopped liver, prepare the Passover seders, and cook the Chanukah latkes. By the time she was born in 1942, Doris had only one grandmother, and she died when Doris was three.

"My bubbie (grandmother) lived with my Aunt Sarah, and I was always told that I could dial her number on the phone and complain that my mother had given me stale bread to eat when I refused more nourishing fare. Her picture sits on my desk, and I have another of the two of us looking very much in love. Funny enough, I never asked what I called her and was never told, but recently I found a birthday card to me signed 'Bubbie.' Can that sound have stayed with me all these years? Is it in my very genes? My two-year-old grandson now calls me Bubbie."

Bubbie embroidered and created exquisite needlework designs; for years her handiwork lay in boxes, but now her beautiful creations fill Doris's home. "I continue the tradition as I knit sweaters, jackets, hats, and scarves for my own grandchildren. In my wallet, I carry a note that accompanied some small diamonds I got from my Bubbie that I have passed to my children. The note reads,

> Darling Doris,
> I hope this little token leads you to
> independence in your future and life.
> This is your grandmother's wish. Amen.

"Independence—how forward thinking! I wonder how this woman who helped her husband in a shop and mothered three daughters knew how to give me such a valuable abstraction. My children have told me that she must have known I would have a hard time with her daughter, my mother. My independence came late; I did have a hard time with her daughter, but suddenly everyone is dead and I am indeed independent. Now I am the oldest family member, and I want to pass on some of our history. I want my children and grandchildren to know about our family beyond what they inherited from my not very spiritual or faithful parents."

The first thing Doris did was to find and tend her grandparents' graves. It was difficult to find her father's parents. The paper she found cited a Brooklyn burial ground. She called the historic society and Brooklyn synagogues, but it wasn't until a distant cousin remembered Myrtle Street that she located the cemetery. "My grandfather's stone is tall and ancient looking; I never realized that he died in 1920, only a few years after emigrating to America, and twenty-two years before I was born. His picture, taken in Russia, before he had his beard cut by a barber at Ellis Island, shows clear features. My nose bridge and eyes are exactly his, although we are separated by worlds and time. My little grandmother, not even five feet, lived until 1941; she died a year to the day before my birth. Dora—I am named for her."

As a child, Doris remembers being taken to the cemetery against her will, viewing it as an alien and scary place. Her family always stopped to take an old man into their car and paid him to say the prayers for the family. Now she visits both sets of grandparents often and has learned to say her own prayers. "Independence? I carry the prayer booklet in the glove compartment so that I can stop for a visit when I feel my need or theirs. In fact, I imagine that they nudge each other as I draw near, saying, 'She's here. She didn't forget.' Perhaps this kind of independence means joyfully remembering one's obligation."

There was not much spirituality in her home growing up. Her parents forgot the religion and tradition of the old country as they became Americanized into the "high life"—card games, parties, cruises, and caretakers for the kids. Her father observed the High Holy Days; he fasted on Yom Kippur, carrying his tallith (the ritual prayer shawl) in a blue velvet bag adorned with a gold Jewish star. "My mother, sister, and I met him at the synagogue, the one farthest from our house, and raced in our high heels to be on time for a sermon by a rabbi who lectured a congregation he saw only yearly on their sinfulness. For the women, it was 'showtime,' and as each mother-daughter combination entered the sanctuary, there were nods and once-overs from the females already seated. Only in later years did I realize that Yom Kippur was a day of looking inward. More independence: the realization that I had to learn for myself what was really sacred."

Roots

The docent leads art lovers past early Chagall paintings,
tells them Chagall embraced the avant-garde.
In Paris he experimented with a new form.

But it's the same old shtetl,
Jewish life in Russia,
Human form flying over the chaos.

The Czar's stamp on an official form
allows Hillel Kompaneitz, his wife, and four sons
Passage to America on the "Kursk" leaving Russia September 30th, 1913.

They, not the Czar, knew when it was time to go.
Hillel, in old-fashioned garb, died 1920 in Brooklyn.
My eyes and nose-bridge identical to a photo of my unknown Zeyda.

Dora, Bubbie, lived somewhat longer,
Name-giver to her granddaughter,
Devorah Frima, keeper of the Sabbath, Doris Fern.

Henoch, youngest son of Dora and Hillel,
Victim of a lifelong depression,
Needed the touch his mother could not supply.

After witnessing the death of her parents
At the hands of some Cossacks.
Saturday night fun in the shtetl.

Chagall's lovers fly over their home.
The fiddler crouches on the roof playing his song.
My Bubbie and Zeyda must certainly be dancing to his tune.

—Doris White

How do you pass on what hasn't been nurtured in your own life? Before anything else, there has to be an awareness that something has been missing from your life. How do you know this? The simplest way to access this information is by tracking how you feel through your senses. Paying attention to the way in which you most comfortably process what happens around you, identify what sensory modality you utilize most often. This may be through observing, by watching how others interact, and by seeing how others are nurtured. You may become viscerally aware that something is missing—a sinking or hollow feeling, an underlying melancholia, a sense of disappoint-ment, or the recognition that something is deeply desired yet not present. What you hear—the language, the words, the tone—may provide valuable insights to your understanding. Chances are that, without your conscious knowing, one or more of your senses has been heightened and developed to give you important clues and information about the world around you.

If your life is rich with tradition, what gifts given to you by your elders would you like to pass along to the next generation? Creating a family history book that shares the memories and traditions of your own family, or con-structing a family tree and filling in as many blanks as possible, are fruitful ways to provide a living history and can serve as important references for future generations.

Over the years, I've observed a curious thing about human nature—qualities and values often seem to skip a generation. A grandchild may enjoy the same things a grandparent does, perhaps certain talents, gifts, and inter-ests, something that a parent doesn't share. A special bond with another sig-nificant adult family member, especially at a time when children are looking to separate from their parents on the way toward establishing their own inde-pendence, can provide much-needed comfort and safety for a young person's healthy development. As we've seen, Els' connection with her grandmother continued into adult life, when her choice of doing healing work mirrored what she had seen her grandmother do. Her grandmother's connection and reverence for nature helped Els define for herself what was really important and meaningful to practice.

Sometimes, though, it is not a specific person but rather a group that we feel a need to relate to. Sylvia knew that reconnecting with her ancestors ceremonially would ensure a positive forward movement after her divorce. Developing her creative process helped Tuija gain access to what she intu-itively grasped: a desire to connect with other cultures, the world, and the strength and creativity of women through the ages. Dalila understood the deep desire and need to reestablish her connection to her heritage and to her ancestors.

Aside from friends and family—those related by blood as well as those special few chosen to be family—others can function as community as well. Mentors, teachers, and coaches provide support, guidance, and wise counsel, encouraging and inspiring us to be all we are meant to be. Religious commu-nity often fulfills a deep spiritual need, providing a sense of belonging to something bigger. Self-help groups and twelve-step programs may provide exactly the right kind of community in times of need or crisis. In past times, before the advent of technology and before advances in transportation made moving from place to place easily possible, most people lived out their lives in small communities of extended family and friends. Imagine today returning to the notion of community in its purest sense, a community where people actually choose to live together, their daily activities shared and their personal lives inextricably intertwined. Barbara's home is in a small cooperative community nestled in the rolling hills of the Sonoma countryside. The community members form eleven units, including families, couples, and even single residents who vary in age from young child to elder. They come from different backgrounds and religions and have various life experiences. The community's mission and purpose guides the unfolding of daily life. Activities such as communal dinners and business meetings, and jobs essential for the efficient running of the community, are shared in kind by the adult members, with the children performing age-appropriate chores.

Rituals are a regular part of community life and are performed in a specially designated space—a circle of redwoods. Communal gatherings often begin and end with singing. Each of the members takes their turn creating and performing rituals, some around existing holidays, others around rites of passage, and even some designed to meet the special needs of a specific member or of the community as a whole. The emphasis is less on the formality of the ritual and much more on the creative spirit. Setting the intention for the community, clearing a space for everyone to freely express themselves within the context of the group, is the single most important element of the ritual process.

While the process of successfully learning to live together is ongoing and difficult at times, the rules of conduct that strengthen and affirm communal bonds are simple: "Own your own judgments. Assign no blame. Do no harm." Although the rituals and rites performed in this community respect and honor the sanctity of the individual, it is the collective spirit that drives and supports everyone.

The Fire of Fifty

Sometimes a milestone event is an exceptional opportunity to create a rite of passage that includes not only a formal ceremony but a celebration in community as well, as Elise's fiftieth birthday was. Every element was personally designed with a specific purpose in mind. Although it was a ceremony to mark a major transition in her own life, Elise invited all of the women who would be in attendance to consider, several months before the event, how they would participate as well. In this way, she created a communal rite of passage yet tailored it for each individual woman.

"The celebration began as a pushing from inside. I needed to mark this birthday, and I knew I needed to do it with friends. I wanted them to know who I was in the context of where I had been—what it took to be me."

There is a special place, a valley in Wyoming, and a special group of women who meet every year to play and get back in touch with who they are without husbands and children. Elise chose them as her witnesses, along with some other special friends, to be part of her ceremony. She sent an invitation to perform a fire ceremony, a ritual where the individual requests fire to take to God what no longer serves them. "Gone with the flames are old perceptions of yourself, beliefs or attitudes that block you from giving your best to the world, keeping you from being who you are meant to be.

"As women, when we move beyond the biological function of bearing children, we need to give birth to ourselves, igniting our creative power in new and different ways. I asked everyone to give thought to what they personally need to give to the fire, with the actual ceremony being optional. I asked that a symbol of this be made to be consumed by the fire. Since our society worships youth to such a degree, I also wanted to acknowledge and honor the beauty of elders. I wanted to establish a sense of tribe. My family of origin was so dysfunctional; I needed sisters of spirit. So out of my needs and longing this celebration of passage was born."

The rite began with a greeter at the door and a smudging with local sage for purification, as well as to help carry prayers to God. Each of the women took a Native American name, a powerful way to mark this shift, making them recognizable to each other within the tribe. Elise asked her friends and sisters to pray for her as she entered the role of shaman, calling the seven directions—east, south, west, and north; below, Mother Earth; above, Father Sky; and within, our souls. Local spirits and ancestors were invoked as well.

"I set the intention for the ceremony—to witness the sacred life passage, to unite us as tribe, to heal the fire parts of ourselves, to give away inauthentic parts that no longer serve us, and to become fuller, freer adult women. I spoke of the times when God was seen as a woman and asked my sisters to focus on the feminine aspects of God, the wisdom of Sophia, who knows what is right within her heart."

Then Elise read *Phenomenally Woman* by Maya Angelou. Fifty is the beginning of a woman's greatest power; we give ourselves permission to be who we really are. We take responsibility for our own happiness. We give the serious attention to ourselves that we formerly gave to others. Elise invited all of her friends who were already fifty to stand and have wreaths placed upon their heads by younger women. "You have lived long. You have years of earthly experience. You are a treasure to our tribe." How seldom we honor our female elders in American culture. How right to do so.

Elise spoke of the passages we all go through: childhood, where we learn the rules; adolescence, where we break some and see the foolishness in some others; acceptance of the rules, where we grow children or careers, taking our place inside that context; and then there are the passages where we find out who we are and make our own rules, often following the compass of our hearts.

"By forty, women change; we say what we want. By fifty, we do what we want. We have had some success, some failure. We did not die from either one; we gain a most valuable thing—perspective. We silence ego enough to have a word with ourselves. The bloom of youth leaves us for something earned and more valuable. Life is lived on our own terms. Some of the false self is shed. Things we tolerated become unacceptable. Some unacceptable things soften in the light of compassion and understanding. We try things we never did before."

Then Elise told her story—where she began, the challenges of her childhood and her motherhood, what it was like to be a wife, and the passages she has come through. "All pieces of who I am—nothing wasted. My witnesses cried for me. I cannot tell you how that changed me; the compassion, the deep honoring of who I am and how it has come to be that I am this. My gratitude for this is in me. It was not easy to hear, not pretty or cleaned up, but as raw as it all was—the truth of me. They sat and listened. This was my rite of passage: to be seen, loved, and accepted. It washed away the shame I carried and opened the dark secrets to the light and the air where the wounds get healed."

A significant element of this rite of passage was the fire ceremony. As we journey through life, we may have some regrets, hold grudges, and carry some heavy old baggage. There are burdens and anger attachments, bad habits, excuses, stuck places, faulty definitions, and old expectations. We keep bumping into these things, hurting ourselves on them. These are things we need to let go of because they no longer serve us. Each woman approached the fire in her own time and gave the effigy to be burned.

The talking stone was passed; only the one who holds the stone is allowed to speak. "Be silent witnesses for each one who speaks, honoring her words. In this way we give the gift of unconditional love, the love that transforms.

Let each woman have full range of joy or pain. We are not here to minimize or fix, but to support with love and empower each other. Speak only if you wish to. We will honor words or silence."

The women concluded the solemn ceremony in a celebratory mode— "Amazing Grace," a very enthusiastic rendition of "We Are Family," champagne, and chocolate.

"The energy goes on for me. I continue to drop things that do not serve me. I have repeated the fire ceremony again and again, feeling how essential it is to do this, to mark and share the process with others. To have a woman's divinity to pray to so I can see how I, too, am part of the God energy that walks in beauty. What is uniquely mine is the ability to bring this to others. The themes are universal. I would like to shift the Feminine today by honoring both the male and female aspects in every one of us."

If the fire ceremony resonates with you, determine what symbols of your life you could release into the fire. This could be pictures; any document of finished transactions (mortgage, student loan, etc.); remnants of clothing; or anything else. Jill went to a dollhouse store, bought a tiny valise (old baggage); several miniature books, each representing a decade of her life; and a gilded birdcage (minus the bird). These were her "fire offerings." Although a fire ceremony is one powerful way to release old business, there are many other ways to create a "rite of release," including washing away the past with water (rivers, streams, or waterfalls); letting the past fly away (off the top of a mountain, building, or the like); or burying the past (actually burying these pieces in the earth).

Renewal in the Desert

Beyond personal celebrations of significant birthdays, anniversaries, and events commemorating special milestones, there are other occasions when individuals come together with a common purpose in mind and magic happens. Sometimes the magic remains long after the event is over, influencing the way we live thereafter. At times, a vast number of people, perhaps a whole generation, may be impacted, or there may even be global consequences. Many of us remember Woodstock, or the "Summer of Love," or "I have a dream." Beyond the meadow, or the season, or the speech, something unique and inexplicable happened that managed to catapult a collective unconscious forward.

Sometimes our individual experience takes place within the context of a small, intimate group, as it did in Elise's rite. It could be a spiritual retreat, a pilgrimage to a sacred site or shrine, or a reunion that serves as the catalyst, promoting a sense of communitas, that total departure from one's ordinary life to enter into the realm of the extraordinary.

In 1973, Tucson, Arizona, hosted the Southwest Feminist Retreat. Various women's groups advocating for the health and welfare of women and children came together in an act of unity to share their information and insights. The intention for the convocation was to create a powerful vehicle to effect change. But beyond the formal agenda, the workshops, and the discussions, Debby remembers that "an unbelievably celebratory thing happened in the desert."

The year 2003 saw the thirtieth anniversary reunion of many of the women who had been there in 1973. Debby's friend Pam offered her home in the desert so that a group of about forty-five women could meet in a joyous commemoration of that original event and era. Many of these women had been "lost" along the way, having fallen out of touch with each other, so coming together after thirty years was not only a collective reunion but a vehicle for the individual women to rediscover and reconnect. "There was a need to gather, to make sense, to give meaning to what had persisted in all of our lives for the past thirty years. This was a way to honor our youthful passion, what we had built. We also remembered those who had died, those who were ill, and those who had struggled."

For about six hours, the forty-five women sat in a giant circle, each in turn telling her own story of the past thirty years. This rite of passage honored the memory of a special time long ago, but more significantly it served as a rebirth of community, acknowledging and reestablishing the power that is possible when many join together for a common goal.

The Circle: A Living Symbol of Healing

Humans are deeply intrigued by the form of the circle; its power lies in its ability to fill a longing within us. Every culture and every religion has used this symbol to express its deepest sense of connection and harmony. As energetic containers, circles offer boundaries, protection, and safe space. The wholeness of the circle implies that we are each whole unto ourselves, as well as integral parts of a greater whole. Linking multiplies the power of the individual, bringing together accumulated knowledge and collective wisdom, making it readily accessible to all people. Symbolically, the circle represents the wholeness of life, and beyond that, the interconnecting circle of life.

Since the birth of civilization, "the collective of village and city is a symbol of the Feminine. Their establishment began with the marking of the circle, the conjuring of the Great Round."[6] Knowing the strength of the circle itself, ancient matrifocal cultures defined life and communal living in the round; "gate, enclosure, and cattle pen"; round houses and hearths; and fences and fortresses offered the warmth of companionship and protection for all members of the community living equally together.[7] Inherent in the Great Round, all things circumscribed by its encompassing security became sacred to society. People who lived within a circle understood its wisdom from the inside out.

Many women find the circle, gathering together for the ritual of sharing and witnessing one another's stories, to be a powerful element in a rite life. A recent study concluded that "circles of women have begun to emerge spontaneously within widely divergent cultures and . . . these circles seem deeply meaningful to their participants."[8] When women gather in the ritual process, they frequently join in a circle, each woman equidistant from the center, eliminating hierarchy and promoting compassion and a sense of community.

For women, the circle not only defines sacred space: It can become sacred space itself, adapted as a sanctified place of initiation. "When we enter the circle, it is said that we enter 'a world between the worlds,' a sacred liminal space where it is possible to enter into communion with the divine, step into the mythic and actually alter the fabric of reality."[9] The form is inclusive; women gather together in ritual, opening the circle wider and wider to allow everyone to enter in. Whatever gift each member brings is uniquely valuable; the power is in the sharing, in both the giving and the receiving, in which we are all made whole.

Community of the Spirit

Finding community, with emphasis on the spirit, seems to be a common thread through women's lives. The labyrinth in Patricia's backyard has become the focus of worship and meditation for the "spiritual midwives" who come together for many different kinds of occasions. For Sister Joan, the religious order to which she belongs is community, all members sharing the desire and the sacred obligation to serve the greater community through devotion to God.

Several women I've spoken with have created organizational vehicles not only to satisfy their own spiritual needs but to establish a forum for other women to access and explore ways to enhance their own spiritual lives. Lisa's International Friends helped women from abroad to network and acclimate to life in the United States, while Joyful Life teaches how to create personal power and achieve desired goals. Elise cofounded Ravenwalk, an organization that presents workshops designed to promote and teach healing and that helps women create personal rituals and rites of passage. Rita's grassroots organization, We Care USA, provides aid to those in need abroad. It emphasizes the sacredness of life everywhere and reminds us that we are all connected.

As a result of treating patients for many years, I became increasingly aware that some people's issues and conflicts were far more than psychologically or emotionally related; they were indeed crises of the spirit. What to do? How could I be an effective healer if I chose to dismiss these issues out of my own ignorance, or if I arrogantly insisted that a psychological answer or cure was the only solution? My own spiritual life has been enriched and enhanced since becoming an interfaith minister several years ago, and I believe that my ability to be helpful to others has increased as a result of this.

My studies in pursuit of this goal had been a largely solitary experience. Entering a small interfaith seminary, I continued my practice while making the time to do the reading, research, and papers that were required for the course. The immediate events leading up to my ordination in 2000, however, provided a pleasant, if totally unexpected, surprise. The members of the class, living all over the country, were required to participate in a retreat at a spiritual center near New York City for a few days prior to ordination. Initially, I saw this as a huge inconvenience, but once I resolved myself to the inevitability of it, I managed to just settle into the process.

Over forty of us gathered for two days in the heat of August, housed in small dorm rooms without air conditioning and sharing communal bathrooms. We spent time together, ate meals together, did early-morning yoga together, and got to know each other. Each of us was required to speak for ten minutes on a topic of our own choosing; every story encapsulated a significant part of an individual life, providing an intimate bird's-eye view into each soul—the things people had gone through just to arrive at that time and place.

As I listened hour after hour, I became aware that there was no desire or need for any of us to fix anybody else; everything was right just as it was. Someone taught a song, or a chant; an amazing amount of joyful singing throughout the time we spent together seemed to lift us all up. Our rehearsal for the actual ordination ceremony was brief, yet each of us grasped exactly where we were supposed to be and what we were supposed to do. This sharing in spiritual community, so different and apart from my regular life, felt like a rite of passage to me. I was already changed by the time we parted, going our separate ways once again. At ordination, the sacred ancient ritual of anointing with oil symbolized and solidified the new identity I had already assumed.

A key component of any rite of passage is removal from the ordinary and familiar. A movement toward something new—whether representing an external or physical change, an "outer passage," or a psychological or emotional one, an "inner passage"—requires some kind of shift to occur for the transition to be truly effective. For "outer passages," rites don't just signify a change or shift—they are part and parcel of that change. The use of symbols and symbolic gestures, essential parts of the enactment, actually comes to embody the shift. What is far more difficult to grasp perhaps, because of its intangible nature, is the accompanying psychic shift, the "inner passage," which heralds a change in the persona and helps accommodate for an outwardly changing role. These are powerful rites of passage as well, although they have not been acknowledged as such traditionally.

Vision quests, Outward Bound programs, and retreats of all kinds, including spiritual or team-building experiences, provide opportunities to test who we are in new and often challenging circumstances. When you leave behind the self that you usually identify with and strip away pieces of yourself that no longer serve you, you are better able to focus your attention on what is currently presenting itself as important for you to know. But it's not always an easy thing to take yourself out of ordinary life. Many don't have the luxury of the time and money it would take to remove themselves to a place where they could have an optimal threshold experience. So it is ultimately up to each of us to innovatively design ways to create rites that honor the threshold experience. Remember Hilary's silent home retreat or Sylvia's preparation, both external and internal, for the consecration of her home.

The Beloved Community

You must be the change you wish to see in the world.

—Mahatma Gandhi

Angela's story is about fully engaging life. Action and interaction best describe how she chooses to live in the world. *Open: One Woman's Journey* is her personal story from an Asian American perspective. As teacher and lawyer, as social advocate and political activist, as friend, and as ordained Zen Buddhist priest, Angela has learned to just allow life to unfold free of expectation. Simply being asked to help others triggers the "rite" action. Helping to build the beloved community is her mission.

"The world feels as though it is moving in directions that are altogether chaotic. Yet something deep within me says that the possibility still exists for calm to be found in the midst of it all."

While Angela doesn't know exactly where her journey is leading her, she does know that as she approached the fifty-year mark, she seemed to gain a greater clarity about where it's taking her. "It is not about a career or raising a family. Nor is it about finishing a project that will someday go out into the world as an expression of my intellect or spirit. I am living with deep appreciation for having the chance to meet many different kinds of people—sometimes to teach, sometimes to represent them in a crisis situation, and sometimes simply to help build what Dr. Martin Luther King once called the beloved community. How did my life come to this place? There were many markers, many rites of passage."

The rites have included the conventional and the extraordinary: helping to birth a baby with a close woman friend who was alone when her son decided to make his entry into the world, becoming a public voice through trial by fire when Los Angeles imploded in 1992 as a consequence of bearing witness to the most tragic and horrendous taking of two human lives, taking part in an ordination ceremony where she became a priest in the Zen Buddhist tradition, and sitting at dinner with the president of her nation and the president of her ancestors' nation one winter evening in Washington, D.C.

"It was not always clear that these were rites of passage. But in reflecting on all of them, they emerge as exactly that. For each experience, another layer of who I am was simultaneously added while parts of me were stripped away. In the birthing of a child, there was a letting go and an embracing of a new life, all at once. In the implosion in Los Angeles, the immediate aftermath was genuine concern, openness, and caring about the entire city, not just about the interests of the rich or influential. The long term brought greater cynicism, hardness, and deception. In the murder case, it was realizing that the tragedy was a product of dysfunction, not just in the lives of those directly affected, but dysfunction that exists in our society as a whole. And in the ordination, it was the shedding of one life only to take on another that is filled with even more unanswerable puzzles."

Many things shifted in each situation—psychologically, physically, emotionally, and spiritually. Sometimes it was literally the gaining or shedding of physical weight, or the experience of uncontrollable sobbing, or the sense of complete helplessness and therefore complete fearlessness. These responses could not have been contrived or planned; they simply were part of the events that took place. In the ordination ceremony, however, there certainly was a ritual. "But I have since learned that in the Zen tradition that I follow, rehearsals are nonexistent. Aside from the public lectures I deliver (which are never written in advance), the only others who perform formal ceremonies without rehearsing in advance are the priests of my temple.

"For the most part, my rites of passage were unplanned. I can say that in many instances it was asking me for help that triggered my engagement. Then I brought forth my best effort without a preconceived notion of what I needed. Rather, the entire focus was on what was needed from me. My engagement was clear, focused, and sincere. Sometimes the outcome was favorable; other times not."

Angela offers these simple axioms:

- Rites of passage come in many forms and at many different points throughout a lifetime.
- Treat these times as sacred.
- In your participation, don't look to accomplish any particular outcome; rather, make sure that you savor what may seem to be the confusion and chaos of the moment.
- The calm emerges soon enough.
- Nothing in life is an accident.
- You can waste a lot of time thinking, planning, and strategizing so that things turn out just so.
- You may even think that your plans were executed to perfection.
- Be prepared for surprises.

I and Thou: Beyond Time

> We are the mirror, as well as the face in it.
>
> —Rumi

Often it is in looking in the mirror that we see ourselves most clearly. This is especially true when, bearing witness to someone else's pain, we ourselves are catapulted into our own rite of passage. In working to help heal the flood of emotional trauma after 9/11, Christine, a psychologist, found herself pulled into the emotional undertow only to reemerge stronger and more resolved.

EMDR (eye movement desensitization and reprocessing) is an innovative therapy that organically processes, and ultimately releases from the body, trauma long held in the psyche. In this work, whether revisiting childhood states or subsequent traumatic events, we can find a way for the broken self to pick up the pieces in order to heal. In essence, the brain simultaneously remembers and creates images, both imagining and reimagining wholeness.

In Christine's case, helping to reassemble the broken spiritual shards of a New York City firefighter who marched into the hell of 9/11 helped her to piece together parts of herself long missing. As in all true healing work, it is a two-way street; both the healer and the one healed are transformed in the process.

"It isn't every day that you get to work in the eye of the hurricane. For me, working with New York City's bravest after 9/11 had devastated their ranks but not their spirits allowed me to bear witness to that emotional whirlpool and gave me access into the psyches of these amazing heroes. As I helped them process what they had gone through, it was with the hope of ultimately healing the unimaginable pain."

As her work unfolded, two major shifts occurred within Christine. The first was the result of being in this eye of the hurricane, being present in the moment with a specific individual, knowing his experience and what actually happened to him. Imagine that your normal, everyday life is captured on film, each frame giving way to the next in a logical progression. When severe trauma hits, it's as if the film breaks, and you keep reliving the same image over and over again. EMDR splices the film, gently and effectively healing layers of psychic injury in a relatively brief amount of time.

"So when I had the opportunity to see an actual video made while the towers were falling, I was able to experience the impact that EMDR had on one specific firefighter, the man I happened to be working with. The experience of that was like a video too—recording a moment frozen in time, watching the scenes unfold, knowing that he had been one of the last men to make it out alive. I felt a desperate sense of wanting to change history—it was as if past, present, and future were all there at once, and if we could somehow change the past, the future could be changed. Beyond merely witnessing this, I felt as if I was there helping him hold and carry the pain he was feeling. Seeing him on tape before he entered the soon-to-fall World Trade Towers was almost an out-of-body experience—realizing that we all have access to that 'beyond' time, to that place where, in the not knowing, we know all."

As Christine worked with this man, a door seemed to open for a moment, and she experienced all of the things she had intuited. The most common experience for the firefighters who lived through it all is survivor guilt, feeling that they didn't do anything, that they didn't do enough, with the underlying message being "I should be dead instead of my brother."

"I was, and will always be, profoundly humbled by being in the presence of courage so strong that it makes a healthy person voluntarily run into a burning building. As I watched these men run into the World Trade Center on the videotape, knowing that the buildings might well collapse, I understood the notion and felt the direct feeling of the experience—someone was going in to save people just because it was the right thing to do. Being near someone who would willingly die for you is a life-altering event—these individuals performing the ultimate sacrifice and helping us feel safe in the presence of evil. These men form their own family, so much so that they spent nearly a year after the tragedy tirelessly searching for any possible remains, living the motto 'Never leave a brother behind.'"

As Christine worked with this extraordinary group that had exhibited true courage and strength under enormous pressure, another shift occurred within her—she found her own healing grace. "This work mirrored an earlier trauma in my life—a rape I had experienced decades ago—seeing horrifyingly up close the full force of the worst we can be, of human evil. In working with these men, I had the exact opposite experience—viewing the best we can be. I am constantly awed by just how capable we humans are of always seeking, and finding, richer, fuller expressions of who we really are.

"In the last decade, and most profoundly in the last few years, I have found my way firmly onto my path, honoring my calling to communicate from the depth of me and to nurture hope, even when all seems hopeless. I know now that the only way I can do this is to be constantly reminded of the potential that we all have to create hope. The firefighters, and everyone I see striving for wholeness, are the physical embodiment of that; they are 'the possible human.'"

As we grow, and hopefully evolve, there may still be little "lacunae"— empty spaces that we somehow grow around but that nevertheless still remain. What would it be like if you could go back and fill in the missing pieces of your life? Most of us believe that what is in the past can't be changed, that what has happened is irrevocable, fixed in history. But you *can* change your life, not only as it moves forward into the future, but also by reaccessing the past based on what you know now, based on your perceptions in the present.

You can actually rewrite your past by changing your attitude or belief system. Moving forward from a past event often helps us fill in the blanks, gaining a new perspective and valuable insights about what happened and why it happened the way it did. The more we come to know about ourselves as we move through our lives, the better we are able to understand and analyze our past. Think back to an event in your life that impacted you significantly. Can you understand why what happened to you then had to happen the way it did? Can you see that the way an event unfolded may have been necessary in order to pave the way for future integral growth? Does acceptance of this now help you forgive yourself and heal the past?

One need not be a therapist to bear witness to someone else's life. When the next opportunity arises for you to be with someone in crisis, try this: just sit and listen. Don't assume that what you think is appropriate will be good for the other person. Don't try to fix anything. Don't give advice, interpret, or judge. Enter into dialogue only if you are invited. Since this is not something most of us are readily taught, it may turn out to be one of the most difficult things to do.

Tragic events in our lives, however devastating, may bring positive growth opportunities if we allow ourselves to remain open enough to see them in this light. Strength of character lies in the desire and the willingness to overcome adversity, unmasking the pain and allowing for healing resolution to occur. As we gain insight into ourselves, we increase our capacity to intuitively understand what is in our best interest, and we deepen our ability to develop empathy for others.

Throughout our lives, most of us are part of at least one community, but more often than not we are part of several. We take our own special place in community, assuming different roles at different times. Our participation and energetic involvement contribute to the creation of something essential, alive, and vital to us individually and to the lives of the group as a whole.

Everything exists in community. The great designer of the universe saw to this. Stars to snowflakes, atoms to ants, humans to blades of grass—every intricate detail, every subtle nuance, everything joining together and collaborating for the common good. A united effort, a unity in community of others like itself, a holy communion. Imagine, then, a world where a consciousness equal to the task of the grand design matched its perfection.

Common Ground

- You are a part of everything.
- Give of who you are.
- Do whatever you can.
- Whatever you can do, do it now.
- When you serve another, you serve yourself.
- It takes just one . . . and then another and another.

CHAPTER TEN

Conclusion: Connecting the Dots

We are pain and what cures pain, both.
We are the sweet cold water and the jar that pours.

—Rumi

We all have our own life themes or leitmotifs—those really big, recurring issues that figure in a major way in our lives, repetitively insinuating themselves and forcing us to take yet another look. For some, this may revolve around the family of origin—problems with parents and siblings; not fitting in; not being appreciated, loved, or understood; or even being totally cut off. For others, the key issue may be about financial and material success—never being able to "get out from under," or feelings of never having enough, always wanting more but finding abundance elusive. Problems with authority from any source, or religious or spiritual conflicts and crises, may present as the main issue for some, while the search for a significant other or a life partner may be the driving force behind others' lives. You can be sure that whatever your own life's theme is, it will continue to engage you, finding ways to be recognized and persisting until you get it.

Repetitive struggles with any of these can leave a person feeling like a victim, misunderstood and unresolved, and incapable of controlling his or her own fate. If, however, the lessons of these themes are understood and mastered, they are capable of helping to move one toward personal growth and empowerment.

In the ideal world, a healthy individual has fully integrated all aspects of the self—mind, body, and spirit. Part of life's mission is to aspire to, and ultimately achieve, this goal. As we go through life just trying to figure things out, we inevitably, and more often than not unconsciously, choose one of

213

these aspects to express ourselves in the world—a preferred way through which we process and enact our life themes.

For some, to think is to "know." Life is filtered through the practical, logical, and analytical mind. Data is collected, deemed useful or not, collated, and finally integrated or tossed out. These individuals frequently spend a lot of time "living in their head." Overintellectualizing, however, has its dangers; oversimplification, rationalization, and rigidity of thought leave little room for an emotional and spiritual perspective.

For others, to feel is to "know." The first line of communication with ourselves and others is through the world of the emotions. Here, the feeling tone rather than the fact seems to count the most. But exaggerated, sustained, high emotion can prove exhausting, and roller-coaster emotions can deplete us on every level as well.

For others still, to move is to "know." Our physical packaging, our container for a lifetime, our bodies, may serve as the vehicle through which some individuals "feel," how they best commune with the world around them. Because our physical body is noticed most immediately and most readily identifies us, perhaps too much emphasis has been placed on this aspect of expression. There is an unnatural preoccupation with working the "container," attempting to reshape and fix our external appearances to create what is considered to be the ideal. Conversely, many individuals are oblivious to their bodies, seemingly anesthetized from the neck down. Or, worse yet, they are abusive to themselves in one way or another.

Perhaps that ideal we may be striving for lies in simply being, in entering into a place where "to be"—just as we are, without judgment or agenda—is to "know." But, easier said than done. Just "to be" is probably one of the hardest things to learn. It requires acceptance of who we are through the process of tough self-examination, honest introspection, and hard analysis of how we interface with what life hands us. It also requires trust that we are being partnered by spirit. This is a difficult concept for many of us to acknowledge, let alone grasp. So is surrendering to a higher power, something most of us are not readily taught. Those who have learned to surrender have often done so when things have gotten really bad, when they have hit a wall or rock bottom and have no other place to go. That most of us would give up control and give ourselves over voluntarily in this way without any kind of assurance or guarantee of having a better outcome is simply not the norm.

Life themes are a tangible shorthand way to teach us about our movement forward in time. Rite and ritual, which help to bring the unconscious to consciousness, can aid us in the process of sorting through and making sense of life themes. The feared danger posed by any painful period—be it physical illness, paralyzing depression or anxiety, or spiritual crisis—is that we will be pulled down, sinking into the muck and mire of it against our will. We no longer see it as a separate entity; rather, it becomes part of the self. Enacting a rite of passage, or a series of these, is a tangible, practical way to see the difficulty as something one is passing through, not as an essential piece of one's identity. Performing rites around our pain helps us to encapsulate it, moving us forward to the next destination on our journey. If we are open enough, it may be that the invisible thread binding everything together in the universe weaves its way through our life, tying our own individual experiences together and ultimately creating our own spiritual practice.

Our lives carry patterns. This simple exercise will help you identify what they are. Here we are using numerology as a tool rather than as a predictive methodology, as you often see in magazines. Your own "number" is just a vehicle to help you chart the decades of your life. On a sheet of paper, note the date of your birth, with day, month, and year written in numerals. Then just add all the numbers together, finally reducing them to the lowest number. For example, January 10, 1960, would be written 1/10/1960; then, broken down, it would look like this: $1 + (1 + 0) + (1 + 9 + 6 + 0) = 1 + 1 + 16 = 18 = 1 + 8 = $ (final #) 9. The first year on your sheet is the year you were born. Next to that year, put the number you have just added and reduced—for example, 1960 and the number 9. Make a list of every year after that until you arrive at the current year. The cycle of numbers you will observe is from 1 to 9. Whatever number you arrive at as the first, complete the cycle to 9 and then start all over again.

Now note important events that have occurred in every year—things you began or completed, milestones in your life, illnesses, challenges, triumphs, and the like. When you are done, see what patterns emerge. Are "1" years beginnings? Are "9" years endings? Are there repetitions in patterns for each of the numbers, or do some numbers appear more frequently? Are there cyclic repetitions in each decade or in only some decades? Begin to notice that what may appear as random incidents may in fact have their own natural order. What do these patterns have to teach you? What challenges or opportunities do they bring up? What accomplishments do they outline? Whatever the patterns show, just be open to new understandings and insights. Each time a pattern repeats itself, you are being given another opportunity to grow from the wisdom you have gained from past experiences.

The stories in this concluding chapter illustrate the concept of life themes and demonstrate how, for each of the women, one or two major themes thread their way through the life, defining and shaping the existence and eventually helping to tell the story of each person's life mission or purpose.

A Work in Progress: A Lesson Plan for Life

By projecting yourself into the future, you may come face to face with the problems and with the issues of living that confront you. Using imagination and intuition at any time in your life may help you short-circuit your projected issues, helping you to transform your future life in the here and now. Taking charge at any time, especially when you feel stuck and need a life "jump start," can help set and correct your course.

Clearly stating her intention and defining what her ideal life would look like, Monique set down a blueprint for her own path, literally creating a "lesson plan" for her life. The goal of this exercise is not just about seeing life unfold in exactly the way you think or fantasize it should. Rather, its true value is revealed through a constant process of reexamining, redefining, and reframing the life you're in in order to gain mastery over the life you want to create.

Since we are all "works in progress," most of us tend to move forward through our lives. As we do so, we lay down the "dots" (all of the significant things that happen to us) that we will ultimately try to connect. In this way, we gain perspective on our lives by looking backward, through retrospective review. This unique exercise encourages us to "create the dots," which we will eventually connect along the way, before we've lived them.

"At some point in your life's journey, you may decide, 'This life is not working for me.' This realization may be accompanied by a creepy onset of panic, resentment, guilt, fear, frustration, or depression. You may even become immobilized by the awakening that much of what you know about yourself—how you spend your time and how you do the work that you do—is fundamentally rooted in the definition or direction of well-meaning parents, a spouse, friends, or others in your familial or social circle.

"It was at the age of twenty-two, on a vacation in Switzerland, that a tsunami of such feelings came over me while I was seated in a charming cottage window seat overlooking the hills of the village. Frustrated and unhappy with my life, I wanted to stay nestled in that seat forever. In that moment, I vowed to begin to take responsibility for my life's choices and their consequences. While relentlessly challenging, it was, and remains, an exhilarating resolution."

Monique knows people, as many of us do, who ask at thirty, forty, and fifty years old, "What do I want to be when I grow up?" They giggle outwardly, but inside they are not laughing. The mythical midlife crisis isn't a myth at all. While physical and mental capacities seem to diminish slowly as we age, time to create a fulfilling and engaging work and life relationship is also running out. Bored, unhappy, and counting the days to retirement, or wishing they could win the lottery and quit their jobs, many of her friends are reflecting on what they perceive to be lost years and question their life's choices.

"My advice to others, while it may sound simple and even naive, is to choose to do what you love, and not to give up until you do. It is your right to do work that expresses and fulfills your needs, talents, and passions. It is your right to identify ways to harness your courage, overcome fears, take the little risks that make the big risks possible, and become an individual whose work results in self-expression, growth, and love."

Frustrated by the complaints of friends who did nothing but moan and groan about their life and work, Monique made a silent commitment to choose instead to do work that she loves. Inspired by self-help books that encouraged the reader to "have it all," she conspired to create a plan that would bring her happiness in every aspect of her life, unrealistic as it seemed at the time. For a couple of weeks, she wrote and rewrote her plan, mindful to ensure that what she was creating was truly what she wanted.

"Day and night, I reread the words that clearly spelled out my expectations for how I wished to experience my life, emotionally, physically, spiritually, financially, and professionally. I held nothing back. The plan, which I have saved to this day, was jam packed with every daydream, fantasy, and aspiration I could imagine. I edited the plan as appropriate along the way, and my life has become a continual 'work in progress,' continuing to evolve in extraordinary and unexpected ways. My dedication to the plan never wavered, and I was inspired, if not divinely so, to make choices to facilitate its fruition. Strengths and uniqueness were uncovered that I never knew I had, and overcoming obstacles took place with greater ease."

But everyone needs a coach. A sister encouraged her to leave the safety net of their small town in Bucks County, Pennsylvania, and move to New York City. A former spouse underscored the importance of education. A boss provided kindness and encouragement and spurred her professional growth. A husband, grounded in integrity and common sense, taught her about respecting abundance and generosity. A friend honored and respected time spent away from their relationship. "When the student is ready, the teacher will come." She has been fortunate to have many.

"Don't wait for midlife or a vacation to faraway places to examine your rights, reengineer your expectations, and revisit the kid whose dreams may have been left unattended, ignored, or in the dust so many years ago. Pause now to reflect on what you value most, how you spend your time, and whether you truly are living the life and doing the work you intended. Taking ownership and responsibility for what you know to be true and necessary for you in an effort to be truly happy in your life is a rite of passage, and in the end, a privilege."

Anticipating what might happen as life unfolds may serve you well as you project yourself into those times and *change them now*. Literally, we can change the trajectory of the bigger picture of our lives by the actions we take moment to moment. If you are not already doing what you love, examine what you are passionate about. Then write down a few aspects of your life, either real or hoped for, that truly excite your imagination and creativity. Very often, what people wish for and their current realities are nowhere near as far apart as imagined.

Today, in this moment, you can begin to take a new level of responsibility for your own life. Write a life plan that includes everything you want, realistic or not. Choose one goal from the plan and set it in motion. Take time every day to either take an action or to give some focused thought to how you will achieve what you desire. Revise your plan in six months, and again in a year. Feel free to make changes in the interim, replacing outdated ideas with ones that more accurately reflect where you are and where you want to go.

As an interesting aside, I took some of the women through the meditations that appear earlier in the book. You may recall that, aside from the visual content of the meditation, there were questions to answer and remember for future reference. Visualizations, guided imagery, experiential writing, and even reading shapes of clouds or tea leaves are all creative modalities to access information about ourselves not available through discussion and analysis. Free-associating often removes inhibition. Not surprisingly, the women's responses shed a lot of light on each of them individually, illuminating their style of relating, how they process what happens to them, and how they adapt—in general, encapsulating how they walk in the world.

In the "Gifts of the Darkness" meditation in chapter 5, we were asked to get past the guardians of the castle and find a way inside. Responses included flying over their heads, bypassing them by swimming the moat, or gaining trust by "seeing eye to eye." Monique confronted the guards in a cordial but businesslike manner by shaking their hands and introducing herself. This is very much the way you would find her in person as well. So take some time to go back over your own responses and reflect on what your answers tell you about yourself.

Safe Harbor

Every individual has to find a way to have a healthy relationship with themselves before they can successfully enter into relationship with another. This is somewhat counterintuitive in a culture that pushes love, romance, and that special someone as the ultimate goal toward which we all need to aspire in order to be happy and complete. Unfortunately, there is no course 101, "The Essentials of Me," teaching basic life skills, survival techniques, and essential ways to learn self-love and acceptance anywhere that I know. No wonder most of us go scrambling a bit, and some of us more than that, early in our lives. Theodora's life was dominated by her search for "safe harbor," a powerful metaphor stemming from early childhood memories of the sea, recalling happy times and a feeling of safety. Only after a series of painful, unfulfilling relationships did she discover that the solace and comfort she was seeking had been there all along—just not where she was looking for it.

"From college through the end of my twenties, part of me felt like a leaf that was blown about by whatever breeze seemed safe and welcoming. Although grounded in work and responsibility, I was lost in terms of my own sense of self and how that would be received in a romantic relationship. Inexperienced? Maybe just desperately hoping and trusting that the man I might be with would not hurt me. I was very much like a child that way—seeking out the safe harbor."

After her first long and important relationship ended painfully, Theodora felt lonely and depressed, flawed and unlovable, but not sure how she'd gotten that way. The following two years were spent in two relationships that were very wrong for her. The first man was kind, but he had an extremely troubled recent past, including alcohol and substance abuse. The desire to rescue probably kept her engaged longer than she should have been. Sadly, years later, this man's path led to death in a car accident.

The second man, a recovered alcoholic, appeared more stable but turned out to be no better as a partner for her. When Theodora became pregnant and chose to have an abortion, her safe harbor came not in the form of this man, but from her dearest girlfriends, who helped her through all levels of this ordeal. The man treated the event as if it meant nothing, and so she chose never to see him again.

"At this point, my life slowed down enough to allow my mind to quietly take stock. For a while, I had been searching for my spiritual path, but I had not been able to find the right fit; fortunately, that was about to change. Events led me to move to Los Angeles, and I was given guidance from a woman I had known only a brief time. She directed me to a beautiful outdoor temple with a lake, overlooking the ocean. One day, I wandered onto the quiet grounds of this sacred place and felt tears flowing down my cheeks. Something very deep inside told me that I had finally come to my safe harbor. Here I would find my inner strength, and peace. For the first time, I felt loved, unconditionally, from the source of boundless love, wisdom, and joy. Gigantic exhale.

"In the years since, I have followed a path of peace and Eastern spiritual practices, and I have observed a slow and graceful self-transformation. Life continues to throw its life lessons in ever-changing patterns, but I am no longer completely at the mercy of the wind. I can anchor myself in self and continue to soar."

A healthy relationship is one that is reciprocal, equitable, and balanced. At times, one partner may need more than the other, but when does one's need cross the line into rescuing territory? Is being needed a primary way for you to express love? What if your partner is self-involved, troubled, selfish, or unable to give? What is emotionally and energetically left for you?

Consider five relational themes with a current partner or a partner from the past. For every theme, write down your partner's position on the issue. Next to it, write your own position on the issue. In a third column, write one word to describe whose position dominated—self, partner, or equal. This is not a tit-for-tat checklist but rather a way to see if one person has overshadowed the other in a relationship, and it offers a way to identify how to find equality and create balance. If you determine that there is inequity repetitively in the relationship, write down three suggestions for each issue. Finally, and perhaps most importantly, take the time to discuss or negotiate how to remedy the problem and how to heal the relationship if possible.

The Container of a Lifetime

Sometimes, even when things seem to be going well, we may suffer a disconnection with ourselves. Although enthusiastically participating in what is most significant to us, we may not be able to acknowledge the importance of our role or of our essential presence in what is being accomplished. Lisa had fought her whole life to be heard. "I never felt good enough or believed I was as talented as my creations proved." Her studies at the Institute for Transpersonal Psychology (ITP) brought her a greater clarity and a depth of understanding of the process of self-acceptance and of the importance of expressing the diverse aspects of herself. To mark the end of her first year of studies at ITP, she created a piece of art that was very representative of her journey.

Prior to enrolling at ITP, Lisa had already begun to fully stand up for herself and to truly appreciate her strengths. Her work there provided a forum and format that awakened the recognition of other strengths, the support of like-minded people, and the powerful transpersonal energies that we all have at our disposal. "After a year of experiential coursework, I was much closer to being no longer willing to be stifled. I knew I had a voice and much more confidence to express what I wanted or needed. I believed in myself. This was powerful work.

"Our final project for the yearlong course was to create a container to honor our work and ourselves. I understood the importance of ritual from my studies, but I don't think I understood the significance of this particular project until I was well into it." Lisa took a Japanese tea box and decorated all four sides and the top with images that represented things she had accomplished or learned over the past year. It was a very emotional experience for her to finish the box, a symbol of her life's creative projects. "I sat on the floor and cried, overwhelmed at the growth and accomplishments that I so rarely acknowledge or appreciate. I felt extreme gratitude."

Each of the five sides helps her to summarize and honor her experiences. She looks at the box daily, reminded that she has many gifts and talents, even if she doesn't always use them all. "There are periods that are my time in the cocoon, growing and evolving yet again. I do know, from my box, that my experiences in life have happened for a purpose and that I will be incorporating all my skills together sometime in the future. These are the major themes and symbols of my life:

The Tree and My Family. My family is sacred in my life. They stand at the foot of my tree. I am so proud of my children and their accomplishments. I never took credit for their accomplishments because I do feel they have earned their accolades by themselves. But I must admit that part of my owning my accomplishments must include that, along with my husband, I have raised two amazing children. I honor a job well done as 'MOM' and am so grateful to be blessed with them.

Work and Volunteer Accomplishments. This side honors the businesses and organizations I have created from the love in my heart. Ten stepping-stones to power and joy, Joyful Life, honors my childhood dream of helping people be the best they can be. A club I started several years ago called International Friends brought women together from around the world (then living in the New York metropolitan area), bringing community and compassion to many who otherwise might feel lost and alone when they arrived in this country from overseas.

The Snake. The "wild woman" energy is something that is just emerging in me. This snake, and the flames surrounding it, represents my inner fire that is coming out!

My Vision. This side is covered with my thoughts, poems, and artwork. A personal collage illustrates my vision of my future work and reflects my transformation.

Native American Images. Since I was a child, thanks to my parents, I have had a love of Native American culture. My power animals—eagle, butterfly, and buffalo—appear in various forms to give me guidance.

I find that expressing myself creatively helps to honor the deep emotional work that I do; getting images or words out on paper is very grounding. The most essential thing, however, is to let go of my expectations that this needs to be great art. Sometimes I can just let things flow, allowing the images and words to simply come through me. That is the best, when I truly feel connected to spirit. It may not be accepted by many in society, but I am less afraid of that now than when I was growing up. I know now that I need to express myself. All women need to find their own voice. We need to believe in ourselves and begin seeing ourselves so that others have the opportunity to see us as well."

What images and symbols resonate with you individually, providing your own personal shorthand language for how you relate to the world? Recall when you first encountered these. Were they always present, or was there an immediate recognition and affinity when you realized your connection to them? How have these influenced and shaped your life? If you have not been aware of these, take the time to free-associate to any idea, image, or symbol that comes into your imagination. They need not be logical or obviously meaningful. Just allowing them to be present sets the intention for them to keep working on your psyche and spirit. How they translate into your creative life will take its own shape in its own time.

My Body: The Substance of Spirit

Using her body as the vehicle for expressing herself in the world, Dunya has found that it literally has become the container of her being. From a classically trained dancer, forcing her body to move in often unnatural ways, she ultimately transformed herself into a practitioner and teacher of the mysteries of belly dancing, Sufi dancing, and creative movement. Dancing to her own innate natural rhythms has become Dunya's spiritual practice.

"My husband and I separated three days before 9/11. Since then, I've been in 'a fullness of myself,' able to experience all of my feelings and perceptions of self, no longer censoring aspects of my existence. In a silent workshop that I give for women, I recently noticed all of us moving in consonance, with very few clues beyond a gentle indication from my own movements. Afterward, one woman commented that you could actually see the moment when each woman would step out of where she was and seemingly walk through a doorway into an unknown place. For myself, when I go through one doorway, there's yet another one beyond. Each one reveals the next one right away; it's not so much an epiphany as an opening. As a younger woman, I used to be into the 'aha' epiphany, but as I've matured, so has my experience of what is just there—something far more real to me."

At this point in her life, Dunya recognizes that there are substantial changes happening that will definitely not reverse themselves. Her body is changing; she has entered menopause. Her parents are aging; she's talking to them about death. "There is something about menopause that is changing the way I see time, as if I'm coming out of the surface of my life, rising from the deep interior. Now, when I'm with someone I'm going to be intimate with, they have to be present, to be whole with themselves. I can't lose time with myself and my life by being with someone who isn't there, someone who needs me to be something other than who I am. I wish I had understood this when I was younger. If only I'd recognized that my own company was so valuable, I'd have spent more time with myself."

Since childhood, Dunya understood that she was seeking something, but she didn't know what it was. "In fact, throughout my life, when I hit upon something, I *knew* it. A constant currency of awakening, sequential awakenings, defines my spiritual path. I've always known that it would all 'just happen.' I'm realizing that I am part of the evolutionary force. You make humankind evolve by doing your huge small things. I feel like the fearless guide. That feels good; there is no fear about opening, about death. I have fears about wasting time, fears that I might slide back a little. But you slide back, and you move forward."

In the past, Dunya used her body addictively, forcing it to make unnatural movements, literally escaping from herself through professional dancing. Her body was her power, but, by manipulating it like a marionette, it also became her punishment. She now senses that she's coming to a place that is much more receptive, feeling that it is her dharma to provide an environment where this can take place. The first ten years of Sufi work were spent just trying to feel her body. "I would do my practice naked in front of a mirror. The first years were hard; then I totally fell in love with my body. What I discovered was that the better I felt, the more my body became what I had always wanted it to look like. The more I did movements that felt delicious, the more my body became its ideal."

In a subsequent relationship, Dunya found herself in the process of holding on to her newfound sense of self in the negotiations, saying to him, "I want my body more than I want you. I have to have me, or else there is nothing to give you." The body is the substance of spirit for her on this plane. "I respect what it is doing, what it is trying to tell me. It is this internal relationship with my body that needs negotiating."

In one of her workshops, there was a circle of women doing a "hand dance," the hand movements that accompany belly dancing. "You could see that each person was so unique, so different, yet we were all ostensibly doing the same thing. Over and over again, doing this dance is a rite of passage, one's own true essence expressed through the common form."

A key element in Dunya's story is not only about finding our highest selves, but holding on to this hard-earned knowledge when we join in relationship with others. This seems to be an essential theme for women, weaving its way through many of the interviews and conversations I've had. While being in relationship is an essential and healthy goal for most of us, we still need to invest a fair amount of time and energy being with ourselves, working on our own development. After all, relationship with another, although a big slice of life's pie, is certainly not all of it.

Some of us make excuses for not making enough time for ourselves. Some of us may even experience anxiety when we are left to our own devices and so may avoid being alone, much to our own detriment. Think about things you once enjoyed, or might enjoy, doing alone. If you are having trouble identifying these, go back to your childhood, or to a time when you were single, or without children. Is there something you promised yourself you would do if you only had the time?

Unfortunately, all too many women can relate to Dunya's experience of feeling alienated from her body. Developing body knowledge and a realistic concept of your own physical being is an essential element for a healthy, balanced sense of self. Performing movement of any kind, be it dancing, gymnastics, tai chi, or chi gong, provides yet another vehicle through which your body might choose to express itself. The idea is to simply explore modalities of all kinds to help you expand your knowledge of yourself and the way you experience being alive.

Medicine Buddha

In loving memory of a dearly beloved friend and fellow journeyer.
May her life be as an eternal blessing.

Barbara's very recent passing leaves all who knew and cherished her sad for the loss of her loving and radiant presence, but deeply grateful that she is released from her physical burden. She died as she lived, with total integrity, with deep belief in the divinity of spirit, and fully aware of the eternal nature of soul.

Not only can the body become our own spiritual practice by teaching us how to honor what we are given, learning to live comfortably in our own skin, but it can also teach us how to live with spirit when the body falters, breaking down and failing us in some way. Learning how to deal with illness is an inevitable challenge, but finding spirit within the difficulty may provide the opportunity to dip deep inside in order to find the gifts of healing grace.

Utilizing both traditional and alternative modalities for healing, Barbara became a thoroughly "informed consumer," ultimately helping to create her own positive outcome some twenty years ago. After this life-threatening crisis, Barbara experienced several other major health crises. Each in its own turn has served as a rite of passage, a transformation toward healing, deepening Barbara's spiritual belief and practice. She has encouraged and inspired many others to rise to meet their own challenges through their own healing crises. And she has taught about living the sacred life every day.

"In October of 1985, I had terrific pain across my midriff, and intercourse was becoming painful. I was a hiker and sometimes a jogger. Did I strain myself? On the first visit to the doctor, I was diagnosed with PID (pelvic inflammatory disease). Knowing that this was ridiculous, I took the pills anyway, as I was obligated to return to San Francisco where I was working in the jewelry business. Pills didn't help—back to doctor. Oops, wrong pills. Try again. Now Christmas and New Years, my stomach is bloated; I'm miserable. 'Get me another doctor.' Finally, February 6, 1986, I'm diagnosed with late stage-three ovarian cancer. No encouragement. Heads are shaking. Sorry. Wow! What do I do now? Do I go with my training (as a hospice caregiver) and die gracefully? I was offered a 'debulking' operation and chemotherapy. Swell!

"Bill and I took three weeks to explore options before agreeing to medical procedures. I increased meditation practices, started visualizations and acupuncture, changed diets, went into deep therapy to help remove blocks to healing, and contacted alternative medical folks and lay practitioners for advice. I called on Medicine Buddha, the great healer, and Green Tara, the compassionate protector, for guidance and help. I was busy! We, with the wonderful guidance of a compassionate oncologist at Kaiser, San Rafael, decided to opt for chemo first, no cutting."

Barbara credits three major transcending events for greatly influencing her recovery. She began meditating at around 3 a.m., since that is when the body is the least active, which in her mind meant that the least healing occurs. During one session, a deceased friend appeared before her and said, "You have everything you need to heal," and disappeared. Barbara's inner core knew that John's message was true, and it was up to her to explore what was available, embodied all around her. "Angels that I had prayed for to come forward with their knowledge were all here, already present and willing to help. Bill, my partner, feeding, washing, clothing, and loving my emaciated body, comforted my fears, an angel for sure. Even a later oncologist did his part, yawning his boredom, which sent me further into alternative and Eastern healing processes. Friends 'laid on hands.'"

The second occurrence was during a meditation, where her teacher's deceased guru, Rudi (Rudrananda, the founder of Grace Essence Fellowship), sat in front of her and "ate" her disease. Not knowing what this practice was, Barbara described the event to another teacher, Ellen Galford, and Ellen continued the practice.

The third big event was during a therapy session where hypnosis was induced to take Barbara deep into her body. "I looked around and found no cancer, only beautiful sparkling jewels. I ended the session with a deep conviction that I was cancer free, so I quit the devastating chemo treatments. Then came a five-plus-hour operation to remove damaged organs and tissue and to search for other cancers. I was *clean* and have been ovarian cancer-free for almost twenty years.

"Today, I'm in my seventies. I married Bill, my wonder angel and partner of many years, just a few years ago. We live in a cooperative community, sharing our lives with ten families on sixteen acres in the Sonoma country-side. We enjoy meaningful relationships with people of all ages, travel, walk regularly, pay attention to diet, play games, see a lot of the grandchildren while fitting in lifelong-learning classes at Sonoma State University, and try to amend world injustices. It's a great life!

"My greatest gift that keeps giving: follow your intuition and heart, and know yourself well enough that you can't be talked into something that doesn't fit or feel right. Speak up and question, question, question. You don't have to be Ms./Mr. Nice to accommodate other people's sensitivities. When in trauma, this is your moment to gain the best healing available, your big chance to bring your body and soul into full being-ness. Healing of many dimensions awaits you. Honor it; go for it."

Lessons of the Primal Wound

Our life lessons often come from themes that are not of our choosing. For many of us, it is hard enough as adults to acknowledge that something monu-mental is happening and then to make and incorporate the appropriate changes that the particular passage may require. Imagine what it must be like when someone is too young to appreciate and understand and may be little equipped to handle the impact of major life transitions, especially when they present outside of the normal rhythm of the life cycle. Then imagine what it must be like to experience many such out-of-sync transitions.

"This year marks the fortieth anniversary of my mother's death . . . and the twentieth anniversary of my brother's death . . . and it is the year my nephew died. But all of these losses, and everything that's come out of them, are still really about the loss of my mother when I was sixteen years old. All that I know comes from having her and then losing her. Her loss was the most radicalizing and critical event of my early life, shaping everything else after it."

Debby describes her mother as an angel, a truly extraordinary human being who was faced by the harsh reality of life from an early age. After living in an orphanage, where she suffered early childhood trauma, she managed to pull herself up and out, eventually receiving a scholarship to nursing school. The strong anchor of her family of six, she exhibited a capacity for extraordinarily profound compassion and sensitivity for others. But, at the same time, she was unarmored; the idea of cruelty and of anyone being hurt was "primitively intolerable" to her. Debby's grandmother and aunts all struggled with mental illness, but for her mother, the struggle ended when she committed suicide.

"My mother was an amazing mom, especially to us as young kids. The truth is that I had the best parents of anyone I ever knew. Although I have the essence of my mother in me, I've chosen to pattern myself after my dad, who manages much better in the world. Because of her death, I understood at a very early age that people get a stock idea about things, their own picture of what something means. People felt profound pity for us, but they didn't understand. Suicide is often seen as crazy, and she wasn't. I accept that she did what she had to do. I made an early discovery too—that when people die, they don't really leave you."

Debby was the oldest of three children and the oldest grandchild. Although a kid, she was always "old." Sometimes bossy, sometimes a leader, other younger people looked up to her. On the day of the death, Debby found her mother and attempted to resuscitate her, but it was already too late. Arriving home from work, her father enlisted Debby's help, now as "the adult," to tell her brothers what had happened.

Her mother's death in January 1965 came about one and a half years after the death of John F. Kennedy. That collective loss had become the paradigm for how to grieve. For Debby, what cushioned and protected her was found in the cultural icon of how to behave, how to be. At the funeral, she remembers an unbelievable crowd of people present, watching the family. Outwardly, she was Jackie Kennedy, brave and courageous. But, seeing the coffin, she had a visceral sense that it was too small, that her mother couldn't fit in there. The surreal moved in to fill the void left by a total lack of reality.

"For a death, especially of this kind, you simply don't know what to do. It is impossible for a sixteen year old to experience grief in the moment. I've learned since then that the power of ritual is so important because it contains the grief. Along the way, I've had small opportunities to do this and have seized these times to create rituals that are meaningful for me personally, and sometimes for the community of which I am a part. This is why telling my story is so important. There are private rituals that I do on the anniversary of my mother's death every year. With gratitude, I use this day of remembrance as a life marker, a time to evaluate how I'm doing and to assess what I need to do. Over time, more and more insights come.

"In January 1985, my brother and I were hiking in Muir Woods on the anniversary of our mother's death, and together we were having conversations about her. You have to know that my brother didn't have a spiritual bone in his body, but there, on our path, was a deer with eyes like my mother's, looking right at us. My brother and I both said "Mom" at the same time. Three months later, my brother's relentlessly progressive melanoma had metastasized to his brain. While he was dying, I dreamt about deer. My mother and brother are buried next to each other in Providence, Rhode Island. When I come back east, I visit their grave sites, bringing stories and letters I have written for each of them. After John died, I had a dream: a mother deer and her son walking toward me on a beach."

For Debby, intimacy and loss are profoundly connected. Every intimate relationship has been challenged by fear of loss. Unresolved adolescent grief reemerged after a significant relationship breakup, and the feeling and expression of grief after this breakup felt worse than after her mother's death. Her capacity for both intimacy and grieving have deepened as a result of her personal experience as partner and mother, as well as in her professional life as a clinical nurse specialist with an important part of her work being in the field of mind/body practices with breast cancer patients. Debby's ongoing challenge has been to learn to trust intimacy again. "If you remain locked in your losses, you can't have intimacy. Allowing yourself the *possibility of loss* opens you up to intimacy."

Growing in the Darkness

Robin's journey illustrates just how fragile life is, but also just how resilient the human spirit is. Issues emerging from her family of origin set the stage for the many roles she unwittingly chose to undertake in her adult life. As the wife and mother of addicts, enabler and rescuer, she had little time or energy left for herself. After years of struggling to reclaim her own identity, growing beyond her negative programming, she rediscovered who she was apart from anyone else and reestablished her own connection to spirit. "Everything, all that I am today, is a result of the adversity I've been through. This adversity allowed me to see how far I'd gotten away from myself, to seek help, and to reconnect with who I am."

Robin grew up with an emotionally distant father, which made it easy for her to marry someone who was very similar. But this nice girl didn't know what to do with her husband's alcoholism. She was very repressed in her marriage, having learned from her family of origin that a woman's primary job in relationship was to "keep it together." Her brother got to do things she couldn't do, essentially because "girls don't do those things." Since her parents had only enough money to send one of their children to private school, they figured the better investment was their son. The messages from home were mixed: it's okay to be smart, but in the long run, women just get married.

Her parents divorced when Robin was twenty-four, supposedly because of her father's affair, something her mother had chosen to largely ignore for a fair amount of time, instead making excuses for him. Robin's own crisis came when her children started acting out the severe dysfunction that was ever present in her home. But, instead of dealing with it, she made excuses as well. In denial around her husband's issues, she became physically cold, even distant from her own children.

Eventually her husband went into rehab, but by then serious damage had already been done. Her daughter, Lynne, made a suicide attempt at the age of twelve. After this, Robin found her way to Al-Anon. "In the beginning, I wondered, 'Why should I have to go to a program? He's got the problem!' But I was given this advice: 'Mind your own business. This program is for you.' Through Al-Anon, I learned about taking care of myself. Dancing, always a love of mine, brought me great pleasure, as did yoga. In short, I found many ways to express love to myself."

Eventually, Robin asked her relapsed husband to leave. "I felt as if I'd been released from prison when he left. His leaving gave me permission to do what I had held captive deeply within myself." However, this newfound freedom at age forty-one took the form of acting out like a teenager, making up for lost time. In the meantime, Lynne, who was then fifteen, fell out of a window during a blackout and finally ended up in a psychiatric facility. Eventually she came home, only to relapse. The solution for Lynne came in the form of attending a boarding school run on the principles of twelve-step programs.

"I continued to get help for myself in the form of breath work, sound work, and other forms of healing. Over time, my daughters recognized my transformation from doormat to strong healthy woman. My choices became healthier around my children as well; I was no longer acting out my frustration and anger toward them. Lynne wanted to be in my presence, following me around, doing what I did. She'd say, 'Mom, every three months you have a rebirth.'"

Her other daughter, Corinne, had had her own fair share of problems. Having graduated from the same school as her sister, she moved back in with Robin, and for three months they were best friends and roommates. Then, sober and just really beginning her life, Corinne and two friends were tragically killed in a car accident. "When she died, I was at a place in my life where I was closer to my 'gut' than I had ever been before. At the memorial service for Corinne, there was an open mike so that people could just get up when they wanted to say or do what they felt. I became the director of this event of songs, prayer, poetry reading, and many wonderful words about Corinne from teachers and friends."

After Corinne's death, Robin almost lost Lynne, who relapsed several times. "I told her, 'You know what you need to do, and you'll do it when you're ready.' When Lynne decided to leave town, I went to the Al-Anon office and offered to volunteer. On the brink of death, Lynne called out to Corinne and found her way to her father's home. She was ninety pounds and strung out, but she's come back from that. Now we have such fun, go to ball games, and have fabulous times together. This is a miracle."

Teaching eighth grade, dealing with teenagers at school and at home, Robin realized that there was no way she could keep doing this kind of work until retirement, and so she started looking into other options beyond teaching. At a Baha'i retreat, she heard Hawaiian chanting for the first time, and the sounding of it resonated so deeply within her that she knew she had to do something with it. This turned out to be the practice of Lomi Lomi, an ancient Hawaiian body massage that was ritually performed at the time of puberty. About three to six kahunas worked on initiates, both boys and girls, for any length of time, from six hours to six days, creating the space through ceremony to help them effectively pass from adolescence to adulthood.

Rites existed as well for special occasions such as weddings, and there was a "family" Lomi Lomi practitioner to keep everyone healthy. Today people come for sessions at birthdays, changes of season, and initiations. "The trainings are about giving and receiving. When I found Lomi Lomi many years ago, my experiences were intense; these were huge emotional releases. Now when I dance and there are powerful emotions expressed, I just accept it as, 'This is a woman who has lost her child. She might cry at any moment— expect it.'

"In my younger years, I was told that my 'gut' was wrong. Amid the chaos and calamity of my life, this theme of intuitive knowing has threaded its way through, informing me about something quite different from what I was told. I used to have a thought and then deny it, saying, 'That's not what I'm supposed to do; that's not the way I'm supposed to be.' I had no one to confirm or validate my feelings, and there was no one to share the joy of creativity— not until I dated a musician in high school who allowed my creativity to shine. Later, my relationship with David gave me the jump start, allowing me to be able to run on my own. Although I am grateful for being with him on and off for seven years, I finally realized that I needed to find myself, not in the context of a relationship, but in my own life."

Robin stayed in a sixteen-year marriage because that was what she was "expected" to do. She doesn't do the "supposed to" thing anymore, instead relying on her own intuition to tell her what is right for her. "Since Corinne's death, I don't have any time for bullshit. If it feels wrong, I'm out of there. I trust my gut, having so much more of a sense of who I am and what I want."

Another huge life theme for her is "letting go." The Buddhists say, "You can't fix your mind with the mind that broke it." Robin had to look outside of herself to find modalities of healing that would work best for her. Her denial and defenses ran so deep that she knew she would talk circles around the issues in psychotherapy. Body therapies seemed to work far better, especially the practices of Amma bodywork (once a week for a year), holotropic and transformational breath work, and "nontalking" therapy, where she was able to vent her frustration and sadness, screaming her anger at her father and husband. "Letting go has become a practice. Just when I think I've let go, more things come up. Letting things go, letting people go, letting someone go to the other side, I have no anger. I feel that Corinne is very close, guiding me a lot of the time. It's a sense that I have of someone waiting for me on the other side.

"All of this darkness had to happen to get me to see who I really am. Keeping the focus on myself has helped me to see what my part is." Robin feels that she's finally on the right path for herself, choosing to simplify her life, leaving a secure job, and making choices about what she wants to do. "My life is very rich now. It's funny, but when I had money, I didn't feel rich. Now it's time to receive more. On the day that Corinne died, a dragonfly landed on my newspaper. The Native Americans have a belief that dragonflies are the soul of the departed. Dragonflies are about possibilities."

As a postscript to this story, turning a possibility into a reality, Robin recently founded Dragonfly Healing Arts, which promotes healing through spirituality and the arts. Lynne recently graduated from college with a degree in music therapy and intends to become a nurse specializing in emergency medicine.

We all have situations or events in our lives that are difficult to cope with at the time they're happening. Choose a few of these to work with. What lessons or insights have you gained as a result of going through these hard times? If it's difficult for you to see the gifts you received, try looking at a similar situation that may have occurred later in your life, a situation that you handled in a better way, perhaps because you'd already experienced something like it once before. What shifted within you to help you cope more effectively? You can take this one step further. Design a small ritual, alone or with friends or family, to honor the good that came from a tragic or difficult event. Sometimes it is only the passage of time and the distance from an event that permits us to see the gifts of this darkness.

Have you reenacted your family drama in significant future relationships—marriage, business partnerships, or even social situations? What are the repetitive patterns you've noticed through these? How could you become more conscious of your own process, thus enabling you to move beyond learned behaviors? If you're feeling really ready to solicit an outside perspective, enlist the help of trusted family and friends in this exercise, asking them to share their observations and insights about your patterns and choices. Keep an open mind to what others tell you about yourself and what their experience is of you.

Have the labels that have been thrust upon you, and the behaviors that these imply, kept you stuck in negative patterning—for example, being an enabler in an addictive relationship? Were you always the peacemaker or caretaker in your family, never thinking about making peace with or taking care of yourself? Did others' opinions about what you were "supposed to" do affect your ability to define your own way? What obstacles still block your road? As you sort out whose ideas and limitations you've adapted as your own, keep the ones that serve you, while letting go of those that don't. Once you realize your own part in the drama, seek out support groups, friends, and therapists that will help you stay present in your own life, learning to shift the focus to yourself. If this is an issue that seems to pervade your life, keep a daily journal of "things to do for me." Perhaps you can even place reminders of self-care around your home, ways to remember that you come first.

People often feel the need to "find" themselves through rebellious acts, which are really meant to create separation but more than likely will create ill will without providing real resolution. Design a "rite of separation" that allows you to maintain a healthy role within the family while declaring your intention to create a mature, separate identity for yourself. This may manifest as a physical separation or as simply a shift in family patterns. For example, choosing to speak to or visit with relatives every few weeks instead of weekly or even daily may give you much-needed space to process things in a different way without the usual influences. It could also mean setting boundaries and parameters about which issues and discussions are permissible and which are definitely off limits, again creating space that consciously honors your own rhythm, instead of continuing to unconsciously march to the family's drumbeat.

From childhood, we know this game; along with our coloring books and crayons, these pages of dots are an exercise in discovery. Little hands learn to draw lines, connecting one dot to the next until we are done, and a familiar image reveals itself. Earliest man observed the heavens—billions of sparkling dots in the pitch black sky. Eventually early astronomers saw the pictures, naming the constellations, dot by dot, star by star, revealing mythic figures—the ancient and eternal, the now and forever, showing us the way.

Reflections on Connections

Choose to see the bigger picture. When you are lost in the woods—a theme of fairy tales as well as the tales of your life—you cannot tell the forest from the trees. Imagine now what it would be like to be able to look down from a nearby mountain and watch yourself trying to navigate through the forest. From this vantage point, you would be able to see where you are, decide where you want to go, and choose the path that might best lead you out of the woods. In other words . . .

Broaden and value your perspective. The nineteenth-century neoimpressionist artist Georges Seurat developed pointillism, a method of painting pictures dot by dot. Standing up close to the canvas, all you see, all that your mind registers, is a field of dots that reveals subtle gradations and nuances of color, light, and shadow, and that is all. Perspective is only gained by stepping far enough back so that the entire picture is revealed.

Identify what is most important to you. Whether it's your purpose, your mission, your passion, or your bliss, it's ultimately about connecting what you know with what you feel.

Recognize that your intuition is your personal bridge to the grand design. Let your instincts, your gut, your inner knowing tell you if you're on track and in sync with where you need to be.

Trust in the grand design. Whatever you believe in, whatever you call that greater something—destiny, fate, kismet, or karma—know that it is there, organizing and driving your life. Trust that your dots will connect.

Make your life happen. Life isn't about "finding" yourself. Life is about consciously creating the best of who you are from what is already there.

~

Epilogue

If I am not for myself, who is for me? And when I am for myself, what am I?
And if not now, when?

—The Sayings of the Fathers

While the "happenings" of our lives seem to happen ever more quickly and
with more intensity, society may have reached a critical juncture in its evolution. Having conquered so many frontiers, where do we go from here? Perhaps the final frontier lays not "out there," in vast universes beyond our own,
but in our own "inner space," those potential openings into our own great-
ness. Grimes, a prescient voice in rite and ritual, suggests that "today ritual
helps integrate and attune life on an increasingly globalized planet."[1] As the
world shrinks and our consciousness expands, rites of passage and the ritual
process provide essential road maps and compass settings, pointing us in the
right direction and marking the course of our lives, and ultimately the life of
the species. But if we are truly at a precipice, maps and compasses may no
longer be enough; it may well take a leap of faith into a consciousness, a
belief that we are far more than we now imagine ourselves to be.

Although seen as a "savior" by so many yearning for salvation, technology
can only take us so far and must be viewed with apprehension as we strive to
integrate its power into our evolutionary spiral. "If we do not birth or die
ritually, we will do so technologically. . . . Technology without ritual (or
worse, technology as ritual) easily degenerates into knowledge without
respect . . . a formula for planetary annihilation. It matters greatly not only
that we birth and die but how we birth and die."[2] Instead of simply careening
along the information highway on autopilot, we need to slow down and map

out our trips, finding personally valuable ways to breathe spirit back into the everyday aspects of living.

Somewhere between the habitual nature of life and the unconscious meandering of our minds lies the middle road. Rites of passage help us awaken an essential wisdom within us that, when heeded, allows us to really live each moment of our lives. Realizing the impermanence of everything wakes us up to the need to be ever mindful and present. Life, that temporary condition between birth and death, beckons us to participate, with every breath of energy and in every aspect of our lives. By taking our "death" into our own hands through the process of rites of passage, we ensure our life. It is our responsibility to "die" before we die, and as we do so, through each successive rite of passage, we come to realize that within this death lies our true life.

Cultural historian Richard Tarnas believes that modern civilization is presently engaged in a collective rite of passage. We are currently at the "threshold" of the death/rebirth mystery. He sees this passage as a "transition to a new world view, a new vision of the universe and our selves in it."[3] Our task is to create a modern mythology that genuinely mirrors our world today, incorporating mindfulness and respect for what is ever changing and yet eternal. We have an imaginative tool, in the form of rites of passage, that is capable of bringing us to a more elemental core of our being. Rites of passage are mythology in action. The form is eternal; the spirit is the new life that we breathe into it to fully reflect and express where we are now.

Notes

Introduction: Opening the Door

1. Daniel Levinson et al., *The Seasons of a Man's Life* (New York: Ballantine Books, 1978), 324.

2. Paul H. Ray and Sherry Ruth Anderson, *The Cultural Creatives: How 50 Million People Are Changing the World* (New York: Harmony Books, 2000), 264.

Chapter 1: Defining Passages

1. Arnold van Gennep, *The Rites of Passage* (Chicago: University of Chicago Press, 1960), 3.

2. Ibid., 3.

3. Bruce Lincoln, "Festa das Mocas Novas: The Cosmic Tour," in *Emerging from the Chrysalis: Rituals of Women's Initiation* (New York: Oxford University Press, 1991), 50–70.

4. Ronald Grimes, *Deeply into the Bone: Re-inventing Rites of Passage* (Berkeley: University of California Press), 7.

5. Ibid., 5.

6. David Leeming and Jake Page, *Goddess: Myths of the Female Divine* (New York: Oxford University Press, 1994), 66–71.

7. Ibid., 59–66.

8. Tom F. Driver, *Liberating Rites: Understanding the Transformative Power of Ritual* (Boulder, CO, 1998), 185.

9. Grimes, *Deeply into the Bone*, 4.

Chapter 2: Passages of the Body

1. Clarissa Pinkola Estes, *Women Who Run with the Wolves: Myths and Stories of the Wild Woman Archetype* (New York: Ballantine Books, 1992), 235.

2. Will Durant, *The Story of Civilization*, vol. 4, *The Age of Faith* (New York: Simon & Schuster, 1950), 363.

3. Barbara Walker, *Restoring the Goddess: Equal Rites for Modern Women* (Amherst, NY: Prometheus Books, 2000), 118.

4. Estes, *Women Who Run with the Wolves*, 437.

5. Ibid., 435.

6. Arnold van Gennep, *The Rites of Passage*, 42–43, a description of the ceremony "Village We Leave" of the Todas culture of India.

7. Ibid., 43–44, a description of childbirth in the Hopi tribe of Arizona.

8. Robbie Davis-Floyd, *Birth as an American Rite of Passage* (Berkeley: University of California Press), 305.

9. Grimes, *Deeply into the Bone*, 19.

10. Ibid., 19.

11. Benig Mauger, *Reclaiming the Spirituality of Birth: Healing for Mothers and Babies* (Rochester, VT: Healing Arts Press, 2000), 123.

Chapter 3: Passages of the Self

1. Joseph Campbell and Bill Moyers, *The Power of Myth* (New York: Anchor Books, 1991), 8–9.

2. Ibid., 8–9.

3. Louise Carus Mahdi, Nancy Geyer Christopher, and Michael Meade, eds., *Crossroads: The Quest for Contemporary Rites of Passage* (Chicago: Open Court, 1998), xvii–xviii.

4. Barbara Walker, *Women's Rituals: A Sourcebook* (San Francisco: HarperSanFrancisco, 1990), 264.

5. Ibid., 264.

6. Ibid., 265.

7. Ibid., 265.

8. Nancy Newton Verrier, *The Primal Wound: Understanding the Adopted Child* (Baltimore, MD: Gateway Press, 1993), 6.

9. Lesley A. Northup, *Ritualizing Women: Patterns of Spirituality* (Cleveland, OH: Pilgrim Press, 1997), 56–57.

Chapter 4: Passages through Loss

1. John W. James and Russell Friedman, *The Grief Recovery Handbook: The Action Program for Moving beyond Death, Divorce, and Other Losses* (New York: Harper Perennial, 1998), 9.

2. Ibid., 116.

3. Margaret Coberly, *Sacred Passage: How to Provide Fearless, Compassionate Care for the Dying* (Boston: Shambhala, 2002), 116.

4. Maxine Harris, *The Loss That Is Forever: The Lifelong Impact of the Early Death of a Mother or Father* (New York: Penguin, 1995), 280–81, a description of All Saints' Day as a recognized time to honor the dead in some cultures.

5. John O'Donohue, *Anam Cara: A Book of Celtic Wisdom* (New York: Cliff Street Books, 1997), 13–14.

Chapter 5: Myths and Symbols

1. Mircea Eliade, *Rites and Symbols of Initiation: The Mysteries of Birth and Rebirth* (Woodstock, CT: Spring Publications, 1995), xv.

2. Anthony Stevens, *On Jung* (Princeton, NJ: Princeton University Press, 1999), 63.

3. Joseph Campbell, *The Hero with a Thousand Faces* (Princeton, NJ: Princeton University Press, 1973), 25.

4. Ibid., 11.

5. Joan Chamberlain Engelsman, *The Feminine Dimension of the Divine*, 2nd ed. (Wilmette, IL: Chiron Publications, 1995), 16.

6. Marion Woodman, *The Pregnant Virgin: A Process of Psychological Transformation* (Toronto: Inner City Books, 1985), 81.

7. Engelsman, *The Feminine Dimension of the Divine*, 17–18.

8. Ken Wilber, *Up from Eden: A Transpersonal View of Human Evolution* (Wheaton, IL: Quest Books, 1996), 142.

9. Marion Woodman and Elinor Dickson, *Dancing in the Flames: The Dark Goddess in the Transformation of Consciousness* (Boston: Shambhala, 1996), 18.

10. Leeming and Page, *Goddess: Myths of the Female Divine*, 3.

11. Angeles Arrien, *The Four-Fold Way: Walking the Paths of the Warrior, Teacher, Healer, and Visionary* (San Francisco: HarperSanFrancisco, 1993), 91–92.

12. Jill Purce, *The Mystic Spiral: Journey of the Soul* (New York: Thames & Hudson, 1974), 29.

13. Rachel Pollack, *The Power of Ritual* (New York: Dell Publishing, 2000), 139.

14. Salman Rushdie, *The Wizard of Oz* (London: British Film Institute, 1992), 21.

15. Ibid., 10.

16. Ibid., 21.

17. Estes, *Women Who Run with the Wolves*, 222.

18. Ibid., 222.

19. Rushdie, *The Wizard of Oz*, 42.

Chapter 6: Exploring the World

1. Victor Turner, *Dramas, Fields, and Metaphors: Symbolic Action in Human Society* (Ithaca: Cornell University Press, 1974), 197.

2. Ibid., 46–47.

3. Ibid., 168–69, a description offered in Malcolm X's autobiography about his pilgrimage to Mecca

Chapter 7: Ritual and Creativity

1. Catherine Bell, *Ritual: Perspectives and Dimensions* (Oxford: Oxford University Press, 1997), 264.

2. Lesley Northup, *Ritualizing Women*, 24–27.

3. Ibid., 29.

4. Ibid., 38.

5. Ibid., 42.

6. Bruce Lincoln, *Emerging from the Chrysalis*, 118.

7. Ronald Grimes, *Deeply into the Bone*, 43–44.

8.Teresa Norman, *A World of Baby Names* (New York: Penguin Putnam, 1996), 1, naming customs of the Yoruba.

9. Ibid., 217, naming customs of the Hawaiian culture.

10. Mark Thurston and Christopher Fazel, *The Edgar Cayce Handbook for Creating Your Future* (New York: Ballantine Books, 1992), 205.

11. Grimes, *Deeply into the Bone*, 310–15, a discussion of *mizuko kuyo* (the water children rite) in Japan.

Chapter 8: Religion and Spirituality

1. Emile Durkheim, *The Elementary Forms of the Religious Life* (New York: The Free Press, 1915), 52.

2. Arrien, *The Four-Fold Way*, 113.

3. Erich Neumann, *The Great Mother: An Analysis of the Archetype* (Princeton, NJ: Princeton University Press, 1991), 61.

4. Robert Graves, *The Greek Myths* (Baltimore, MD: Penguin Books, 1955), 1:13–16.

5. Ibid., 16.

6. Jean Shinoda Bolen, *Goddesses in Everywoman: A New Psychology of Women* (New York: Harper Perennial, 1984), 289.

Chapter 9: Community and Family

1. Woodman, *The Pregnant Virgin*, 24.

2. David Moberg, *Aging and Spirituality: Spiritual Dimensions of Aging Theory, Research, Practice, and Policy* (New York: Haworth Pastoral Press, 2001), 21.

3. Ibid., 22.

4. Ibid., 22.

5. Ibid., 25–27.

6. Neumann, *The Great Mother*, 283.

7. Ibid., 283.

8. Nola Lewis and Marilyn Schlitz, "BeComing—Women's Circles, Women's Lives," *IONS: Noetic Sciences Review* 53 (September–November 2000): 34–35.

9. Northup, *Ritualizing Women*, 59.

Epilogue

1. Grimes, *Deeply into the Bone*, 13.

2. Ibid., 13.

3. Ray and Anderson, *The Cultural Creatives*, 251.

Bibliography

Akeret, Robert U., and Daniel Klein. *Family Tales, Family Wisdom: How to Gather the Stories of a Lifetime and Share Them with Your Family.* New York: Morrow, 1991.

Anderson, Sherry Ruth, and Patricia Hopkins. *The Feminine Face of God: The Unfolding of the Sacred in Women.* New York: Bantam Books, 1991.

Arrien, Angeles. *The Four-Fold Way: Walking the Paths of the Warrior, Teacher, Healer, and Visionary.* San Francisco: HarperSanFrancisco, 1993.

Artress, Lauren. *Walking the Sacred Path: Rediscovering the Labyrinth.* New York: Riverhead Books, 1995.

Baum, L. Frank. *The Wizard of Oz.* New York: Grosset & Dunlap Publishers, 1984.

Bell, Catherine. *Ritual: Perspectives and Dimensions.* Oxford: Oxford University Press, 1997.

Biziou, Barbara. *The Joy of Ritual: Spiritual Recipes to Celebrate Milestones, Ease Transitions, and Make Every Day Sacred.* New York: Golden Books, 1999.

Bolen, Jean Shinoda. *Crossing to Avalon: A Woman's Midlife Pilgrimage.* San Francisco: HarperSanFrancisco, 1994.

———. *Goddesses in Everywoman: A New Psychology of Women.* New York: Harper Perennial, 1984.

Borysenko, Joan. *A Woman's Journey to God: Finding the Feminine Path.* New York: Riverhead Books, 1999.

Bowie, Fiona. *The Anthropology of Religion: An Introduction.* Malden, MA: Blackwell Publishers, 2000.

Brodzinsky, David M., Marshall D. Schechter, and Robin Marantz Henig. *Being Adopted: The Lifelong Search for Health.* New York: Anchor Books, 1992.

Cahill, Sedonia, and Joshua Halpern. *The Ceremonial Circle: Practice, Ritual, and Renewal for Personal and Community Healing.* San Francisco: HarperSanFrancisco, 1992.

Campbell, Joseph. *The Hero with a Thousand Faces.* Bollinger Series 17. 1949. Princeton, NJ: Princeton University Press, 1973.

———. *Myths to Live By.* 1972. New York: Penguin/Arkana, 1993.

———. *Primitive Mythology.* 1959. New York: Penguin/Arkana, 1991.

Campbell, Joseph, and Bill Moyers. *The Power of Myth.* 1988. New York: Anchor Books, 1991.

Chodron, Pema. *The Wisdom of No Escape: And the Path of Loving Kindness.* Boston: Shambhala, 1991.

Coberly, Margaret. *Sacred Passage: How to Provide Fearless, Compassionate Care for the Dying.* Boston: Shambhala, 2002.

Cunningham, Nancy Brady. *I Am Woman by Rite: A Book of Women's Rituals.* York Beach, ME: Samuel Weiser, 1995.

Davis-Floyd, Robbie. *Birth as an American Rite of Passage.* Berkeley: University of California Press, 1992.

Dispenza, Joseph. *The Way of the Traveler: Making Every Trip a Journey of Self-Discovery.* Emeryville, CA: Avalon Travel Publishing, 2002.

Driver, Tom F. *Liberating Rites: Understanding the Transformative Power of Ritual.* Boulder, CO: Westview Press, 1998.

Durant, Will. *The Story of Civilization.* Vol. 4, *The Age of Faith.* New York: Simon & Schuster, 1950.

Durkheim, Emile. *The Elementary Forms of the Religious Life.* New York: The Free Press, 1915.

Eisler, Riane. *The Chalice and the Blade: Our History, Our Future.* 1987. San Francisco: HarperSanFrancisco, 1995.

Eliade, Mircea. *Rites and Symbols of Initiation: The Mysteries of Birth and Rebirth.* 1958. Woodstock, CT: Spring Publications, 1995.

———. *The Sacred and the Profane: The Nature of Religion.* 1957, 1959. New York: Harper & Row, 1961.

Engel, Beverly. *Women Circling the Earth: Guide to Fostering Community, Healing, and Empowerment.* Deerfield Beach, FL: Health Communications, 2000.

Engelsman, Joan Chamberlain. *The Feminine Dimension of the Divine.* 2nd ed. 1987, 1994. Wilmette, IL: Chiron Publications, 1995.

Estes, Clarissa Pinkola. *Women Who Run with the Wolves: Myths and Stories of the Wild Woman Archetype.* New York: Ballantine Books, 1992.

Fisher, Helen. *Why We Love: The Nature and Chemistry of Romantic Love.* New York: Henry Holt, 2004.

Gimbutas, Marija. *The Goddesses and Gods of Old Europe: Myths and Cult Images.* 1974, 1982. Berkeley: University of California Press, 1996.

Graves, Robert. *The Greek Myths.* Baltimore, MD: Penguin Books, 1955.

Grimes, Ronald L. *Deeply into the Bone: Re-inventing Rites of Passage.* Berkeley: University of California Press, 2000.

Harris, Maxine. *The Loss That Is Forever: The Lifelong Impact of the Early Death of a Mother or Father.* New York: Penguin, 1995.

Hayton, Althea. *Not Out of Mind.* Berkhamsted: Arthur James, 1998.

Herford, R. Travers. *The Ethics of the Talmud: Sayings of the Fathers*. New York: Schocken Books, 1962.

Hollis, James. *The Middle Passage: From Misery to Meaning in Midlife*. Toronto: Inner City Books, 1993.

Hopcke, Robert H. *A Guided Tour of the Collected Works of C. G. Jung*. Boston: Shambhala, 1992.

James, John W., and Russell Friedman. *The Grief Recovery Handbook: The Action Program for Moving beyond Death, Divorce, and Other Losses*. New York: Harper Perennial, 1998.

Kaufer, Nelly, and Carol Osmer-Newhouse. *A Woman's Guide to Spiritual Renewal*. San Francisco: HarperSanFrancisco, 1994.

Lao-tzu. *Tao Te Ching*. New York: Vintage Books, 1972.

Leeming, David, and Jake Page. *Goddess: Myths of the Female Divine*. New York: Oxford University Press, 1994.

Levinson, Daniel J., Charlotte N. Darrow, Edward B. Klein, Maria H. Levinson, and Braxton McKee. *The Seasons of a Man's Life*. New York: Ballantine Books, 1978.

Levinson, Daniel J., and Judy D. Levinson. *The Seasons of a Woman's Life*. New York: Ballantine Books, 1996.

Lewis, Nola, and Marilyn Schlitz, "BeComing—Women's Circles, Women's Lives," IONS: Noetic Sciences Review 53 (September–November 2000): 34–35.

Lincoln, Bruce. *Emerging from the Chrysalis: Rituals of Women's Initiation*. New York: Oxford University Press, 1991.

Mahdi, Louise Carus, Nancy Geyer Christopher, and Michael Meade, eds. *Crossroads: The Quest for Contemporary Rites of Passage*. 1996. Chicago: Open Court, 1998.

Mauger, Benig. *Reclaiming the Spirituality of Birth: Healing for Mothers and Babies*. Rochester, VT: Healing Arts Press, 2000.

Miller, Laura J., ed. *Postpartum Mood Disorders*. Washington, DC: American Psychiatric Press, 1999.

Moberg, David O., ed. *Aging and Spirituality: Spiritual Dimensions of Aging Theory, Research, Practice, and Policy*. New York: Haworth Pastoral Press, 2001.

Neumann, Erich. *The Great Mother: An Analysis of the Archetype*. Bollingen Series 46. 1955, 1963. Princeton, NJ: Princeton University Press, 1991.

Norman, Teresa. *A World of Baby Names*. New York: Penguin Putnam, 1996.

Northup, Lesley A. *Ritualizing Women: Patterns of Spirituality*. Cleveland, OH: Pilgrim Press, 1997.

O'Donohue, John. *Anam Cara: A Book of Celtic Wisdom*. New York: Cliff Street Books, 1997.

———. *Eternal Echoes: Exploring Our Yearning to Belong*. New York: Cliff Street Books, 1999.

Osbon, Diane K., ed. *A Joseph Campbell Companion: Reflections on the Art of Living*. New York: HarperCollins, 1991.

Peck, M. Scott. *The Road Less Traveled: A New Psychology of Love, Traditional Values, and Spiritual Growth*. New York: A Touchstone Book, 1978.

Pollack, Rachel. *The Power of Ritual.* New York: Dell Publishing, 2000.

Purce, Jill. *The Mystic Spiral: Journey of the Soul.* New York: Thames & Hudson, 1974.

Ray, Paul H., and Sherry Ruth Anderson. *The Cultural Creatives: How 50 Million People Are Changing the World.* New York: Harmony Books, 2000.

Rinpoche, Sogyal. *The Tibetan Book of Living and Dying.* San Francisco: HarperSanFrancisco, 1993.

Rumi, Jalal Al-Din. *Say I Am You: Poetry Interspersed with Stories of Rumi and Shams.* Translated by John Moyne and Coleman Barks. Athens, GA: Maypop, 1994.

Rushdie, Salman. *The Wizard of Oz.* London: British Film Institute, 1992.

Sheehy, Gail. *New Passages: Mapping Your Life across Time.* New York: Ballantine Books, 1995.

———. *Passages: Predictable Crises in Adult Life.* New York: Bantam Books, 1974.

Stone, Merlin. *When God Was a Woman.* San Diego: A Harvest Book, 1976.

Stevens, Anthony. *On Jung.* 1990. Princeton, NJ: Princeton University Press, 1999.

Tarnas, Richard. *The Passion of the Western Mind: Understanding the Ideas That Have Shaped Our World View.* New York: Ballantine Books, 1991.

Thurston, Mark, and Christopher Fazel. *The Edgar Cayce Handbook for Creating Your Future.* New York: Ballantine Books, 1992.

Turner, Victor. *Dramas, Fields, and Metaphors: Symbolic Action in Human Society.* Ithaca: Cornell University Press, 1974.

Van Gennep, Arnold. *The Rites of Passage.* Chicago: University of Chicago Press, 1960.

Verrier, Nancy Newton. *The Primal Wound: Understanding the Adopted Child.* Baltimore, MD: Gateway Press, 1993.

Walker, Barbara. *Restoring the Goddess: Equal Rites for Modern Women.* Amherst, NY: Prometheus Books, 2000.

———. *Women's Rituals: A Sourcebook.* San Francisco: HarperSanFrancisco, 1990.

Westwood, Jennifer. *On Pilgrimage: Sacred Journeys around the World.* Mahwah, NJ: Hidden Spring, 2003.

Wilber, Ken. *Up from Eden: A Transpersonal View of Human Evolution.* 1981. Wheaton, IL: Quest Books, 1996.

Woodman, Marion. *The Pregnant Virgin: A Process of Psychological Transformation.* Toronto: Inner City Books, 1985.

Woodman, Marion, and Elinor Dickson. *Dancing in the Flames: The Dark Goddess in the Transformation of Consciousness.* Boston: Shambhala, 1996.

Index

About the Author

Abigail Brenner, M.D., attended New York Medical College, becoming a physician in 1977. Her internship and residency in psychiatry were completed at New York University–Bellevue Medical Center in 1981. Dr. Brenner is a board-certified psychiatrist in private practice, a Reiki Master, and an ordained interfaith minister. She lives and works in New York City.

CPSIA information can be obtained at www.ICGtesting.com
Printed in the USA
LVOW07s1626220914

405270LV00017B/1351/P